MINDWORKER®

MAYBECK

THIS BOOK IS THE PROPERTY OF:

STATE _____
PROVINCE _____
COUNTY _____
PARISH _____
SCHOOL DISTRICT _____
OTHER _____

Book No. **One**
Enter information
in spaces
to the left as
instructed

Paul August

ISSUED TO	Year Used	CONDITION	
		ISSUED	RETURNED
St. Mary's			
St. Leanders		'48	'56
St. Liz High		'56	'60
Gap year		'60	'61
St. Mary's College		'61	'65
San Francisco State		'65	'66
St. Liz - teacher		'66	'72
Maybeck High		'72	'73

PUPILS to whom this textbook is issued must not write on any page
or mark any part of it in any way, consumable textbooks excepted.

1. Teachers should see that the pupil's name is clearly written in ink in the spaces above in every book issued.
2. The following terms should be used in recording the condition of the book: New; Good; Fair; Poor; Bad.

MINDWORKER® MAYBECK

Paul August

MINDWORKER PRODUCTIONS, LLC
NEVADA CITY, CALIFORNIA

Mindworker Productions, LLC
208 Providence Mine Road
Bell Tower, 223
Nevada City, CA
(510) 928-5750
www.mindworker.net

MINDWORKER ® is a registered trademark. (MW) ™ is a logo in anticipation of a trademark.

Ordering Information: Special discounts are available on quantity purchases by corporations, associations, and others. For details, contact the "Special Sales Department" at the address above.

MINDWORKER: MAYBECK/ Paul August. -- 1st ed.
ISBN 978-0-9904766-7-2
Library of Congress Control Number: 2014916716

All footnotes are now endnotes, and are at the end of the book.

Cover illustration: Susan Mathews, Maybeck School teacher
Interior & cover design: Ruth Schwartz, thewonderlady.com
Printed in the U. S. A.

MINDWORKER®

Mind'work'er [mynd wurk'er] *noun*: 1) A teacher who values truth, caring and helping students above bureaucrats, school boards and power mongers at school sites; 2) Inner-city teachers who cope with stoners, gangstas, and abused students from broken homes; 3) Teachers who defend students' rights and work long hours for low pay and little recognition; 4) Teachers who provide instructions, directions, information, and knowledge, in addition to caring for the students' emotional, psychological and physical well-being.

Note: This word is a self-designation. Not all teachers are Mindworkers but all Mindworkers are teachers.

Table of Contents

Introduction

ONE PURPOSE OF THIS BOOK is to help eradicate the antiquated cliché: "Those who can, do. Those who can't, teach."

Mindworkers today face life and death situations in their classrooms. Abused children. Missing parents. Drugs and alcohol. The days when teachers could work fewer hours and have summers free are long gone. Today's mindworker struggles to maintain medical benefits, a decent salary and a reasonable retirement for his or her family. Sadly, when my college-bound students see the way their inner-city teachers are treated by administrators, troublemakers, and a few parents, they delete teaching as a career option.

Here's the origin of "mindworker." I attended the annual convention of the National Education Association in Washington D.C., in 1980, to receive the Hilda Maehling

Fellowship to produce an album of teacher songs. All the state delegations had slogans, banners, or signs to represent teachers from their state. The Pennsylvania teachers were the most impressive. They proclaimed in bold letters: United Mind Workers. Their nomenclature inspired my fellowship project. I titled the main song and the album: *Mindworker.*

Mindworker: Maybeck is the first in the series of five books about my teaching life. In this first part, we got fired from a Catholic school so made a bold move in 1972. Have you, my dear reader, ever read a story about teachers who try to start their own school? It always begins with a lot of promise, potential, and possibilities. Then it just fizzles out. This is about the inception of a school that began a journey to success. Unlike other start-ups, however, this story continues in the second book of the *Mindworker* series.

The writing of this book has a history of its own. I wrote the first draft of this book over 40 years ago. It's been revised, transformed into fiction, converted back to nonfiction, and now it's part of my fictionalized autobiography. It's based on actual events but "fictionalized" because—to paraphrase Sarah Silverman, an up-and-coming comedienne—many names have been changed so I don't hurt anyone's feelings or get sued.

These pages also reflect how events influenced my original songs. A few of my lyrics from selected songs make that connection. Almost all of the dialogue is accurate but the characters are composites. I feel uneasy about quoting real people, dead or alive, when their words could be embarrassing. Many conversations were not intended for publication. Most of the actions, behaviors and events, however, have been well documented or have witnesses. The sequence of events has been modified to accommodate the flow of the story. If this book was a film it would be a docudrama.

The manuscript spent decades in storage. I'd revise it at times, attend writing classes, work with a writing coach and eventually send it to publishers and get rejection slips. They considered this book to be only regional, merely a local story. After one freelance editor worked on an early manuscript, I drove to Los Angeles and brought my work with me. In Huntington Beach, someone broke into the trunk of my Toyota and stole my new carrying case with the revised manuscript. There was no copy of that edited work but a previous version still existed. At that point, since the book contained criticisms of Catholic nuns and priests, I wondered if God was on their side. *Bad omen*, I thought. *This book may never be published.*

Around 1988, I gave up and put the manuscript on my retirement shelf to revise it later. By retirement in 2004, I was tired of *Mindworker* and didn't want to relive my past. I still had a future full of fresh ideas and monthly newspaper writing for immediate gratification. We moved to the Sierra foothills where I fell in love with Mother Nature by day, and sang my original songs in coffee houses by night. One evening, around 2010, I stumbled across an old 1984 manuscript revision. It was much better than I remembered it to be. Also, back then, there were no such things as eBooks and print-on-demand. Now, no more rejections from agents, editors, or publishers. I'd do it myself.

I began to resurrect the manuscript, searching my storage bins and sometimes finding only carbons. Before the advent of my first Mac SE II, all my writing was done on typewriter paper. Much of this dusty paperwork was re-typed into the computer by Kristi August, my oldest daughter, who helped me fix it and make it flow.

Then came a significant realization. Several teachers who inspired composite characters recently died. This was the ultimate deadline: a death line. I'm compelled to give my gratitude to those who inspired this story but never lived to read it. I realized my colleagues were dying and they had no way to refute, accept or validate this account.

That motivated me to finish this book before I joined them.

This gave me a new sense of urgency. The story expanded from there. Another event shaped these pages. On the eve of sending this final work to press, I found the first half of another version of this manuscript edited in pencil and assumed those changes had been incorporated, over the years, into my final version. I checked and found none of those valuable edits. So, I made those last minute changes, which were suggested by Bill Chapman, professor of journalism at San Francisco State, thirty years ago.

Don't expect to find a bunch of educational polysyllabic poppycock or pedantically appropriate pontifications here. I prefer KISS—Keep It Simple and Short. Oscar Wilde once said, "The difference between literature and journalism is that journalism is unreadable and literature is unread." Let's hope this is readable. It was worth writing. You decide if it's worth reading.

Paul August, Mindworker, 2015

Cast of Characters

Paul August: Me. I tell the story of how I returned to teach in the same school I attended as a teenager.

Stan Cardinet: History Department chairman and resident radical at St. Liz, a Catholic school in Oakland.

Jim Kelly: Math and science wiz who uses a search for UFOs as a way to motivate students.

Jack Radisch: A former football coach who takes law school classes at night and tells the students too much about their rights.

Father Edward: The principal priest who hired me and enjoyed his role.

Muriel August: My wife and mother to our three children who joined me on the picket line.

Gil Dixon: The lay principal who takes over from Father Edward.

George Baljevich: Also a former St. Liz student, he taught at St. Liz, left to coach football elsewhere, but has since returned.

Sister Marie: Mother Superior of the nuns' convent and one of my favorite teachers when I was a student.

Mike Santos: A new "hippie" style teacher who resists the status quo.

Jorge Stokes: The union rep who helped us organize less than half the teachers at St. Liz.

Father Farley: The apologetic vice-principal to Dixon.

Sister Clem: An outspoken nun who resisted the lay teacher's union.

Sister St. Francis: A gentle, but not intellectually gifted, nun.

Sister St. John the Baptist: A cold, outspoken, and opinionated nun.

Father Bart: A frustrated little guy with an apparently racist soul.

Mrs. Presho: The leader of the parents who supported the "radical" teachers and mother of the Politeo sisters.

Father Bill O'Donnell: An activist catholic priest with the flatland fathers.

Lisa Politeo: Student activist.

Betty Board: School board president and respected community activist.

Bob Howard: Baseball coach, teacher, and union supporter.

Marge Hardy: St. Liz bookkeeper and respected staff member; friendly, helpful and inspiring.

Martha Dunwell: St. Liz graduate and girl's PE teacher who supported the administration.

Bud Johnson: School counselor and another St. Liz grad who lost his job.

The Bishop: Spiritual and business leader of the Diocese of Oakland.

Dallas Williams: The first female black teacher at St. Liz. She was fired with us.

Father Boomer: Drama teacher and advisor to the principal who supported the administration.

Curt Levinson: English department chairman who supported the teachers.

Dave Kinstle: The conscientious objector to the Vietnam War who came to Maybeck as a volunteer teacher for two years then became an innovative, Maybeckian trailblazer.

Stuart Haynes: After graduating from U. C. Berkeley, he joined us in creating Maybeck High.

"With trepidation..."

The Ancestors

When my mom was only six months old, the San Francisco police found her mother—my grandmother—next to her crib dead, with a bullet in her chest and a gun next to her body. The cops called it suicide. My mother's father, an abusive alcoholic, drank himself to death six months later in the summer of 1913. So, I never knew my maternal grandparents, Wilson and Aida Lyons.

My mother, Kathleen Lyons, had one older sister, Aida, and four older brothers: Bill, Bud, Harry, and George. These orphans were rescued by my great aunt, Elizabeth B. Goodman, always known as "Goody," who took all six children into her home in San Leandro and raised them.

On my father's side, my great-grandfather boarded an English whaling ship off the coast of the Azores around 1860.

He spoke Portuguese, not English. Since he came aboard during the month of August, the English sailors called him "August," which is how I got my family name. The original name was Bixco. August got into a conflict with the first mate who threatened to kill him. Later, my dad's grandpa took a club from the ship's deck and killed the first mate while he was sleeping. If it were reversed, I wouldn't exist today.

Joseph August sailed for seven years and came around the horn to San Francisco. His son, William August, married Marianna Crabbe, the daughter of a South Bay businessman. The August five-acre cherry orchard and farm can be traced back to the Peralta family, who obtained it in a land grant directly from the King of Spain. My dad inherited three-forth of an acre and I grew up on that royal soil.

My Catholic Childhood

With trepidation and my ancestor's legacy of murder and suicide, I entered this world five days after the Japanese attacked Pearl Harbor to bring us WWII: Dec. 12, 1941. One of the nurses who cared for me in the East Oakland Hospital liked my Irish head of red hair because it reminded her of her missing son who was on the battleship Arizona that sank at Pearl with most of the crew. If I believed in reincarnation, then in a previous life I was that redheaded sailor.

My mother self-described herself as jolly but bossy. She had an outgoing Irish demeanor, a dazzling smile, and twinkling eyes with red hair and brown eyes. As the youngest of the rescued brood, she was a little spoiled but loved to be the center of attention, singing, practicing the piano, and playing the church organ (with errors) at Mass on Sundays when the regular organist couldn't make it. She liked to write letters to the editor and put religious words to her own music on the piano, such as the prayer of St. Francis, which she played frequently. Her favorite pop song was the Irving Berlin classic, "What'll I Do," which she played obsessively. She dreaded housework. She'd mop the kitchen floor, throw down old newspapers to keep it clean but never picked up the papers until the next mopping. My friends laughed about our kitchen being always littered with newspapers but I thought it was normal.

Mom, a good Catholic, married a "fallen-away" Catholic, Clement "Clem" August, a Portuguese part-time farmer and blue-collar wage earner. He bundled newspapers at the Oakland Tribune. Dad was born on the San Leandro farm and Grandma gave him the land where he built our three-bedroom home and maintained his farm with a multitude of fruit trees and vegetables. He was a hot-and-cold type guy. He could be generous, giving and kind, to a fault. He always gave away tons of tomatoes, flowers, melons and apples, even pumpkins. We picked and sold cherries to pay for the taxes so he could keep the farm. If Mom told me, "Wait 'til your father gets home," I sometimes got a strap to my ass for my misbehavior, but not often.

My first jobs were helping my Dad on the farm. I picked cherries and went to market with Dad who sold them for three cents a pound. I trimmed dead boysenberry vines in autumn and sold corn for 35 cents a dozen during the summer. In later life, I wrote a song memorializing my Dad's mini-farm called "**Country Boy, City Blues:**"

*Dad grew an apple tree out by the boysen-
    berries.*
*Red, green, yellow apples, all from the same
    tree.*
*Even though Dad was a high school drop-
    out,[1]*
*Folks from the University came to Dad to
    see,*
*And study his farm, and learn about his
    magic apple tree.*

The parish priests had allowed my Catholic mother to marry my non-Catholic Dad—a "mixed marriage"—on one condition: send the children to Catholic schools. So, they preordained my Catholic schooling for me and my sister, Patricia Ann. When I was baptized, the pastor put my name on the waiting list of Saint Mary's, a brick elementary school in San Leandro, a suburb on the south side of Oakland. I entered the second grade there.

My first day led to trouble. I dropped my orange peels on the playground, just as we did in the first grade of public school. The other boys and girls at my new Catholic school warned me. "You're not supposed to drop any peels on the ground." Sure enough, Sister Mary Yardmonitor caught me and I began my first of many after-school sessions picking up trash in the yard.

After spending my first grade in a public school, I wasn't up to second grade level. When the nun put math problems on the chalkboard, I simply copied the numbers. I didn't know how to add or subtract. They put me back in first grade.

Throughout these early years, the nuns usually found me guilty of minor mischief. My third grade nun caught me in the fourth grade yard and ordered me to empty my pockets while a crowd of classmates gathered to watch. Out came a handful of dreaded, illegal firecrackers. The nun gasped, as if they were sticks of dynamite. A batch of wooden matches came out of my other pocket.

"My goodness," the old nun murmured. "He has enough matches there to burn down the school."

But even worse, I dropped a toy silver bullet, a prize from a penny gumball machine. The old nun thought it was real. Her eyes widened. She had a real thug on her hands. Only Sister Mary Principal could handle this. The young spectators, in their uniform of maroon sweaters and gray pants or skirts, expected that the nuns would expel me for potential arson and ammunition activity.

Fortunately, my godmother, Goody, who paid my Catholic tuition, commanded great respect from the church. Her daughter, the vice-president of an Oakland branch of the Bank of America, a generous donor to the second collection, had financial clout. I would have been gone, but the nuns "had mercy on me." After a brief suspension, they put me on a year's probation.

As a kid, I often stayed after school to play football or other sports on the playground. I'd also go over to the Boy's Club across the street to play pool, basketball, or make plastic crafts. I didn't like to go home after school because I went in the wrong direction, along the railroad tracks, below the tracks and between the tracks. We had the Western Pacific Railroad to the east of us and the Southern Pacific to the west of us. Friends sometimes came by my country place and we played war-in-the-jungle games in San Leandro Creek and swung on tree ropes like Tarzan.

I had games I played alone. When a southbound freight rumbled over the SP trestle, I ducked under the bridge, walked on the tar-stained planks underneath and held on for dear life as the bridge moaned, creaked, and cracked until I feared it would collapse. Then I'd run back off the bridge to the creek soil and safety. Intellectually, I knew the bridge had been inspected and wouldn't fail, but emotionally I surrendered to my anxiety.

Our family sometimes spent a week's summer vacation at a resort in Guerneville on the Russian River where I swam, caught frogs, and swung into the water from a swing. I also watched as a little girl fell off an inner tube and began to drown. My dad kicked off his shoes, stripped to his underwear and swam like hell to save her life. I imagine she later got married, had children, and grandchildren thanks to my dad's rescue. No one ever thanked him.

On alternate summers, we stayed at the Dew Drop Inn, perched on a cliff above Martin's Beach near Half Moon Bay, south of San Francisco. It had giant waves, a treacherous surf, riptides and undertow. The old cabin belonged to Grandma August's family who let us use it occasionally. The coast guard showed up one Sunday with their long boats, trying to paddle out through the surf to save three folks who capsized about 200 yards off shore. They were never found. I was limited to wading, finding starfish, and playing in the caves at the south end of this dangerous beach. Over many years, the beach slowly eroded and a new beach appeared north of it called Maverick's, a surfer's world-class destination.

My parents never took us more than 100 miles away from the San Francisco Bay Area in any direction. We took the ferry across to Marin County, north of San Francisco, to visit my aunt Aida and Uncle Clayton's apple farm in Sebastopol. More than once, Dad drove us south to Santa Cruz to enjoy the boardwalk games, salt-water taffy, and the scary but thrilling wooden roller coaster rides. Dad drove us through California's Central Valley so we could enjoy a big box of Modesto's free stone peaches, which Mom complained about as she sweated over a hot stove in summer to cook preserves that we enjoyed all winter long.

In school, I made progress in the sixth grade where Sister Teacher was more human. I wrote weekly classroom comics, acted up, and clowned around. My problem with nuns seemed to come and go, depending on their personality.

When I entered the seventh grade, the Catholics changed our school's name from Saint Mary's to Saint Leander's. Our new teaching nun didn't share my sense of humor. She intercepted one of my friendly written messages, which featured a popular phrase by TV star Jackie Gleason: "One of these days, pow! Right in the kisser." She read it, shook her head in disappointment, and solemnly informed the class that, "The kisser is a sacred thing."

By the eighth grade, I had developed a sense of rebellion. I learned how to stoically accept slaps from rulers on the back of my hand and how to use carbons to write, 1,000 times, "I shall not talk in class." I learned excuses for anything short of Christian perfection. The eighth grade Sister Principal asked me to send her a telegram if I ever turned out to be anything other than a bum. She has since left the nunnery and married. This book is my response.

St. Liz High School as a Student

My godmother insisted on sending me to a Catholic high school. I refused to go to nearby Bishop Sheen's because it was considered a school for snobs. They didn't even have a football team. I took the long bus ride through Oakland to St. Liz where I managed to find myself in the usual minor troubles.

When I smuggled an anti-authority editorial into the student newspaper, I was sent to student court. When I contemptuously walked out on my judicial peers, an old priest brought me to an empty classroom, pulled out a leather strap and ordered me to bend over and grab my ankles. Then he belted my ass. Tears rolled down my face, but he kept swinging until I couldn't bend over any more.

"Does it hurt?" he asked.

"Yes," I said.

"Well, I don't feel anything," he laughed and belted me again.

Punishment wasn't always physical. When the guys generally got too rowdy, Father Emery, the principal, called special sessions in the auditorium for only the boys. Emery would describe the misbehavior, call out the name of the culprit, and order him to the front to drop his pants, bend over, and get paddled. One time, though, he called Mundo, a big, easy-going guy: 300 pounds of fun. But when Mundo dropped his pants, the entire placed roared. He had holes in his sagging underwear. The public humiliation was far worse than the paddle spanking he received as each whack echoed in the big gym.

There were lesser, non-physical penalties. When the old social hall across the street was demolished, it came down with a loud crash in the middle of class time. I yelled, "Somebody dropped something." The class all roared with laughter but I stayed after school alone. And at the school assembly, when the snow trip committee said we were going to Heavenly Valley, I yelled, "It sounds like hell." The student body roared. I went to Saturday detention: a two-hour work detail to pick up papers, sweep classrooms and paint school walls. I also spent hours sitting in detention, mindlessly copying rules. This was my introduction to the essence of being a journalist: sit and write.

In all fairness to the nuns and priests, their guidance was often sensitive, individualistic and left a lasting impression. I remembered one class when Sister Marie gave us a brief lecture on manners. She said that it was rude to hold your bread in your hand while you buttered it. I had never heard of this. I always held my bread in my hand to butter it. I felt as though I had been ignorant all my life. From then on, as a kid, I remembered to always put down my bread. As I grew up, I discarded much of that mannerly stuff but, to this day whenever I hold a piece of bread in my hand to butter it, I think of her.

By my senior year, I was on probation again. I decided to get revenge with a more positive tactic. I hit the books with a vengeance to become the only student simultaneously on the honor roll for grades while on the probation list for bad behavior.

In the hall, I approached our principal priest during my senior year. Father Emery Tang shaved his head and looked every bit like the Chinese Korean leader he was. Tough but fair. Intellectual and compassionate. Perceptive and forgiving. He could have been the CEO of a New York corporation. After he quit running schools, he managed a successful media project in Los Angeles for his religious order.

"Look, Father," I said to him. "I made the honor roll." I pointed to the list posted on the glass outside of the school's main office.

"Good, Paul. I knew you could do it." He turned to go in the office.

"But wait, Father. Look at this." I pointed to the other list. "I'm also the only honor roll student in the school who's on probation."

"What?" Father Emery did a double take, laughed, and said, "As of now, you are off probation and I know you'll never be on it again." He was right.

I regarded my Catholic experience as a good primer for a writer, rebel, and abstract thinker. From the first grade and beyond, we discussed spiritualism, mysticism, infinity, eternity, good and evil. Standard Catholic classrooms included a crucifix, rosary beads and rituals like prayers and the sign of the cross: no American flag, no Pledge of Allegiance, no national anthem, no American Dream. It was all very cosmic and impractical. I loved it.

The Gap Year

After high school, some students take a year off to travel, work or kick back for a year before beginning college. I had nowhere to go. I didn't go to college because my parents couldn't afford the Catholic campus where my classmates enrolled.

Paul August
Honor Roll 1; Varsity Track 2; Block S.E. 3, 4; Class Assemblies 1, 2; Junior Jamboree 3; Choral 4; Thuringian 3, 4; Federation 4; Cheerleader 3, 4; School Play 4; Class Teams 2, 3, 4; Federation Talent Show 3; Pep Club 1, 2; Vice-president 3; Organizer 4; Christmas Ball Committee 4.

The yearbook photographer caught me while I was clowning around during the class of 1960 photos. My real graduation picture had an exaggerated caption. I portrayed "The Imaginary Invalid" from Moliere's classic comic farce.

PAUL AUGUST

I was determined to earn enough tuition money in one year to get me started so I could work my way through college. I also needed a higher education to learn more about life than what little I learned in high school or from my working class family. Dad worked at the Oakland Tribune in circulation, bundling newspapers on the third floor. He got me a full-time job in the basement pressroom where, as a "flyboy," I helped my co-workers maneuver giant rolls of blank newsprint into the presses. They came out as the day's newspaper. I came out of the pressroom each day with ringing ears from the cacophony of the presses and coughing up black phlegm from the news ink in the air of the stuffy basement.

I had music in my blood. Dad pounded drums in a marching band as a kid. Mom made me take piano lessons in the 5th grade where I learned the basics, but quit practicing to play flag football as a receiver for our team. Musically, I was raised on Top 40 radio, rhythm and blues, and 45 rpm rock 'n roll records. My uncle chastised me for listening to the "jungle music" of **Little Richard**, **Chuck Berry**, and **Elvis Presley**.

After high school graduation, my classmate Jerry Wall and I decided to promote rock 'n roll dances every Sunday night that summer, at the Eagles' Hall in Castro Valley, a suburb about ten miles southeast of Oakland. They had the prettiest girls around. We broke even the first night. I didn't quit my day job at the Tribune.

Jerry didn't want to continue because we made no money. I wanted to continue because we lost no money. So, I decided to go it alone. The dances were successful because the teen audience followed my main attraction, **Little Jimmy Cicero**, a singing piano player with a drummer, hot guitarist, a bass player who owned a music store and a fan club full of young women.

In September, I expanded to Friday nights. I later opened dances at the Spanish hall in San Leandro where I hired off-duty policemen to patrol the weekly event. I got to know one 31-year-old personable cop as he showed up each week to keep the peace. He was popular with all the kids. Then, one Monday morning, at a newspaper rack, I saw the headline about a San Leandro cop: slain. Officer Fred Haller, the son of the police chief, had been shot seven times as he sat behind the wheel of his patrol car. His gun was in his holster. Friday we were talking. Then he was gone. This was the first person I knew to be killed by gunfire, but not the last.

I stayed out of college that year after high school (1960-61) promoting dances on weekends and working full-time for the Tribune where my dad and uncle worked. The biggest dance I held featured **Jan and Dean** on New Year's Eve of 1961 before they became surfers. Their manager was a guy named Lou Adler who went on to produce the **Mamas and the Papas**, win Grammy awards for Record and Album of the Year, and enter the rock music Hall of Fame. I had a chance to stay in contact with him but I didn't. Something else was more important. I needed to go to college and become the first one in my family to earn a college degree.

Rock 'n roll dance concerts offered fast money in one night. I had cutthroat competition. I hired **Richard Berry**, the writer and original artist of the great party song, **"Louie, Louie,"** to appear at one of my concerts. A competitor, who owned a big Bay Area record store, threatened to stop selling Richard's records if he played in the East Bay for anyone but him.

Richard returned half of my deposit then I never heard from him again. At least I can brag that I got stiffed for $75 by the original **"Louie, Louie"** songwriter. I also expanded dances to Sunnyvale, which would become Silicon Valley, where no one showed up— my first flop. At the armory in Concord, we had too much trouble. Drunks crashed the dance, picked fights and created violence for fun. That night, after the dance, I really got a jolt.

A frightened Filipino janitor came running to me, his eyes wide in terror. "Mr. August. There's a body in the men's room."

I opened the stall. A motionless body knelt forward with the head in the toilet bowl, but not in the water. I reached out and touched him. He groaned.

"He's alive," said the janitor, still upset.

"Yeah. Just passed out drunk," I said. "But I don't need this." As much as I loved music and rock 'n roll, I wasn't cut out to be a moneyman in the entertainment industry. These dances gave me a bitter taste of reality. I stayed on my course to get into college a year late. I wanted to move out of the blue-collar culture and into the professional realm.

In the summer of 1966, I took a Spanish class at U.C. Berkeley to get a taste of the university, and I tried, unsuccessfully, to read Plato's *Dialogues* on my own. I needed a teacher and classmates. In late July, I took a part-time job at St. Mary's and became a temporary janitor. The regular custodians assigned me to washing out garbage cans behind the school cafeteria. This was my initiation to college life.

Saint Mary's College

My former St. Liz classmates knew the admissions officer at Saint Mary's College and convinced him to let me in on condition that I maintain a "C" average. I began as an outcast—out-of-place with a low rider '50 Merc and a leave-me-alone attitude. Having been held back in the first grade and then taking a gap year, I was almost 20 years old and I felt out of place with my 17-year-old preppie freshmen classmates. I had been successfully self-employed and made enough to cover the tuition for the first couple of years. I hung out with the sophomores and took extra classes to catch up with my classmates. That heavy schedule only lasted a year before I accepted my fate with the class of '65. At Saint Mary's College, in Moraga, a small town about 20 miles east of Oakland, other students showed me how to play folk guitar and blues piano. I wrote songs, learned rock guitar and organized a surfing band in my senior year, The Tappa Keggmen. Tap a keg of beer and we'd perform at dances for all the beer we could drink. I wanted to be a rock 'n roll star, like the Beatles, not a fringe character in the music business. My band played, and I sang, **"Twist and Shout"** at a bowling alley near Saint Mary's College for 13 straight hours. We still didn't break the world's record supposedly held by Tibetan monks who started chanting and singing around 1954 and never stopped.

I worked my way through college doing odd jobs: pulling weeds from ice plants in the nearby luxury homes, building cement birdbaths, delivering baskets of California fruit at Christmas for Mission Pak, and filling in as a fry cook at T-Bones, a fast food joint near campus. I also worked in the college cafeteria, as a server and dishwasher, and by my last year on campus I ran out of money for room and board so I slept in the attic of St. Augustine's dorm and arranged to work at the cafeteria morning, noon and night for food. In addition, I slowly slipped into debt with student loans.

One summer I worked at Simmons Mattress Factory in San Francisco. I almost got crushed when a bunch of metal tables, leaning against the wall, fell over on me. A big, burly black guy caught the tables and saved my ass. The summer of my junior year, I spent time in South Lake Tahoe making change for slot machine players at Harrah's. At night, I strummed my electric guitar and sang the most popular song of summer, the **Rolling Stones's "Satisfaction."** I was the hit of the parties, which continued every night. During one surrealistic week, my ex-military roommates and I watched Watts burn on live TV. I couldn't believe my eyes. We were watching from a Tahoe paradise while rioters burned parts of LA.

My experiences at Saint Mary's paralleled significant incidents in American history. In November 1960, I took my first and only job with the national media. NBC-TV hired a bunch of college kids to do exit polls after people voted in the Kennedy vs. Nixon election. I was one of them. In October 1962, I watched JFK on TV along with a crowd of students in the De La Salle dorm lobby. It was the Cuban Missile Crisis. The next day, I stopped by the chapel to say a prayer to Saint Anne that no atomic bombs detonate in America.[2] The small church was packed. Everyone was scared. This is the closest we ever got to nuclear war.

On Nov. 22, 1963, as I walked out of Dante Hall and headed back to my dorm, a student coming to class yelled, "Hey, somebody shot Kennedy in the head." I knew JFK was in Dallas. I entered the dorm lobby and turned on the TV. Walter Cronkite had it covered. The word spread about the TV and the room filled. I had a part-time job and I needed to get to T-Bones in Rheem, just over the hill. I knew I'd be late, but I had to know what happened to JFK. When Cronkite announced his death, I sat there stunned and felt tears rolling down my face before I left for work.

As a feature and editorial writer for the Collegian, the campus newspaper, I once got accused by the Dean of Studies for plagiarism because I used some obvious quotes from T. S. Elliot. In our discussion, I mentioned that my editor didn't object and, "even T.S. Elliot had an editor—Ezra Pounds." He softened when he realized I knew what I was doing.

Coming from a working class background, I learned more about the great American mainstream culture from my classmates and roomies than I did from any books. As I was shaving with my electric shaver one morning, a guy going down the hall came in and couldn't believe what I was doing. He came back with a razor and literally taught me how to shave: "Feel the warm water. Now the smooth creamy foam. The close thin blade so close to the skin." My father always lathered up and used a razor but I always thought it was old fashioned. My classmate showed me it wasn't.

The same preppie classmate dropped in while I was out on the deck reading, facing a wall of green trees and grasses on the western slope. "Whoa. Look at that. All those incredible colors," he said.

I knew he was an art major but I didn't understand. "What colors? It's all green."

"No," he replied. "Infinite shades of green. Look at those redwoods. Dark green. The oaks. Lighter green." He gave up naming the trees and merely pointed: "Yellow green. There. Brown green. Look, dark green deep in the tree with a yellow tint around the outside."

And suddenly it all came into my vision. I saw the different shades of green. It was truly an epiphany. After living on my dad's farm for 19 years, I thought of the palm trees, the cherry trees, the tulips, the artichokes and the boysenberry vines. Now I could see them differently. Amazing.

For a while, after I junked my '50 Merc, I had a '51 Chevy with a rip in the convertible roof that tore off when it got hit with a gust of wind on a cold winter night on the Nimitz freeway in Oakland. I bought a 250cc Yamaha motorcycle and buzzed up to Tahoe that summer only to be greeted by a snowstorm in June coming into the Tahoe Basin from Donner Summit. I learned to check weather reports before embarking on any long journey.

Politically, I sympathized with the liberals and the ban-the-bomb protests on campus, but I still maintained an individuality in my beliefs. I refused to picket against the great conservative orator, William F. Buckley, Jr., who came to speak on campus. I opposed censorship of any kind and I supported freedom of speech for any speaker. Buckley was one of the greatest, even if I disagreed with everything he said.

Saint Mary's seminars helped me bring together the Catholic experience in my mind. I had seen too many of my friends leave Catholic high schools with an "either/or" mentality. Either they were blind faith Catholics or they became bitter atheists who complained that they had been "brainwashed." By the end of my four beer-drinking years, I became temporarily converted into a rah-rah cheerleader and wannabe intellectual with a surfing band on weekends. College can sure screw up a guy. It took me years to get back to my rock 'n roll wage-earner roots. I came to understand the Catholic Christian tradition as a logical extension of Greek mythology and philosophy. It all made sense to me, within a historical context.[3]

The College Graduate

After I graduated from Saint Mary's College in June with a degree in English literature, I headed for Tahoe on my motorcycle where I trained for, and became, a dice dealer in the casino for the summer. That's where I met Muriel, the beautiful brunette Keno girl with the Tahoe tan that lit up her dazzling blue eyes. We met where we worked, at Harrah's in South Lake Tahoe at the orange bar.[4]

Muriel wasn't one of those Tahoe party dolls. She lived in the Sierra[5] foothills near Nevada City, California, 50 miles northwest of Tahoe. She loved the outdoors, adored animals, and had a British two-seater MGA sports car. We spent time together all summer and we both knew that summer would end but our relationship would not. As summer wrapped up, I left for San Francisco to attend graduate school in English at San Francisco State. I lived in a Sunset District garage loosely converted to student housing. The commute to Muriel in the Sierras was a 300 mile round trip.

On October 30, 1965, Muriel and I got married in St. John's Catholic Church in North San Juan, Muriel's hometown (population 125) in the gold country of the Sierras. She came back to the Bay Area with me, to an apartment I found in Colma, a suburb of San Francisco where there were more dead people (two million) than live ones (two thousand). After the 1906 earthquake, when rebuilding the City, civil officials decided to move all cemeteries out of San Francisco to make more space for living souls.

We both came from country backgrounds and we felt like sardines in an apartment with people living above us, below us, on both sides, across from us, and up and down the hall. Muriel missed being surrounded by trees. She found a job at Macy's in Stonestown, a San Francisco upscale mall. I continued at San Francisco State with my classes in literature and clinical psychology. I decided to apply for an MA in Psych but their policy dictated that I spend too many hours each week in an undergrad psych lab studying fat lab rats. I declined, but the experience inspired one of my original psycho songs:

Get a fat lab rat and feed him LSD
Put this fat lab rat in a big rat maze.
Slip those electrodes into his cranium.
Watch for synaptic sparks.

And when I finished research on that fat lab
*   rat,*

MINDWORKER: MAYBECK

I didn't know much about myself or anybody else.
But I collected a massive amount of data,
Irrefutable, statistical, psychological conclusions,
About fat lab rats.

Back in 1964, during the Gulf of Tonkin incident, while I was at Tahoe, I realized that I might be drafted for Vietnam. If so, I intended to go to Officer's Candidate's School and enlist as a first Lieutenant. I didn't like being told what to do, but I savored giving orders to others. The war grew by the time I got to San Francisco State in 1965. I was influenced by the campus protests and speakers against the Vietnam War. I became an anti-war proponent because the U.S. supported a dictator against the people's uprising. I had a deferment as a college student. That would change if I needed a job.

That Christmas, we visited my mom and dad and my sister Pat in San Leandro. Dad was jaundiced. He had an aversion to doctors because he had adult onset diabetes, varicose veins, a detached retina from being hit by a car, spinach caught in his esophagus and high blood pressure—more than his fair share of ailments. He said he would go to the doctor after the holidays.

Meanwhile, Muriel became pregnant and we had to figure out what to do next. Before we could, we learned that dad's exploratory operation found cancer from the colon had spread to the pancreas and there was nothing they could do. Back when he was diagnosed with diabetes, he quit sugar and used a sweetener substitute: saccharine. He used excessive amounts of these pills that contained cyclamates, later found to be carcinogenic. The cure may have killed him. He died at the end of January 1966 at age 61. He had paid into Social Security from its inception in 1937 but never lived to collect a cent. My mother, however, received a widow's benefit that would be her only minimal income for as long as she lived.

I dropped out of S.F. State at the end of January so we could move to a duplex in Oakland where I could be closer to helping my mom and sister handle my dad's farm. Now I needed a job.

The job market for rock 'n roll stars was a little tight, but I landed a position with Bob Chatton, a local independent record distributor, as a song promoter. I knew him from 1960 when I produced **Jimmy Cicero's** first record, "**Sherry**," which didn't sell, but I learned how the entertainment business worked. The job was easy enough. I buzzed around all the major San Francisco radio stations in Muriel's little red MGA sports car delivering new 45-rpm records to deejays, pushing indie labels like Chess, ABC, Atlantic, Dot and a few more. I promoted artists like **Ray Charles**, **Sam and Dave**, **Dave Brubeck**, **Pat Boone**, **Percy Sledge** and dozens of others. But much of it was an illusion.

At radio KSOL, "The voice of the black community," I entered and saw a mild-mannered white guy at the studio controls with turntables spinning. "I'd like to see **Dr. Soul**," I said.

"Yeah," said the blonde-haired white guy with a trimmed beard. "Just a minute."

I assumed this was the engineer and he'd introduce me to **Dr. Soul**. Then he flipped a switch, leaned forward and growled into an overhead microphone: "Whoa, baby. 'Dis be doctor soul. De voice of de black community, brothers and sistas. Hold on. I'm gonna give y'all a soul injection. Ooooo ooooo eeeeeee!"

Then he turned to me and said, in a white voice: "Yes sir. How can I help you?"

I was speechless. This white guy, using an imitation black voice, pretended to be the voice of the black community? He was the most popular deejay among all the rhythm and blues deejays in the Bay Area.

KSOL represented the best and worst of the San Francisco music scene. During one visit, I talked with one slender, young deejay who played an old upright studio piano and composed songs he sang over the air between records. With his big afro and his wide smile, wearing knickerbockers and dancing, **Sly (and the Family) Stone** went on to become one of the most accomplished artists of that era. Unfortunately, he fell into the drug pit and never recovered sobriety.

Another deejay at KSOL refused to listen to a great new song by a young artist. That day, when I called the New York record executive with this bad news, he said, uncharacteristically, that he would contact the deejay directly. After that call, the deejay called me immediately. He wanted another copy of the record he'd tossed. I made another trip from Oakland to San Francisco. He listened to one second of it and called it a hit, instantly putting it on the air. I suspected that the bribe (payola) was on.[6]

And when those New York suits tried to give me under-the-table bonus money to push their product above the other indie labels, I told the owner, Bob Chatton.

"If you didn't tell me, I would have fired you," he said.

"I know. That's why I told you," I replied.

The big hot 'n heavy Top 40 San Francisco rock station, KFRC, was controlled by an ex-deejay who floated around his Beverly Hills swimming pool, listening to his chain of national music programs. Record executives in Los Angeles, Nashville, and New York either wanted to grease my palm with payola when I promoted a hit or to chew out my ass if I didn't get airplay for their jive tunes. This was not the path to rock 'n roll success. It was too crass for my '60s-styled "enlightened consciousness." I wanted a meaningful career or at least a day job with more integrity.

Chapter 1

"Subject matter isn't..."

I APPLIED TO TEACH at only one high school—my alma mater where, as a sophomore, my highest grade was a "C." Father Edward twirled the white, knotted rope that dangled from his brown robes as he ushered me into his principal's office. "Paul," he said. "We need a teacher for American history."

I told him, "My college degrees are in English literature and psychology."

"Subject matter isn't too important in Catholic schools," said the principal priest. "It's the commitment that counts."

I didn't even have a teaching credential, so I couldn't apply to the public schools. St. Liz, my Catholic high school in the flatlands of Oakland, seemed to be an inviting option.

"The job is yours, if you want it," said Father Edward lowering his huge frame into the cushioned armchair behind his desk. He raised his bushy eyebrows and spun the rope at his side in anticipation of my reply.

"I'm not sure I really want to be a teacher," I said.

"Why don't you try teaching here for a year or two, until you decide what to do with your life," suggested Father Edward, tactfully.

I needed a day job, so I accepted the position and a big cut in pay.

Going back to teach at my old high school was like regressing to a classroom womb. It was comfortable because I knew the system, the neighborhood, and the spirit of the school intimately. I knew the routine, the philosophy, the campus, and the expectations. It was also uncomfortable because I had to work with nuns who were my former teachers and targets of my adolescent anger and furtive paper airplanes.[7]

Without teaching experience, I struggled through my first year of teaching (1966-67) while taking U. S. History courses at Cal State Hayward at night. I barely stayed one step ahead of my students. By my second year at St. Liz, I was a gung-ho, red-hot young teacher. I organized Friday night summer dances, bringing in "hippie" San Francisco rock groups on the verge of national fame. During the winter, I led ski trips, supervised fund-raising with the sale of the World's Finest Chocolate Bar, and directed "Charlie Brown" skits for assemblies. During the spring parish carnival to raise funds, lower tuition, and keep the school afloat, I shivered in a dunking booth. When Fat Eddy got shot by a rent-a-cop at the parish festival, I wrote it up and got my first freelance article published in *Rolling Stone* Magazine. Freelance writing paid less than teaching. No career change yet.

Students confided in me as an informal counselor. I knew who was on drugs, when the gangs were due to rumble, and how to reconcile a pregnant teenager with her parents. My St. Liz days were filled with bright smiles and talented students.

Muriel and I felt a new responsibility when our first daughter was born—and later came her brother and sister. My Vietnam War draft deferment changed from A-II (married, teacher) to A-III (children). All of our three children were baptized in the nuns' convent at St. Liz. We purchased a big old English row house in the Fruitvale district of Oakland, and I occasionally walked 12 blocks to school. It was all very safe: home, school, priests, nuns, and the security of Father Edward's words: "Paul, we are giving you tenure. You have a job with us as long as St. Liz exists."

About all that was missing at St. Liz was Father Edward's leadership. When the old Franciscan principal raised his cherubic head at a meeting to ask us lay teachers

<u>ROLLING STONE: Sept. 16, 1971</u>

Fat Eddie and
The Rent-A-Cop

Fat Eddie got shot by a rent-a-cop at a church festival in East Oakland. It happened six months after a police squad car was bombed into oblivion at the corner of East 14th Street and Fruitvale Avenue, and five weeks before the blind man killed the kid with the firecrackers.

I'm sitting in the dunking booth waiting for a thrower to hit the target and dump me into a mammoth tub of cold water. This festival inspired my first published article in Rolling Stone: Fat Eddie and The Rent-A-Cop.

what we thought would be a fair salary, we replied, "Parity. The same pay scale as the Oakland Public Schools' teachers get."

Of course, this was an unreasonable demand. Catholic school teachers traditionally are paid 30 percent less than public school teachers because they work in academically-sheltered environments: no behavior problems (kick 'em out), no attendance problems (parents don't pay tuition to let their children cut class), and few academic problems (this kid needs "special attention" so let's dump him on the public schools). When we suggested pay equal to our public school peers, even the more conservative lay teachers gasped in astonishment, not just the principal.

"The church can't afford that," said Herman Gray, one of the conservatives. His balding head, suit-'n-tie and thick glasses went perfectly with his aging attitudes. "St. Liz parish would go broke."

We responded with various euphemisms for "bullshit."

"We know what we need and what we want," said Jack Radisch, a history teacher and defender of individual rights. "Where they get the money is their problem, not ours. The Bishop lives in a mansion in Piedmont. All we want is a decent wage."

Good Father Edward responded with a generous compromise. The parish could not afford the benefits that public school teachers received (medical, dental, vision, annuities, retirement) but he did get us the salary increase. We almost fell over.

"A 30 percent raise without negotiations? We just said we wanted it and they gave it to us!" said an astonished Jim Kelly, a math and science teacher who valued making learning fun.

And that wasn't all. We pushed for, and won, the right to teach a treasury of elective classes. Stan Cardinet, our resident Berkeley intellectual, compared Beethoven to the Beatles and illustrated the life of Joan of Arc with songs from Joan Baez in his humanities course. He also offered a popular course in Nazi Germany. Jack Radisch, who was studying law at night, taught classes that emphasized the legal rights of juveniles.

Kelly, like a mad, happy scientist, organized the Society for Communication with Unidentified Flying Objects (SCUFO). He happened to be from Roswell, New Mexico. Students helped install an observatory with a telescope on the roof of St. Liz to observe the universe on Saturday nights. I introduced a psychology course, with an emphasis on adolescent self-awareness and took over the seniors' marriage (and sex) class from the celibate priests who previously taught it. I often exchanged classes with other married teachers who appeared as guest speakers.

We introduced intersessions[8] for January and June, stopping regular classes to try new experiences. A Spanish teacher rented a bus and drove 25 students to Mexico to spend two weeks. Stan Cardinet took a group by charter flight from San Francisco to Europe. Teachers took P.E. students to Yosemite to camp out. College prep students visited university campuses. Students were making films, writing poetry, attending the ballet and spending whole days with policemen, newscasters, musicians and lawyers.

These were the golden years of St. Liz, a teaching Utopia. But there was trouble in paradise.

Chapter 2

"There are times when..."

DURING MY FIRST FOUR YEARS at St. Liz, Father Edward, a gentle, rather indecisive cherub of a man, enjoyed following fire engines, ambulances and police cars whenever he heard a siren. If a student or a parent died, he would elevate the family tragedy to high drama and blend his roles of principal and priest at the pulpit in funeral oratory he obviously enjoyed delivering.

His blue eyes peered over rimless spectacles. He had a balding head with wisps of grey hair dangling around his ears. Father Edward's smile was natural and easy, but his serious moments always seemed contrived, as if he had to act serious to be serious. Everyone liked Father Edward.

But not everyone liked Gil Dixon, Father Edward's beady-eyed, young vice-principal.

Gil Dixon used computers to figure out things no one wanted or needed to know. He wore plaid sport coats with short-sleeved shirts that exposed his skinny wrists. At faculty meetings, he crossed his legs and exposed shins of pale, hairless skin between his white ankle socks and too-short dark slacks. His usual facial façade was the stern-faced disciplinarian, programmed to follow orders, but when he smiled his infrequent smile, his thin faced transformed into a picket line of teeth. He was a gangling, awkward figure, often unsure of how to react to his immediate surroundings, eyes darting rapidly around in his otherwise expressionless face, as if seeking clues about how to act.

Short, chubby Father Edward and tall, skinny Gil Dixon worked together like a psychological Mutt and Jeff team. Father Edward secretly delegated the more unpleasant tasks to Dixon, who publicly carried out his orders. Then, if the heat got too hot, the loving and merciful principal priest would overrule Dixon in the spirit of Christian charity, brotherly love, and the ecumenical heritage of Pope John. And, of course, Father Edward and Dixon both represented the older, conservative, and religious factions of the faculty as opposed to the young, liberal lay teachers. The writing on the wall came from Father Edward who sent an open letter to the faculty:

MINDWORKER: MAYBECK

Dear Faculty,

Parents do not appreciate faculty members who teach strange or outlandish theories, nor do they appreciate teachers who give the appearance of being, or even siding with, hippies.

There are times when it is better not to teach something than to teach it.

Parents expect, and demand, that our teachers will be clean-cut and neat in appearance. They also expect their children to be taught in an orthodox manner with materials that conform to the normal cultural and social heritage of America. Remember the old adage: "He who pays the fiddler calls the tune."

Edward aimed his verbal darts at us four rabble-rousers. At the bull's eye of the target was Stan Cardinet. One of Stan's favorite lessons, during his history of art class, involved a massive unraveling of blue ticker tape. Entering Room 201, one would find students engulfed in blue paper. Stan stood on top of his teacher's desk dispensing tape. He wore wrinkled slacks, a well-worn jacket, appropriately frayed at the cuffs, and an out-of-style polka-dot tie askew over a blue work shirt buttoned at the collar. Ticker tape lint gathered in his full beard and settled in his shoulder-length blonde hair.

"This is an experience in living art," Stan announced. "We have here the reality of movement, the concept of confinement, a sense of space, the natural inclination for experimentation and the total awareness of the texture of this paper."

Cardinet's depth of academic knowledge balanced his contrived ignorance of the mundane. He knew the music of Mahler, the literature of Goethe, and the art of the Renaissance. But he didn't know anything about the latest TV shows. He'd say he didn't understand why a team would play for hours and then win or lose within seconds. He wouldn't have recognized Dick Clark or known why he should. Stan lived in the abstract, in the intelligentsia, in the Berkeley clouds. Father Edward didn't like that.

Another of the priest's darts hit Jack Radisch, a feisty would-be lawyer who defended the rights of teachers and went too far in teaching the rights of students. Radisch coached football after school and studied law at night. He never really *discussed* anything—he argued everything. He would state what he understood to be your point of view. If you were careless enough to grant him that lever, he would use his facts and rhetoric to demolish you. He talked slowly, but if you tried to break his chain of presentation, he would raise his voice using elongated words and increased volume. For example:

Radisch: "Students have the right to (pause)..."

Opponent: "I don't agree that..."

Radisch: "To pro-tect (loud) them-selves (louder) from un-auth-or-ized ... (loudest)."

When he argued he liked to stand, wearing his dark blue suit, white shirt, and thin tie, all slightly rumpled, as if he had taught all day and studied law all night, which he did. He believed that the law could, "change the hearts and minds of men." He accentuated his points with mild fist blows to the table like a lawyer before the judge of the faculty court. Putting his other hand on his hip, he turned his body slightly, tilting his head as he talked, curling one lip and looking at his adversary with his good left eye because the other strayed at times. Father Edward, a product of the Catholic hierarchy, didn't like Radisch's defense of teacher tactics and student rights.

From Oakland to London: Stan Cardinet and Jack Radisch took 17 students from St. Liz to England during the Easter vacation of 1969. They toured the Tower of London, took a walk along the docks, crossed over London Bridge and visited Fleet Street, according to an article in the *Oakland Tribune*. They did their own fundraising to cover costs.

PAUL AUGUST

I arrived at St. Liz in 1966 and met Stan Cardinet: a blonde-haired, blue-eyed young man. Stan returned from Europe one summer with a beard. The principal wanted him to shave it off. Stan resisted. The rest of us grew beards as a sign of solidarity. The Principal relented. Stan soon became a bearded Berkeley intellectual with long hair, wearing a flower in his lapel. We wore various forms of hairy faces throughout the sixties and beyond.

A third target, Jim Kelly, also fit into the principal's crosshairs. Kelly's thick mutton-chops and beer belly made him look like a young Mark Twain. His physical appearance was consistently careless. He wore a cheap long sleeved light shirt that was too small and only partly tucked into his faded corduroy trousers. His sandy hair was too short over the ears and too long over his eyes. Kelly smoked a smelly cigar and had more expressions and stock phrases than a country politician. He'd lift an eyebrow, lower his head, jut out his chin and twist his open hand, as if throwing an imaginary pitch, summing up the most complex problems in simple terms: "That's a bunch of bunk." or "It's a hurter."

Besides sponsoring SCUFO and taking students to the roof of the school at midnight on Saturdays to scan the universe for flying saucers, Kelly tried to make science fun in other ways.[9] For example, students brought the roses and Kelly dipped them in liquid nitrogen. Then he'd bang the frozen rose against his desk, shattering it. Father Edward was puzzled by such strange and unorthodox approaches to science.

And, of course, I became a target. In my classes we celebrated the feast of the great pumpkin at Halloween and discussed symbolism, allegory, and mythology while distributing pumpkin seeds in candlelight. In psychology, students learned about Freud's Oedipus complex, penis envy, and phallic symbols. Marriage class was always on the brink of scandal. I delicately answered questions like, "Mr. August, what is oral sex?" Father Edward didn't like classes that answered those types of questions.

Jack Radisch, former dean and football coach at St. Liz, returned to teaching students about their rights. He had more fun on a teacher's picket line than relaxing behind an administrator's desk.

Our unorthodox views were tolerated during the years 1966 to 1969. Later, when

Jim Kelly and I enjoy Styrofoam coffee before class. Kelly also went through a hairy metamorphosis.

the school began to experience a shortage of funding, our political positions earned us more opposition, and the tolerance factor went down by several degrees.

Gil Dixon retreated with his computer and came back with this brilliant equation: "Because enrollment is down we must raise the tuition." We mavericks thought the equation should be reversed: "If we lower tuition we will raise the enrollment."

We held a meeting and convinced the rest of the faculty to send Father Edward to the Bishop for help. He did this and reported back to the faculty wearing his most serious mask. He lowered his head. His baby-blue eyes peered over his spectacles as he tucked his arms into his priestly garments and announced: "The Bishop will not guarantee the survival of the school."

Radisch refused to accept defeat. He stood at the back of the library, pounding on a library table to make his points, and presented his case to the faculty-as-jury. "The Bishop builds new schools in the suburbs but refuses to assist our school with 700 inner-city students, almost half of whom are minorities. He has a financial responsibility. He's a businessman. He has to be pressured into helping us. Going in as beggars won't help."

Stan Cardinet agreed and slowly stroked his beard as he suggested, "a march on the Bishop's mansion. As a spiritual leader, he has a moral obligation. One can readily observe that there is more lawn in front of the Bishop's Piedmont mansion than there is on this entire asphalt campus. That is immoral."

"But to march on the Bishop's house— that's his home," conservative Herman Grey said. He sat stiffly upright and his eyes were wider than usual. "I can't believe you would seriously consider such a thing."

"What a farce," said Kelly. He puffed on his cigar, tilted his head, and tossed his fingers toward Grey. "Herman, we don't really have to march. But if we all vote to march, the Bishop will meet with us. I'll guarantee you that."

Father Edward unraveled his shaky arms from his friar robes and raised his trembling hands. "I have done all I can. I now leave this to you. Do as you see fit," he dramatically proclaimed. Then he turned and left the room.

The faculty sat in silence for a few seconds, listening to his wooden sandals clip-clop down the hall and out of the fight. We took that to be Father Edward's tacit approval and, in an unexpected display of unity, even Herman Grey voted to march on the Bishop's house.

The following week Radisch and Stan went before the Piedmont City Council. Piedmont is a small and separate elite city within Oakland's boundaries. It was one of the five richest cities in the United States. Its per capita income ranked with Scarsdale in New York. Naturally, when Radisch stood before the Piedmont City Council and demanded a parade permit to march on the Bishop's home, they refused.

"We arrived there at 7 p.m.," Radisch told the gathered faculty. "They put us last on the agenda. They made us sit and wait until 12:45 a.m.—almost six hours."

I rattled the cages at the Oakland City Hall to get a parade permit to march from St. Liz to Piedmont. They stalled me out and never followed up with me. We set the stage for a confrontation at the border of the Oakland-Piedmont city limits: the poor little minority school students and their teachers vs. the big white bully cops protecting a Catholic Bishop's luxury mansion.

It worked. We got our meeting with the Bishop, but not at his mansion. Bishop Floyd Begin, a grim grey-haired man with sleepy dark eyes behind his black-rimmed glasses, came in late for our appointment at his ornate office overlooking Lake Merritt. He granted us only ten minutes. When he saw Stan's tape recorder rolling, he blew up. "If that's the type of people I'm dealing with," he said as he headed for the door, "then I'm leaving."

Gil Dixon, vice-principal, stuttered and apologized and Stan turned off the recorder. Radisch and I exchanged glances, amused by the Bishop's ploy. But our other faculty representative, Sister Marie, the Dean of Girls, refused to be intimidated by anyone. After the Bishop calmed down, she asked, "Why did you finance a second gym for a suburban Catholic high school, but you won't help to maintain our inner-city classrooms?"

The Bishop replied, "By building a girl's gym, we were able to convert Cardinal High to a co-ed school, take in girls, and increase enrollment. That saved money because we didn't have to build a girl's school. I'm in a terrible financial situation: $2.3 million in bills and only $1.7 million in the bank. That's why I can't help your school."

Radisch stood up, assumed his tilted posture, and bent forward showing his good profile to the Bishop. He pounded the table with his fist. "Bishop, you support the suburbs because they donate more money to your diocese than the inner-city schools. But it was inner-city money that first built your suburban schools. And we know you have money. Your diocese has millions invested in stocks and bonds, and even in mortuaries and restaurants."

By the end of what turned out to be a two-hour meeting, the Bishop agreed to help the St. Liz on a year-by-year basis, giving us $43,000 for next year to repair the heating system in our converted cellar classrooms. But he made sure to let us know that he didn't like the idea of our lay teacher salaries being equal to the public school teachers. His parting shot to us was, "You can't drink champagne on a beer budget." Of course, this was said as he stepped into his Cadillac and his chauffeur prepared to drive him back from his lakeside Oakland offices to his Piedmont mansion.

After we returned to St. Liz with our bone from the Bishop, Father Edward withdrew from faculty meetings and involved himself with puttering around the school. He entrusted Gil Dixon to lead faculty meetings, make announcements and to guide parent committees. The spring term ended on a hopeful note and we all went our various ways during the summer.

Chapter 3

"All those fantastic dances..."

S T. L IZ ON F ACEBOOK (2014): Tère wrote: "Paul August ~ You are the legendary man who is responsible for all of those fantastic dances during the Golden Years. You'll never know how many hundreds of us admire you. Creedence, Santana, Quicksilver, Linda Tillery, Pink Wedge, Sons of Champlain, Loading Zone, Youngbloods, and the Little Princess light show. Paul August could tell us about all of them, along with some wonderful stories behind those magnificent dances!!! How 'bout it, Mr. August?? We cannot ever thank you enough for making our years there so damn unforgettable. Love, Peace, & Happiness My Friend ♥"

Legendary man? Moi?

After my first year of teaching at St. Liz, I needed a summer job. So, I promoted Friday night dances as a fundraiser for the school and a summer job for me. Parents served as chaperones, teachers earned extra cash for helping out, and students looked forward to the dances. I created a summer job for myself that seemed to please everyone.

When Kelly learned that we paid an outside company $50 for light shows, he borrowed the school's audio-visual equipment and his students bombarded the auditorium with high-intensity beams filtered through water and food coloring. Kelly, ever the inventive genius, dunked a wire hoop into soapsuds and pulled up a thin bubble. Then, from the balcony, he reflected a theater spotlight off of the bubble and onto the back screen of the stage. A giant boiling rainbow lasted a few seconds and then burst in a shower of exploding guitar screams, drumbeats and guttural vocals.

While he was principal, good Father Edward enjoyed policing the dances I promoted each summer for St. Liz. He rolled his brown robe sleeves above his elbow, carried a double barreled flashlight and patrolled the parking lot in an old Woodie station wagon armed with two spotlights and a police band radio. During crowded dances, the priest patrolled the inside, chasing gatecrashers, sniffing out marijuana smokers, and blinking his flashlight at horny teenagers making out on the dance floor.

That first year—the summer of 1967—I used local "garage bands" and barely broke even, but made enough on the last two dances of summer to cover my expenses and pay myself a commission. Garage bands were local youth, mostly suburban, who were inspired by The Beatles and other rock, blues, or soul bands. They rehearsed in their parents' garage until they made the big time. Most didn't. The national phenomenon lasted from '63 to '68 when the wannabe rock stars either went to college, got jobs, or were drafted for the Vietnam War.

1968 and '69 were the most successful dance years. My dance committee students went to **Bill Graham's Fillmore West.** They were like talent scouts, and they brought back information on up-and-coming bands who would play local gigs for less than their national rates. My scouts told me about the **Santana Blues Band.** Like many of the bands I used, we hired them just before they were stepping up into the national spotlight. **Carlos Santana** became a Latin music icon and has gone on to win 20 Grammy awards.

Clover, a little country rock band from Marin County, had a lead singer who was undiscovered: **Huey Lewis.** He later placed 19 hits in the top ten, including, **"The**

Power of Love." Another song, **"I Want a New Drug,"** may have been copied as "Ghostbusters." Lewis sued and both parties settled.

A band called **Together** was organized by **Cory Lerios,** who went on to perform with **Pablo Cruz.** They had a couple of top ten records: **"Love Will Find a Way"** and **"Whatcha Gonna Do?"** I can still hear these songs playing all over Lake Tahoe every summer.

When I was at Saint Mary's, my friend John Barreiro and I would go to the Monkey Inn in Berkeley on Tuesday nights to see an impressive rock group called **The Apostles.** We got to know them a bit. When they turned up re-named as **Creedence Clearwater Revival** at Fillmore West, I booked them for St. Liz. **John Fogarty** and friends appeared at our high school just as their first record, **"Suzie Q,"** hit number one in the nation.

During that dance, I talked to two Creedence band members who raved about great new songs coming in from New Orleans. This bayou sound gave these East Bay guys a whole new image. I believe that Fogarty's distinctive vocals and dazzling guitar riffs made that sound. Those songs, like **"Proud Mary,"** would be nothing without his musical style and arrangements.

The Monday after the Creedence dance, a band member called school. "We took Friday night's dance check of $1,500 to the bank but it bounced."

I told him, "This is the most we ever paid anybody. We didn't have enough in the bank because that money is still in the school vault. We haven't deposited it yet."

They said they'd come over to get it.

"Bring a couple of suitcases," I replied. "We got a lot of ones."

When they left school with all that cash, it almost felt like an illegal transaction.

The biggest dance we ever had was **Quicksilver Messenger Service.** Almost 1,000 teens, twice the population of St. Liz, crowded into our auditorium to hear their music, some of which, according to my students, ended up on their "live" album. This band never had a hit record but had a great reputation at Fillmore West for performing live.

After the Quicksilver dance, Father Edward exaggerated a bit when he told a group of parents, "There was so much pot at that dance, I could have made a fortune if I swept up what was on the floor in the corner." I noticed that marijuana, in the late 1960s, mellowed out the troublemakers—no fights. Contrast that to the early '60s when there were bloody fights, during and after many rock dances. As a dance promoter, pot did what I hadn't been able to do several years' earlier: stop the violence.

Contrary to the crowded Quicksilver dance, **Norman Greenbaum** bombed. At the time, he had a number one hit record: **"Spirit in the Sky,"** with a haunting guitar intro. But he never played the Fillmore before appearing at our dance. No one knew about him and we almost lost money on the low-crowd turnout.

The **Youngbloods,** with **Jesse Colin Young**, moved from the east coast to Marin County. Their hit record, **"Get Together"** never got above five on the top ten but eventually sold over a million records. Their lyrics were like an anthem to the peace and love generation: a call to get together and love one another. I was lucky to get them at an affordable price. They lived near Napa in the North Bay and played for less at our school on a night when they had no national booking.

I always liked the **Sons of Champlin,** but they never got the hit record they deserved. **Bill Champlin** became a successful studio musician in L.A. and then spent years with the band, **Chicago.** He resurrected the Sons and kept his band going into the 21st century.

Teens liked the code words in band names. The **Loading Zone,** featuring **Linda Tillery,** alluded to getting loaded on drugs. **Pink Wedge,** a great little psyche-

august 1st · St. Liz. Hi. · 8:00-1:30 · $1.50

April 1970 / KYA Radio Script / The score of the week has to go to the trick pulled off by Paul August, a psych. Teacher at St. Liz High. For a fraction of their usual fee, August landed Norman Greenbaum – for the Friday high school dance. The school opens its doors to all schools, for three bucks a head. By the way, this teacher August is the teacher who once lined up a little group called Creedence Clearwater Revival, and another struggling outfit called Santana, for those dances. With initiative like that, you gotta believe (KYA JINGLE). It's great to be in San Francisco.

delic garage band from Alameda, had a more esoteric allusion to LSD. Then again, one of my favorite garage bands from San Leandro, that included two of our St. Liz students, had an innocuous pun of a name: **the Post Raisin Band.**

> **St. Liz Dances:** These were possible be-
> cause of our proximity to San Francisco
> and Fillmore West during the 60s. Also, a
> dedicated group of students formed the St.
> Liz dance committee. They handled public-
> ity, distributed posters, sold refreshments,
> staffed a coatroom, contacted chaper-
> ones, and handled the lighting and stage
> mechanics. They really ran these dances. I
> booked the bands based on their advice.
> These students deserve more credit than I
> do. Simply put, without them, we would
> have had no dances.

I ran into trouble when I booked **Elvin Bishop** and **Cold Blood** for a concert at the Oakland Theater. Elvin went on the radio and promoted himself as performing at a nonprofit gig in San Francisco on the night of our concert. He played our concert early, then played in The City later that same night at a benefit for a blues guy. It affected our audience attendance. His agents saw nothing wrong with this, ignored my complaint, and got confrontational. It was just a reminder to me to get back to my writing and music and let go of the business end of entertainment.

My primary source of this music came from Bill Graham. He was the first rock promoter I knew of who paid his bands more than union scale.

MINDWORKER: MAYBECK

I tried to blend my rock 'n roll experience with helping students. It didn't always work out. When the Rolling Stones staged their Altamont rock concert (1969) 60 miles east of Oakland, I used my entertainment industry contacts to get jobs for 50 St. Liz students to sell soft drinks. The traffic jammed to a stop near the speedway. We bailed out of our bus and hiked three miles to the concert.

When we arrived, we looked for the seven concession stands. Instead, we found only one confused area with a truck full of cyclamate soft drinks. These carcinogenic sodas, all in the process of being recalled, were not popular. We built a makeshift stand, unloaded the truck and broke up pieces of wood for a fire to cook hot dogs.

By late afternoon, I had a new problem: one guy and two girls on drugs. I remembered that an ambulance was sent to every high school in Oakland one day when a shipment of bad "reds" arrived in the Bay Area. "Reds" are homemade versions of Seconal, a potent sleeping pill. At Altamont, one girl laughed hysterically: mescaline. One guy became depressed: hashish. Another girl simply passed out in the back of a truck: an unknown combination of drugs. We helped two of our strung-out students to the bus. A medic checked our third girl, still unconscious.

"Heart rate's okay," said the medic. "She just has to sleep it off."

By evening, the concert had deteriorated into violence. A cyclist roared through the crowd. A knife fight broke out near the stage but we were so far above and away that the agitated crowd looked like a swarm of ants under the lights. We didn't know, at the time, that a man was being murdered.

Mick Jagger stopped the music and screamed, "What are we fighting for?"

Almost everyone made it back to the bus after the concert ended. I counted heads— one girl missing. I asked the students, "Who saw her last?"

Various replies came from different students: "I think she got a ride with some guys."

"Wasn't she on an acid trip?"

"She ran away from home once before."

"She can take care of herself."

I sent out a scouting party but the students returned. "No sign of her."

The 49 students on the bus were cold and tired. Some were sick. We were already three hours late. Parents worry.

"Come on, let's go Mr. August."

"No," I said. "We can't just pull out and leave this girl stranded 60 miles from home."

"She probably hitchhiked home already."

"Yeah. Don't worry about her. Let's go."

I glanced out again into the dark, empty concert grounds, littered with papers and cans. There was no one out there. It reminded me of the deaf mute student I lost on a ski trip in Tahoe. We sent the ski patrol to find her. She had taken the long route down, in a sudden blizzard, on the last run of the day. On the way home from the snow, after I swerved to miss a boulder on Interstate 80, I decided, no more ski trips. As I walked out to the speedway and searched again for our missing student, I decided, no more student job deals at rock concerts. How do I get myself in these situations? I returned to the bus and looked back into the darkness. Still no student.

"Mr. August, please..."

"Why don't we all just say a prayer and then go?"

"Okay," I said with a sigh. We said the "Hail Mary." Then I nodded to the driver, "Let's go."

The engine started. Diesel fumes drifted through the bus. The driver closed the hissing double doors and unlocked the hand brake. The bus slowly began a U-turn. Its headlights flooded the deserted field.

"Oh, look. There she is in the headlights."

We stopped abruptly. A cheer arose as our lost soul ran toward the bus. Everyone cheered again as she stumbled to her seat. Then a weird thing happened. All 50 teens suddenly became silent. Everyone thought the same thing. We almost left without her but we stopped to pray. The prayer? It worked!

"Hey! Why doesn't somebody say something?"

The weary teenagers burst into laughter as our bus inched its way out of Altamont and back to the flatlands of Oakland. The girl on drugs who had passed out finally awoke, sat up, and got sick in the back of the bus. It smelled terrible. We may have had a miserable trip back, but we all came back. Alive.

Chapter 4

"Black is a skin color..."

SCHOOL YEARS TURN ON A SEPTEMBER to June axis. Classrooms open with a sense of renewal, a fresh start for eager young minds and a new chance for teachers. Everyone bounces about, finding books, learning names and opening reams of paper to crank off purple ditto copies of "How This Class Is Run" and "What You Should Do To Get an A" and "Catholic School Rules and Regulations."

The diligence sustains itself until Thanksgiving, after which students practice holiday songs, tangle tinsel decorations, and write essays on keeping Christ in Christmas. After New Year's, the second semester rolls on at a measured pace and comes to a slow end. Teachers give F's. Students cheat. Parents complain. The year rolls into the nervous pre-Easter crisis season where we're burdened with questions without answers, problems without solutions, and uncertainty about September.

After Easter, school deteriorates. There's an awesome anticipation of summer. School films are booked solid for restless classrooms. Museums and zoos are jammed with field trips. Discipline loosens. Boiling tempers flare into student fights and faculty bickering. School ends in a June whimper of confiscated water guns, empty lockers and trash bins full of knowledge. Summer is freedom, a time for rejuvenation until our cycle begins again next September.

As school began again, I thought about the time the class of '68 invited their favorite teachers to a graduation party. I joined some of our graduates in a poker game. Big Ben, a Mexican student who couldn't write his own address, dealt out low-ball cards. Ben had difficulty telling time and adding or subtracting large numbers in class. He never liked school and never made an effort to learn anything because he was going to be a garbage man like his daddy and make more money than the teachers. He earned a "courtesy" diploma from St. Liz. It was also clear that he didn't have to know how to read to collect garbage.

As the penny bets grew to dollars, Ben wagered quickly, made accurate change and played superb poker. He bluffed us over and over again by playing dumb. His display of math, memory, and betting tactics blew our minds and emptied our wallets. The party got louder and looser. Sally jumped in the swimming pool. Graduates laughed. Teachers kept a poker face.

Then one of the graduates yelled, "Mr. August! Does it make any difference the cops are here?"

"Well, no," I said.

I knew the Oakland Police, some of whom were St. Liz grads. They sometimes changed shifts at our dances. The party music blasted too loudly and too late for the neighbors. The kids turned down the sound.

I also found myself doing informal student counseling because, as the teacher of the only psychology course that I knew of at the high school level at the time, students perceived me as one to confide in about adolescent adjustment problems. One time, a student invited me to a pot party. I politely declined, but I confidentially mentioned the incident to Father Edward to illustrate the good rapport I had with troubled students. Unknown to me, the priest called the weedhound into his office for an FBI-like interrogation. The kid felt betrayed. And rightly so. I had been incredibly naïve. Father Edward suspected me of flirting with narcotics. I learned not to confide in the principal at the cost of losing a kid's trust.

However, I didn't learn enough from my mistakes. Sally Andrews was a tall 17-year-old brunette. One day Sister Marie, the Dean of Girls, asked me to counsel Sally. "She came to me crying," said Sister Marie. "She said she took your psychology class and she wants to talk to you." Sister Marie didn't send Sally to Bud Johnson, the official counselor, because it was well known he couldn't cope with emotional problems as well as he handled academic ones. I, on the other hand, was known to be a sympathetic listener.

Sally also came to me crying, without understanding what was causing her tears. "Mr. August, I feel like dying. I had a terrible dream," she said. "I can't seem to shake it. And I can't stop crying."

"Tell me about the dream," I replied.

"Well, I had these beautiful wings and I was trying to fly but I was suffocating," she said. "In my dream, my head was in my mom's pillow and it was suffocating me."

"How do you feel about your mother?" I asked. That opened the floodgates. More tears, and lots of talk about her relationship with her mom. I used classical dream interpretation to talk about the archetypal clash between the blossoming teen and suffocating parents. Eventually she calmed down and seemed to understand the cause of her anguish.

Later that day, I bumped into Curt Levinson, who was straightening his shelf in the faculty room. Levinson was somewhat out of place at St. Liz. He commuted to Oakland from Sausalito where he lived with his parents. His dad was a retired corporate executive and his mom a socialite. Curt's photo frequently appeared in the social pages of the Chronicle escorting beautiful debutantes to charity balls. He was built like a lifeguard, had a lawyer's moustache and a junior executive's haircut. He always told good stories about recent events, laughed hard, and arrived at the senior ball with a different dazzling woman every year. He knew the best wines, the correct words to say, the right way to act, and the proper manners.

Levinson's only obvious aberration was his teacher's shelf. In the faculty room, all the teachers had large shelves, in addition to their small mailboxes. Curt's shelf was the neatest, most organized area in the entire school. At times, he would be caught unconsciously lining up corners of books, stacking them ever so precisely, nervously tidying up his domain.

"It's only the coffee break and I'm already drained," I told Curt.

"What's happening?" he asked.

"Sister Marie asked me to counsel a student this morning. I used the student's dream as an opening to her feelings," I said.

"That's great," Levinson said. "We're covering symbolism in my literature class. Tell me, how did you interpret her dream?"

"I'd rather not say. It gets very personal and..."

"Oh, come on, August. You don't have to tell me her name. Really. Did you use Freud's phallic symbols?"

"No," I said. He continued to badger me. I finally relented. I described the dream and how I used Eric Fromm's book, *The Forgotten Language*. I used the author's method of leading her to an understanding of the emotions behind the dream. I didn't mention the student's name.

"And keep it confidential," I told Levinson.

Two hours later, at lunchtime, Sally came to me in tears again. This time she knew why she was crying. "I hate you," she screamed. "The whole school knows about my personal life."

"What?" I asked, shocked.

"I hate Mr. Levinson, too. He used the dream I told you about me as an example of dream symbols in his class this morning. He explained to the whole class the dream I had. How could you talk to him about my personal life?"

I felt guilty; I had betrayed a student's confidence. I didn't know Sally had Levinson's class. He didn't know it was Sally's dream. Sally was shattered. Later, when I told him about it, Curt Levinson blushed crimson at his faux pas. It was a mess, and I could only blame my damned naiveté again. Slowly, I managed to rebuild my relationship with Sally, but it was never the same after that. She never fully trusted me again, although I counseled her from time to time.

I began to feel too involved in student life. I needed some distance from the young men and women of St. Liz. Also, I couldn't confide in the principal or the other teachers. No more counseling students. No more buddy-buddy dope raps with the guys. I didn't go to student parties and they stopped inviting me. It was a slow, subconscious withdrawal—simply the way that a young teacher burns out and becomes just another brick in the wall that separates the generations. Or so I thought at the time.

"I have tendered my resignation to the Bishop."

Two weeks before the school opened for the fall semester of 1969-'70, Father Edward announced: "I resign. No series of events or persons brought it about; I've simply done all I can, and my job here is finished. New leadership is needed—someone with different ideas and methods."

With school only days away, the parish school board and Rev. Orville, the pastor of St. Liz's entire parish, had little choice. They did what Father Edward expected them to do and hired Gil Dixon as the first lay principal of a Catholic school in this diocese. Even before school started, the new principal somehow found the money in our bare-bones budget to lease a computer for his office. Change was coming to St. Liz.

When the semester arrived that September, the faculty voted me as their representative to the principal's advisory board, which had some degree of power, and helped the principal make the big decisions at St. Liz. These after-school meetings began to consume my personal life. I sat with the grown-ups, yapping about faculty problems, toying with school finance and inventing new student rules. My students no longer confided in me when they wanted to stop a fight before beginning it. I reluctantly referred crying students to Bud Johnson, the school's only counselor, who spent most of his time changing class schedules, distributing college applications, and collecting letters of recommendation. I lost track of the slang names for narcotics until I didn't know the difference between pink wedge, purple haze, or Panama Red.

Students whom I had previously counseled now gravitated toward Mike Santos, a new teacher from Berkeley who made it his business to know what was happening on the dope, fight, and pregnancy fronts. Santos showed up in September 1970, bushy-haired and bearded, wearing a fringed leather vest and a wide collar shirt, opened to expose his hairy chest. Dixon was clearly puzzled that the former principal, Father Edward, had hired such a character before he left in June. What Dixon didn't know was that Kelly secretly sent his friend Santos to St. Liz for a job. Kelly had directed him to shave, get his hair cut, borrow a suit, and learn how to knot a tie, all of which Santos had done when he applied, but was now forgotten since he'd gotten the job.

Santos's University of California credentials were impeccable: he graduated summa cum laude from the graduate division of the education department. This was the good, upwardly mobile son of a Mexican farmer from Modesto. What no one knew was that the newly hired, clean-cut teacher was an anti-war activist, a free speech advocate, and a protest fighter. At St. Liz, Santos quickly fell in with the radical axis. His black hair blossomed out in a kinky natural. His thick, black beard and small, husky frame made him look a little like Fidel Castro. He wore political buttons like *Free Angela Davis, Make Love Not War,* and *U.S. out of Vietnam*. This blurred the invisible line between student and teacher. His openness earned him trust from the students and distrust from those colleagues who viewed him as a weak link in the mythical united front of teachers and administrators.

This "united" front at St. Liz stiffened as the school population changed to a majority of minorities. For the first time in its history, St. Liz, like many other schools in Oakland, had more minority (Black, Asian and Hispanic) students enrolled than white ones. This situation was not particularly pleasing to the new principal.

Dixon lived in Lafayette. At the time it was a 100 percent white suburb of Oakland where the Third World was still undiscovered. He always smiled as he brought his lunch tray to the faculty table in the cafeteria. During one lunch period I debated his ethnic scholarship policy with him.

"Gil," I said, "Santos told me that when the black students from the University of San Francisco came to you with college scholarships for the black students at St. Liz, you refused the money. Is that true?"

Dixon stopped smiling, gulped down his meat loaf, and the expression drained from his face. He said, "Yes."

"Why?" I asked. My lunch sat on my cafeteria tray. I didn't touch it.

"I can't give out scholarships for only black students. That would be discrimination in reverse," Dixon said. "If someone said, 'Here's scholarships for white students only,' that would be discrimination. So limiting it to black students is discrimination against whites."

"But Gil," I insisted. "St. Liz students can get college scholarships if they are Italian, Irish, Portuguese, or German. Why exclude blacks?"

"Black is skin color, not nationality," he replied.

"That's ridiculous," I said. Dixon's eyes darted around the table, noticing that the usual lunchroom banter had stopped and we were the focus of attention.

"Well," he said, "You're entitled to your opinion." And, as far as he was concerned, that ended the discussion. But I wouldn't give up.

"Then how is a black kid gonna get a scholarship?" I asked. "What nationality is 'black'?"

Dixon simply shoveled another fork full of meatloaf into his mouth and shrugged his shoulders, raising his eyebrows in an I-don't-know gesture. He stopped talking and nothing would make him resume the conversation. No black students received black scholarships that year.

Then, on Martin Luther King Jr.'s birthday, Santos organized an open symposium in the auditorium for students to discuss racism.

One of the black students mentioned: "There is this one prejudiced teacher who calls us Negroes."

"...or just calls us, 'they'."

"One of our brothers couldn't get credit for his story because he used the phrase, 'off the pig.'"

Poor Herman Grey, who was the target of the wrath, turned crimson; the words from the black students motivated him to get up and leave the assembly. The entire event so disturbed the school's equilibrium that Dixon did what he had to do: called an emergency faculty meeting.

Chapter 5

"He carried a loaded .38..."

NORMALLY, FACULTY MEETINGS were dull: long on bullshit and short on substance. Faculty members generally doodled, snoozed, knitted, smoked, daydreamed, corrected papers, read, or amused themselves by enjoying the proceedings as one might enjoy the theater of the absurd: all these "important" people trying to be serious, looking so silly, and spending so much time doing so little.

Lay: In Catholic schools, a teacher or administrator who is not a nun or a priest is considered a lay teacher or a lay principal. In the religious world, the "laity" is every church member who is not part of the clergy.

Today's tempers were boiling. Insurrection. It was the black students. We took our usual places in the library, nuns against the wall, priests in the back, lay teachers along the windows and administrators up front. We sat in a square, facing each other. Dixon called for a prayer. After the prayer, battle began.

Herman Grey, the object of the black students' complaints, asked solemnly to be recognized to speak. He was an English teacher who, year after year, taught the same lessons, used the same books, and gave the same tests in the same courses. His posture was always correct, supported by polished wing-tip shoes, a three-piece suit, solid color tie and white shirt. His oval face had a scrubbed look behind those thick glasses and his receding hairline augmented his decorous attitude.

He allowed himself vices like smuggling a piece of gum into his mouth during class for a cleaner breath or holding a key to the Playboy Club in San Francisco. To get to his San Leandro home, he had to drive his four-door Cadillac through the black section of East Oakland, so he carried a loaded .38 revolver in his glove compartment and he might have been just paranoid enough to use it.

On his desk in class he had a picture of his happy wife and their cute little child. Students claimed he was "uptight," "stuffy," and "snobby." Herman didn't care what students thought. At the meeting, he adjusted the coat to his suit, stretched his neck a little, straightened his tie and peered at the faculty through his thick glasses. "I totally repudiate what those Negro students said about me. That assembly was full of open lies, character assassination, and public disrespect for teachers."

In an equally somber tone, Dixon responded. "It should never have gone this far. I don't know what would have happened if I tried to stop it." As Dixon stood, his lowered head gave his uplifted eyes a look like those of a thin, scrawny bull about to charge a waving red flag. "Therefore, teachers are not to use swear words, like hell or damn. Teachers must report any abusive language. No books containing four letter words are allowed without permission from the principal."

Stan Cardinet reacted: "Frankly, Gil, I don't see the connection between the assembly and your autocratic decrees. I would have hoped that we could profit from some introspection following the concerns voiced by black students."

George Baljevich asked for the floor. George grew up in the neighborhood, graduated from St. Liz, and then taught there for ten years. He quit to coach college basketball but didn't like it, and returned home to St. Liz. He always had a cigar in his hand and a lame joke in his mouth. He wore white tennis shoes, plaid slacks, and a short-sleeved pullover red sweater. George shaved his head completely bald. It shined like a tan billiard ball. His sly smile and thin pointed nose made him look like a worried fox, a resemblance that was heightened during his serious moments by his long, furrowed forehead and bushy eyebrows.

George always categorized everything by numbers before he made his point. "The three most important things in the United States today are the atom bomb, television, and tests." He'd say this before describing the test his class had to take. Many discounted George as a bullshit artist, but no one denied his simple charm.

He pointed out the library window, toward the East Oakland foothills. "There's a change happening in Oakland. It's happening because of three reasons." George held one finger towards the faculty; his eyes narrowed, his smile disappeared and deep lines etched into his tan forehead. "First, the poor black folks in West Oakland are coming over here to East Oakland because of urban development. They've given up. My second point is here in East Oakland. The flatland blacks can see the rich blacks in the hills. That makes for frustration.

"Number three. We have black students here who are affected by what's happening out there. Huey Newton's got guns for the

Black Panthers. There have been riots in public schools. The blacks at this school want to be recognized. They want black history classes. They want black scholarships. They want black teachers. And they want respect."

The meeting left us with the usual results—a lot of talk, no decisions, and bewilderment as to the purpose of these meetings.

Gil Dixon's problems continued. At a student assembly held in the gym, he stood before the microphone and addressed the students in a low authoritarian monotone. "As a new part of our dress code, students will not be allowed to wear tennis shoes to school."

A large "boo" roared from the bleachers, across the basketball court. "Why not?" yelled the students.

Dixon stood motionless, and then lowered his head slightly in his typical bull-like posture, his eyes darted across the student crowd. He folded his pale hands protectively over his crotch before answering. "Because grubby tennis shoes are a distraction, not conducive to learning," he responded.

This, of course, was not a true answer. What he didn't say was that dirty tennis shoes didn't project a good image. So rather than make distinctions between clean and dirty tennis shoes, he banned all tennis shoes. The end-of-school bell rang and the black students began to walk out.[10]

"Stay seated," said Dixon.

The protestors didn't stop.

"No students are allowed to leave an assembly without the principal's permission!" Dixon shouted.

The black walkout had nothing to do with the tennis shoe issue. Months before, at the Martin Luther King Day Symposium, a number of students and faculty left the assembly at the end-of-school bell. They didn't stay because they had after-school jobs, scheduled sports activities, or they just didn't want to stay in school one minute longer than they had to. So, in protest to this, when the end-of-school bell rang at Dixon's assembly, the black protestors walked out.

Later, at an advisory board meeting, Dixon gravely unrolled his computer printouts. The predicted enrollment was so low that Dixon told us we couldn't afford to keep the whole staff. He called on those of us on his advisory board to decide which three non-tenured teachers should lose their jobs, and he suggested that Mike Santos top the chop-list. When the faculty later learned of impeding layoffs, an air of gloom and oppression hovered over St. Liz until Santos sat down and wrote his letter—then all hell broke loose.

MINDWORKER: MAYBECK

In a sweeping, seven-page open letter to principal Dixon, Santos used the rhetoric of the Declaration of Independence, denouncing the "King's prerogative to govern as he pleases." The letter listed grievances, proposed solutions, and subtly threatened open rebellion. Fifteen faculty members signed it, and Dixon again did what he had to do: called another faculty meeting.

Since the letter was addressed to Dixon, the meeting was called to order by Father Jim Farley, Dixon's vice-principal. Father Farley was a thin Franciscan. His brown robes clung to his frame like a gunnysack full of turkey bones. He smiled incessantly, which was particularly annoying at a moment like this. He piled his black wavy hair above his high forehead. With his long nose and thin chin, he bore a striking resemblance to the character in "Archie" comic books named Jughead. He used his oversized hands as a supplicant, to appease people. At the faintest sign of disagreement or criticism, he immediately backed away, holding up his big hands defensively.

He apologized even when he had no reason to because he wanted to clarify himself and bring himself back into good graces. He didn't want to be misunderstood or disliked. So, he wandered the halls with a silly smile, apologizing whenever he could find someone to apologize to. Farley led us in the prayer and then announced, in his own euphemistic way, that we were here to give the letter-writer and his co-conspirators a chance to recant their evil allegations.

Santos began with a high edge to his voice. "Dixon brought the budget to the faculty. Then, when we didn't rubber-stamp it, he said we were only advisory. He presented his own budget to the parish school board. That's not democratic. Now teachers are being laid off."

Sister St. John the Baptist deplored this shotgun style attack on the new principal. She was an odd nun who never talked with anyone socially. She spoke only at faculty or department meetings, or in class. She had a square face that never smiled, except when a priest appeared and then she obsequiously smiled like hell. As with many of the nuns, we never knew what she really thought, what she really believed, or why she was here. Today, she let us know.

"Well, Mr. Santos," the Sister said, with a deadly forward glare in her green eyes, "The principal runs the school, not you or your cronies."

Radisch stood up and beamed his one good eye at Principal Dixon, saying, "You wrote yourself in to have veto power over anything in the school. This flies in the face of all the labor legislation within the last 30 years. We're not your feudal serfs."

Herman Grey came to his principal's rescue. "Does not the principal draw his power from the Bishop and, ultimately, holy mother the church?"

Stan raised his longhaired head, jutted his beard forward, and addressed the nun side of the faculty meeting, "We only have one black female teacher—Dallas Williams. She has been repeatedly called out of class to pacify black students. This is manipulative in nature and it disregards the integrity of both black teacher and student."

"Oh, no," Father Farley said, waving his hands in a stopping motion. "As vice-principal, I often ask students who, on the faculty, they could talk with. Oftentimes a black student asks for our black teacher. It is the student's request, not Mr. Dixon's."

Kelly twitched his fingers in the air, raised an eyebrow, and bent forward with a new issue, "What about this student park fiasco, Gil? The students haven't had a say in it. We have a vacant lot next to school with a promise that it would be a students' park. Hey, why not call it the Principal's Park, eh?" Kelly sat back and chuckled through his muttonchops.

"I removed this matter from the student council because they failed to make any progress," Dixon said slowly, though his eyes blinked rapidly. "I formed a new student park committee."[11]

It went on like that. Santos, Cardinet, Radisch, Kelly and I condemned tyranny, praised the democratic process, and de-

91

nounced the "King" who locked the school, froze finances, squashed students, and manipulated teachers.

Father Farley, Herman Grey, and Sister St. John the Baptist declared their loyalty, defended their principal, and counterattacked the radicals who, they believed, were just trying to save jobs, get pay increases, do less work, and take over the school. The meeting lasted five-and-a-half hours. A mild déjà vu haunted us: another experience where we spent so much time doing so little.

Chapter 6

"SCUFO spent a winter's..."

IXON'S FIRST YEAR AS PRINCIPAL (1970) had begun with a sense of hope. Was he the cure for the financial plague that had been unleashed on St. Liz? The faculty wanted financial stability and an end to the annual question of survival. Stan suggested that we should "lower ourselves to the decadence of other parishes and sponsor bingo games to ensure our existence." Bingo was illegal in California. Radisch researched the legalities and advised us that only a court could decide if our religious, nonprofit bingo game was legal or not. The faculty voted to begin bingo.

Kelly worked with the parents' club, inventing a giant neon bingo board. The legal façade was to be an "Art Show" coupled with a spaghetti dinner. We taped student drawings on the hall walls for art. Parents dished up inedible pasta. The five-dollar donated admission included "free" bingo. It worked. We uncorked a financial bonanza with hundreds of overweight, aging bingo players packing the gym, each trying to win the $1,000 blackout prize.

At last. Temporary relief from financial disaster—"temporary" because we didn't know when the Irish-Catholic Oakland cops would stop looking the other way and close down the success of our smoke-filled Wednesday and Friday night illegal gambling parlor at this little Catholic school.

Gil Dixon declared bingo a success then wanted faculty support to reverse an unfavorable WASC report.[12] The WASC committee (Western Association of Schools and Colleges) evaluates schools. A five-year rating is best. Anything less is symptomatic of a sick school. We were evaluated during our going-to-see-the-Bishop-crisis.

WASC gave St. Liz a three-year probation. It praised the faculty for loyalty to the school, warmth with students, and a dynamic esprit de corps. Its criticisms came in the form of suggestions to relate more to the ethnic community, hire minority teachers and resolve money problems without creating a yearly crisis. The report was a slap in the face to Gil Dixon, who did what he had to do.

That particular faculty meeting was sparsely attended. Some of us were in favor of supporting the negative three-year rating, until Dixon claimed that black students were being hurt by having a second-rate school. In a conciliatory gesture, we supported the principal's appeal. The school eventually received the full five-year unconditional award.

The "radical" innovative teaching continued under Dixon's first year. By now, unusual academic events were commonplace, like Kelly's celestial collision. SCUFO spent a winter's night on the school roof observing a celestial traffic jam, using their eight-inch telescope to view four planets converge in the constellation Sagittarius. Sister Clem supplied adult chaperones with massive amounts of coffee (generously spiked with Irish whiskey).

Sister Clementine, or Clem, as she preferred to be called, was a husky person, big-boned and slow moving. She whistled for your attention, not a thin lip-pucker kind of whistle, but a curled-lip whistle, the kind a hard-hat construction foreman uses to call his crew over the roar of backhoes. She used her facial expressions as a repertoire of her emotions. Surprise: eyebrows up, eyes wide, lips in a circle. Skepticism: complete deadpan. Anger: eyes cold, mouth frowns, jowls down. Disgust: eyes rolling followed by looking away and eventually throwing up her hands and leaving.

Clem was an unusual nun, and like one of the guys: a rock 'em sock 'em nun who's favorite greeting to male teachers and favored students was a tight-fisted punch on the arm—"How 'ya doing, man?" She drank too much, laughed too loud, didn't give a damn, cussed like hell, and lumbered around school twirling her heavy silver crucifix at the end of her black wooden rosary beads exactly like a cop with a Billy club on a chain.[13]

For uncounted years, the good sisters had worn "penguin" outfits and Sister Clem clearly loved the concealment. All you could see was her big face and long hands. Everything else was a mystery. The nuns wore long black habits with white bands around their foreheads. These bands hid the ears and met at a neck covering that looked like the thin towels used in old barbershops to protect men's necks. The nuns' robes fell to their ankles with an additional mantle down the front where the sisters could sneak their hands under their robes to pray the rosary or sit like holy cats, with their paws folded beneath their breasts.

But that year the nuns went modern: fewer robes, more skin. It turned out that Sister Clem had big ears, a chubby neck and a double chin that previously had not been noticeable. She never quite seemed herself after the new outfit revealed her body. She did what she had always done, but with just the slightest hint of hesitation. Sister Clem evaluated Dixon's first year, rolling her eyes in doubt. "Gil started these bingo games, got us a full five-year rating and we still have exciting academic events. But..." she paused, stretched her lips and shook her head. "But I think that trying to fire Mike Santos was a big mistake."[14]

As we moved into our annual spring crisis, Dixon tickled his computers and the printout predicted a drop of enrollment equal to cutting three teachers. The advisory board met to do the dirty work. A crusty typing teacher got cut. No one liked her, so she went easily. Dixon also proposed the axe for old Sister O'Flaherty, a motherly nun who strolled around the library in her shawl, dusting books and signing out movie projectors. She hugged the girls, joked with the boys, and mothered the teachers by baking cookies and making coffee for our faculty meetings in her library. She also quietly said uncomplimentary remarks to trusted teachers about a young 29-year-old principal who didn't like her. The board forced the elderly nun, who had no librarian credential, to retire.

Mike Santos got the axe because of the usual reasons: low enrollment. Less money. Last hired, first fired. We were all assured by Dixon that Santos would be rehired the minute the budget allowed for one more salary.

That spring of 1970, we worked to save teacher jobs. Radisch pooled his personal money with other faculty members to start scholarships for needy students. Parents organized an open house and some teachers took students on field trips to their former elementary schools to recruit freshmen. Enrollment improved.

Then poor Herman Grey quit. His father-figure principal priest had left the school the previous year, losing all effective control. Now, his new principal was under attack by faculty "radicals." Meanwhile, "those ungrateful Negro students" called him racist. Herman closed up his plastic briefcase, made the sign of the cross and took a job in a pleasantly white suburban school. That left a natural opening for Santos to be rehired, but Dixon balked, stalling until the last school day of the year.

Chapter 7

"I cannot recommend him..."

W E WERE STILL ON THE LAST SCHOOL day of the year, 1970, at our last advisory board meeting: I moved to rehire Santos. "We've had an aggressive faculty recruitment drive that increased enrollment. We've got more students and a teacher opening."

Dixon responded, "We promised Santos first consideration for rehiring, but that doesn't mean we have to rehire him."

"What the hell does it mean?" I asked, my voice bouncing off the close walls of the principal's conference room, our secret inner-sanctum.

Dixon replied stoically, "It simply means we consider him for hiring, or non-hiring. I don't have to hire him. He's a menace to the school."

I tried to control my anger. "Dixon, we agreed that if we had the money and an opening, we would rehire Santos."

"Well," Dixon replied, looking forward with an expressionless stare, "you're entitled to your opinion."

"Is it because of the letter he wrote about you?" I replied.

Dixon remained physically still but his eyes dilated, then twitched nervously. "No, that's not it," he replied. "He's a menace to the school because he won't support the administration."

I raised my hands to my shaggy dark red hair. "What, specifically?"

Dixon slowly sat forward, opened a file, shuffled legal size papers and began his charges. "He failed to let the principal know about the black walkout during my assembly, although he admitted he knew of it in advance."

"Santos didn't walk out, the students did. You were the one running the assembly. You didn't stop them," I said.

Dixon listened while he kept his eyes on his paper. When I finished, he continued, without looking at me. "He failed to properly control the Martin Luther King Day Symposium where black students implied that Herman Grey was a racist. He played the role of a drunk in the freshman talent show."

"A drunk?" I replied. "That's ironic. In real life, he doesn't drink."

Dixon continued, "He made a nomination speech for a student running for class office. The student subsequently lost."

"God, Dixon," I said, "a harmless mistake by an over-zealous, first-year teacher, but it's no reason to fire the guy."

"Santos is not only a liability to our school, I believe he is an actual menace." Dixon was winding down, speaking slower and slower, his head still tilted down over his file. Then he looked up and met my eyes for the first time in this conversation. "I will not rehire him. I'm certain I will be able to find someone more supportive of the principal here."

At this point, I was exasperated and incredulous. I asked the other board members to verify that we had promised Santos his job back if an opening occurred.

Father Al Boomer, the drama teacher, was the priests' representative to the board. His small, beady blue eyes looked at the world behind respectable plastic-rimmed eyeglasses and a small, knotted ego lived inside his grandiose manner. He had a bold smile and a bald head. Boomer claimed to have several PhDs in scholarly pursuits like Latin, Christian Psychology, Theology, and French Literature. He never spoke out against anyone, to his face, but reserved his verbal attacks for his disfavored colleague's back. His favorite word was "I," which he emphasized by raising his voice pitch and holding the word like an F-sharp.

Father Boomer announced his allegiance to Dixon by jumping on Santos. "I also object to rehiring this man," he volunteered in a pompous tone. "I have 22 witnesses to the fact that Mr. Santos told his students that I was insecure. When he found out that I had numerous PhDs, he told the students that I must be insecure. I firmly believe that we do not need this man as a teacher. I certainly don't need him."

Bud Johnson, the school counselor, cleared his throat, a sign that he wanted the floor. He wore his slacks pulled up higher than his navel, with a long-sleeved striped shirt, tie, and white loafers. He blinked his blue eyes a lot and when he smiled he expanded his oval face, turning his cheeks into two little red balloons. He swayed when he walked and enjoyed stroking his curly graying hair.

Bud had a slight limp and he was a chain smoker who smoked his cigarettes with flair, sometimes using a cigarette holder, tossing his head back to blow white puffs of smoke upwards.[15] "Well," Bud said as he stretched the word out with his neck and body, "I personally think, for Mr. Santos' sake, he would be more comfortable in a school with a more permissive atmosphere."

"Bud," I said. "Don't do him any favors. Second to Stan Cardinet, he got the highest student evaluation of any teacher here. Students signed a petition to keep him."

"Well," Bud said again, "I saw him in grubby Levis and sandals when he was an assistant football coach. He dresses just like the students! I really don't think this is the place for him."

I turned to Sister Marie, Dean of Girls and our ally in the battle with the Bishop. "Sister, don't you think it's immoral to promise to rehire him and then to break our promise?"

Sister Marie had a majestic aura about her. In the old-fashioned nun's garb, her sharp features gave her a queenly stature. Daughter of a wealthy California family, she held her head high. Her features were perfect. Her humor always dry. The new nun outfit revealed skinny legs, a thin neck and her ears stuck out. I liked the old look better.

"Unfortunately, I don't think Santos, as a probationary teacher, has measured up to our expectations," she said, looking at me. "Paul, when you were a first year teacher, we never had these kinds of complaints about you. Our faculty is already polarized and divided. Santos and his letter widened the gap. His presence hurt St. Liz. I'm sorry, but I cannot recommend rehiring him."

Father Farley perked up when he heard the apology. "Oh, I'm sorry too," he said, holding his hands in a pleading-for-forgiveness pose. He sounded like a parrot to me.

The only support I had on that board came from Tom Rowe, a former football coach, now dean of men. Rowe taught several years in the public schools, but left the difficulties of inner-city school conditions to do some real teaching. His large, light-blue eyes dominated his ruddy face. Wisps of dark hair rimmed his balding head. His roly-poly body seemed to match his mellow approach to problems. And he enjoyed puffing on a pipe while drawing pictures with words, often subtle and indirect words. His ready laugh put people at ease.

Rowe often hesitated as he talked while his lips twitched in silence until his mind matched the exact words for his thoughts. "I would be inclined to think that this board, as the administrative body of the school...I would prefer to believe that we have, in fact, an obligation to Mr. Santos. He was notified that his employment for next year was terminated because of financial reasons. I would tend to assume that if the financial problems were resolved, that his contract would be forthcoming."

Rowe and I were the only sane ones there. The board voted, five to two, not to rehire Mike Santos. The "axe-Santos" meeting took place on the last day of school in June 1971. Rowe and I adjourned to meet our co-conspirators at the Master's, a neighborhood bar and hangout for St. Liz alumni. It has a jukebox that's too loud, a whiskered barfly who is too obnoxious, and a billiard table in a side room too small for trick shots.

At the Master's, we developed our strategy. Rowe: call for another hearing where Santos could defend himself. August: appeal to Father Orville, the pastor of St. Liz parish of which the school was a part. Kelly: arrange a meeting with the teacher's union. Radisch: be our spokesman at the parish school board. Santos: keep students informed. They might boycott the start of school. Stan: make contact with the nuns; try to work the moral issue and get their support.

We made little progress during the summer. Stan arranged a potluck with the nuns. We arrived at the convent and received a tour of their cubicle bedrooms with bare floors. It was a rare chance to socialize with our religious colleagues. Not even Sister Clem went to the Master's. Sister St. John the Baptist wordlessly answered the door then disappeared. Sister Clem laughed and slapped backs. Sister Marie talked with Santos. We accomplished nothing.

Anxiety tainted this summer. Songwriting recaptured a little of my peace of mind.

PAUL AUGUST

The Master's trophy case full of sports
memorabilia from the past haunted my creativity. The glass trophy case held over-
sized St. Liz trophies from a high school
athletic star who now needed the Master's
to dim his mind and fill his belly with beer
every afternoon.

He's our high school athlete.
The greatest to be MVP.
Our high school athletic star.

The trophies that he won and his All-star
plaque are in the back,
The back of Master Mullberry's Bar.
The cheerleaders cheered his bright moves
beneath the lights.
The pom-pom girls looked for him every
play.

His photo's on the sports page.
The greatest teenage athlete.
He always made the teen all-city team.
He won an athletic college scholarship but
blew it.
He got his girlfriend pregnant at the prom.

In our Catholic neighborhood, that isn't very
good.
So, he did exactly what he knew he should.
He married now he plays liars dice every
night.
In the dim smoky light of the bar.

After working in the cannery he comes in to
*   drink TV.*
He knows all the sports.
He's the boss. He's the star.
The star of Master Mullberry's Bar.

Later that summer, Santos appeared at the board and Sister Marie changed her vote, mostly because she wanted school to begin without problems. But the vote was still four to three against Santos. Kelly signed up all of us with the teacher's union. "Let's organize and get Santos rehired. This is all a bunch of bunk."

As the summer edged dangerously towards September, the Santos case remained unresolved. When we took the problem to the parish school board, they said it was a school site problem, not a concern for their making body. The pastor, Father Orville, saw no reason to reverse his lay principal.

Two weeks before the start of school, Radisch arranged a meeting between Dixon's and Santos's supporters. Dixon refused to budge. He presented us with a ditto paper addressed to Stan Cardinet, Jack Radisch, Jim Kelly, Tom Rowe, and me. Dixon ordered us not to picket, boycott or demonstrate. He quoted his new addition to the faculty handbook:

Faculty members should not speak critically of the administration.

I shall accept the decision of the administrative board regarding the Santos incident.

Beneath the last sentence was a blank line for us to sign our names.

Radisch stood up in his tilted way and screwed his good eye in on Dixon. He paused, and then began. "Santos was laid off last April for economic reasons. We recruited students and raised more money for St. Liz. Herman resigned. Now you won't hire Santos because he doesn't support your administration. You are avoiding the true issues and not playing straight with us." Then Radisch stopped, stood straighter, and crumpling up Dixon's ditto sheet, threw it across the room scoring a bull's-eye in the wastepaper basket. "That's what I think of your phony little rules, Dixon!" He headed out the door but looked back in to shout, "If you don't rehire Santos, we'll close this school down." He slammed open the thick door, which crashed against the wall and left a stunned silence.

I stood up and pointed at Dixon. "Gil, you forced us to go union. If you don't rehire Santos, the union will picket registration day and students will boycott school. If that's what you want, you got it." The rest of us walked out as Dixon stood there, motionless, his eyes blinking widely.

The teachers' union here refers to the American Federation of Teachers with 500,000 members nationally, at the time. The biggest union, the National Education Association, with three million members, only represented public school teachers and not private or Catholic schools.

Dixon held out until September first and then rehired Santos.

We won back Santos's job, but it was a costly victory. There had been no chance to rejuvenate that summer. When school started, we were polarized. The St. Liz faculty had become the 15 union teachers vs. 24 conservative nuns, priests, and a couple of non-union lay teachers.

Chapter 8

"The music died..."

PRINCIPAL DIXON DIDN'T LIKE the summer dances. He only saw the illusion of me showing up on Friday nights and dancing away with a sinful profit from a holy non-profit school. He finally put me on a summer salary in 1970 and tightened the dance rules. No sandals, Levis, T-shirts, mini-skirts or tennis shoes. Show student I.D. No one admitted after nine or allowed to leave before eleven. The crowds dwindled and the profits became losses. Within a month, Dixon canceled the dances.

By the end of the summer, the school owed me $300 but Dixon refused to pay because the dances weren't making money. I didn't want to take the new principal to small claims court, so I went to him directly. "We had an agreement," I said. My statements fell on deaf ears.

Dixon gave me his standard response, "You're entitled to your opinion," he said, "but I'm not going to pay you." That was the summer the music died and the dancing stopped at our little Catholic school.

Although I enjoyed sponsoring summer dances at St. Liz (1967-70), going back to school in September was like hopping off the dance-train onto a classroom-train chugging full steam in the opposite direction. The summer Dixon stopped the dances, I had no other summer job. Teachers don't get paid for 12 months unless we thin out our ten-month paychecks. So I played the college-credit-for-money game. I took college classes that give credits for degrees or credentials for more salary.

I encountered "touchie-feelie" groups in psychological classes at Cal Berkeley Extension, laughed through weekend seminars on games and learning at Cal State Hayward, [16] and wrote my way through journalism courses at San Francisco State. I continued freelance writing, doing two more stories for *Rolling Stone*.

As the end of summer melted down to the start of the school year, for the first time in my life, I experienced chest pains. Sometimes I felt a thin stinging in my chest, like a light corkscrew being twisted into my chest. The doctor said it was indigestion, but I felt it was psychosomatic—a somatic reaction to the psychic frustrations of trying to get Santos rehired. I certainly wasn't looking forward to returning to school. After Dixon rehired Santos, I resigned from the advisory board and withdrew from political combat to become the kind of teacher I had previously been contemptuous of, the type who leaves when the last bell rings at 3:15 pm. I went home to write and create lesson plans for my new creative writing classes in the English department.

For a reason known only to him, Gil Dixon reassigned all the union teachers to new classes. Father Boomer took over my Psychology class. He converted it to "Christian Psychology," threw out Freud, added Catholic ethics and morality, and told the students more about homosexuality than they wanted or needed to know.

Radisch lost his forum for teaching juveniles their rights when Sister St. John the Baptist took over his government class. She changed the décor by replacing the American flag with a classroom crucifix. Dixon reassigned Radisch to five different classes in five different classrooms, which meant that he had to leave after every class and haul his huge briefcase to another classroom. Such inconvenience usually falls on a first year teacher, not a seven-year vet. Dixon refused to recognize our union or teacher seniority.

Kelly's higher-level math was reduced to algebra. His science classes were transferred to Farley who subtracted Darwinism and added Genesis. Farley spent a lot of time explaining why Ptolemy wasn't entirely wrong in believing that man was the center of the Universe.

Stan Cardinet found himself again assigned to teach world history. He also found himself undermined by the administration. He wanted to transfer Father Bart out of the history department because of consistent student complaints. His recommendations were ignored.

Father Bart was a little guy who had a nervous habit of hooking his index finger into his Roman collar and tugging, as if the collar were choking him. He did this at moments of embarrassment when his face flushed red and his dark eyes bulged. It seemed as if he tugged to escape that Catholic leash around his neck. He never wore the loose Franciscan robes, only the black suit with its suffocating collar. Father Bart, short for Bartholomew, had a vocabulary limited to clichés and a worldview consisting of racial stereotypes. He'd mimic racial characters, mock minorities, and embarrass everyone in the faculty room, a privileged sanctuary where students were forbidden. While no one found him amusing, neither did anyone confront him about his racism. Father Bart was clearly pleased that the religious teachers were taking over classes previously assigned to the lay personnel.

Radisch cynically suggested that Dixon reassigned us as a vindictive act in retaliation for our victory that forced him to rehire Mike Santos. Stan, a man of integrity, was trusting enough to disagree.

Dixon allowed me to keep my marriage class, which moved like a ship—it either sank or floated, depending on the students in the seminar. With college prep scholars, if I sneezed they'd discuss it; with bored mainstream students, trying to discuss anything was like trying to engage Sister St. John the Baptist in friendly small talk— very difficult. The high point of marriage class was the guest speakers. The students got to question people who came from widely different life styles. When two very different speakers shared a similar view such as "don't marry young"—it had a very strong impact on the students.

That year in my marriage class, my guest speakers included John Thomas, the school's first black male teacher in the newly integrated St. Liz. John Thomas was a tall, elegant, slender man, with short hair and ebony skin. He wore rimless glasses that seemed to magnify his intense eyes as he looked directly at you, unblinking. He spoke carefully, each word precisely enunciated.

His priorities were science and black students. When I asked him to exchange classes with me to speak to my students, I urged this bachelor to tell my marriage class what his views on sex and marriage were and to "tell it like it is."

"Right on," he replied. His eyes sparkled with the enthusiasm of a first year teacher. John Thomas addressed the class on a Friday. The following Tuesday, Dixon kept sending for students from the class to come to his office. When the bell rang, a student approached my desk and asked, "Mr. August, do you know what's going on?"

"No, I didn't know." As usual, the students knew more than their teachers about school happenings.

Other students gathered around my desk. "Mr. Dixon is trying to bust Mr. Thomas," was their consensus.

"Why?" I asked in my naiveté. "What's Thomas done?"

"Somebody finked," said Lisa, a short-haired senior brunette who wore United Farm Worker buttons pinned to her light and dark brown Catholic girls' uniform. "We talked about living together, sex before marriage, virginity and that article from Playboy magazine..."

"I know all that," I cut her off, my irritation showing. "Did he say anything wrong, like the 'f' word or anything like that?"

"No. He was just being honest," said Lisa. "Maybe he said 'bullshit,' but that's no big deal. Mr. Dixon has a whole list of things he says that Mr. Thomas said."

"Jesus Christ, Dixon," I muttered. I left class and found Dixon in the hall.

"Gil, what's all this about John Thomas and my marriage class?"

Dixon's face was expressionless. "You will have your chance to defend yourself," he said slowly.

"Defend myself?" I sputtered. "From what? What's happening?"

"It's confidential," Dixon said gravely. "I will give a letter to you later. I advise you not to discuss this with the students."

"Discuss what?" I said in exasperation.

He shrugged his shoulders and left. I hurried to the faculty room where I asked Thomas, "What's going on?" He held a hush-finger to his lips, told me to close the door, then without a word, showed me the following letter:

OFFICE OF THE PRINCIPAL

March 7, 1972

Dear Mr. Thomas:

The Administrative Board will consider termination of your employment. You are suspended from your teaching duties with pay. You are not to visit the school or talk with students, nor are you to encourage other teachers to talk with students.

Sincerely,

Gilbert Dixon, Principal

Thomas looked at me plaintively, holding his hands up in surrender, shaking his head. "Dixon has not, I am sorry to say, given me his accusations." Thomas paused, put his hands on his thin belly, and his lips quivered as a preface to the best way of explaining what little he knew. "Let me say this. Two of your students, of the more conservative philosophy..."

"You mean, two white kids," I said.

"Yes. One might say that. A young man and a young lady. They approached the school counselor to complain about the rather...er, earthy tone of my sex talk."

"And what did he do?" I asked.

"The counselor went to our principal who, in turn, I would say, has rather drastically over-reacted," said Thomas.

"Now what?" I asked.

"May I suggest that you sit tight, be cool and don't do anything crazy."

"Me? What about you?" I asked.

"We just have to wait," said Thomas. And wait we did.

Chapter 9

"A skinny envelope..."

IN California, March 15th is the traditional RIF (reduction in force) day, when teachers receive notices from their school boards that they might be laid off. That year, 1972, Dixon asked the parish school board to make it March 24th, the Friday before Easter vacation. On March 24th, we arrived at school prepared to fight for our non-tenured teachers. John Thomas' case was still unresolved—like a boomerang tossed out but not yet returned. Radisch cynically thought that Dixon just wanted to give his RIF letters to his victims and leave for vacation. A trusting Stan Cardinet believed that Dixon needed the extra time to analyze results of the freshman entrance exam.

Dixon refused to recognize our teacher union or negotiate with us. He kept his veto power. There was talk of dropping tenure, freezing salaries, and firing teachers. That afternoon we gathered in the faculty room. Dixon's notice on the bulletin board proclaimed that contracts for next year would be granted from his office after school. The three nervous non-tenured teachers went first, clustered together in an impatient group. Curt Levinson beckoned to Santos and Dallas Williams and said, "Let's go pick up our notices." They left the faculty room. We waited.

Stan and Kelly mulled over their never-ending chess game.[17] Kelly memorized strategies, read tactics, practiced techniques and usually won. Stan played with emotion, intuition and perception, and usually lost. Radisch waded through his law school homework.

Finally, Santos returned wearing a big smile and waving a thick envelope. "Surprise," he said. "I got rehired." Curt Levinson stepped in next, with a lively bounce and held up a contract. But Dallas Williams returned with her head held high, fighting back tears. Dallas, a petite woman, had a rare combination of light black skin and hazel eyes that looked like gentle pearls. She joined the union when Dixon tried to fire Santos. Now she clutched a skinny envelope with a one-page lay-off notice within.

Kelly and Stan stopped their chess game and sauntered down the hall to Dixon's out-er office. I followed and waited outside with Kelly while Stan took what seemed like hours to get his contract papers. Kelly and I exchanged quips about Stan's verbosity. Suddenly Stan burst out of Dixon's office. He rushed past us, his face flushed red, his blue eyes dazed, his lips pressed together. He made a simple gesture as he moved past us—his index finger sliced across his throat.

I didn't get it right away. "What's Stan's problem?" I asked Kelly.

"Dixon just fired him," Kelly replied.

"What? Come on Jim! Stan's a tenured teacher. He has seven years of seniority. He's the chairman of the history department. Dixon can't fire Stan."

"August!" Kelly looked at me, twisted his fingers in the air, and raised an eyebrow, "You're out of it. You've been writing too many songs. You've lost touch with reality. I tell ya, he fired him, and now he's going to fire me, too."

Kelly walked confidently into Dixon's office. A slow realization grew within my consciousness. Dixon was using the drop in enrollment to justify cutting teachers who battled him on this issue. If my reasoning was correct, then Radisch, Kelly, and I would all receive a rejection slip.

I turned and followed Stan into the faculty lounge. Kelly was right. Stan received a lay-off notice. There was nothing I could say. Kelly returned to join us. "I got the axe.

What a farce. It's a real hurter." Kelly clenched his fists, jutted his chin, lowered his shaggy head and told me, "Dixon's got two stacks of envelopes. The fat ones are contracts. The skinny ones are rejection slips. I tell ya, it's totally ridiculous."

This was all becoming incredibly curious. Five minutes ago I had a secure job protected by tenure, my status of being an alumnus of St. Liz and by living in the neighborhood. Right now I didn't see how he could dump my partners without nailing Radisch and me.

I entered Dixon's cubbyhole office. Father Farley, sitting in the corner across from the principal's desk, smiled timidly at me. Dixon exchanged glances with Farley, reached for his two stacks of letters, leaned back and gave me an envelope. A skinny envelope. It was a two-sentence purple ditto statement with my name typed in on a blank line.

Dear: Paul August_____

I XX XXXXX regret to inform you that your contract will not be renewed. I will be glad to discuss the reasons for this decision with you.

I was oddly intrigued by the purple ditto form letter with my name typed into a space in black type. It had two typing errors, x-ing out one word and typing over another. The smell of the purple ditto ink reminded me of every test I ever gave. The letter was on our school scratch paper, the backside of surplus Southern Pacific Railroad stationery. Dixon's eyes were glazed and moving slowly. I was sure he was on his tranquilizers.

Father Farley was still looking at me, still smiling his condescending smile.

"Gil, do you know what you're doing? You're firing tenured teachers," I said.

"I'm not really firing anybody," Dixon said carefully. "This is just a temporary layoff due to an anticipated drop in the enrollment. Religious teachers, of course, have seniority over all other teachers."

"What about Levinson?" I asked. "He doesn't have tenure. He's an English teacher too, but I have seniority. And he's been rehired."

"Well, Paul, the parish school board changed the tenure rules some weeks ago. Surely you know that we are a private school, and not subject to the California Education Code. Curt Levinson has departmental seniority. He is the department chairman," said Dixon.

I shook my head. "Seniority applies to employment, not department head. Gil, come clean; this is all a front. You just want to get rid of us because you and the Bishop don't want us to unionize the Catholic schools."

MINDWORKER: MAYBECK

Here I am in the sacred teacher's faculty room looking like a fierce disciplinarian, which I wasn't. At the top is the letterhead on the scratch paper Dixon used to fire us: a form letter. This contrasted to the spring of 1969 when the old principal told me: "Paul, you have tenure. You have a job here for as long as there is a St. Liz."

"No, no, no, that's not it," said Father Farley, replacing his smile with an apologetic gesture.

"I'm sorry, but it is all financial. Truly this is all due to our troubled finances."

I ignored Farley and turned to Dixon. "Gil, this won't work. You've started a battle that might destroy this school."

"Well," shrugged Dixon, "You're entitled to your opinion."

I returned to the faculty room; Radisch knew he was next. "Dixon's enjoying this but I'm not going in there to get canned. Screw him. Let him come to me."

"I can't accept this," I said. "Let's go get a drink."

Stan and I went to The Master's. Kelly and Radisch joined us, laughing.

"What a farce. August, you'll never believe what happened after you left," said Kelly filling his beer mug from our pitcher, and pointing to Radisch.

Radisch stared at me with his good eye and concentrated on his words. "That bastard Dixon just got in his car and left for the suburbs. Farley came in and put a skinny envelope in my mailbox."

"And that's not all," said Kelly, tapping an ash from his cigar. "Guess who else got the axe?"

"Well, certainly John Thomas, because of his sex scandal in August's marriage class," said Stan.

"That's one," said Kelly. "He's still suspended for this year and now he's fired for next year."

"Hell, who else is there?" I said. "He got us radicals and the black teachers. Tom Rowe is still on the administrative board. He's not going to fire himself."

Radisch answered, "Skinny envelopes went to Bud Johnson and George Baljavich."

124

"No way," I said.

"Christ," said Stan.

"Those guys are both St. Liz alumni, like me," I said.

"A hell of a lot it's done for you guys," said Kelly, chuckling.

"George is in our union, but Bud Johnson? Our only counselor? He's not. Why him? What's his offense?" I asked.

Radisch took a sip of his beer and said, "Sister St. John the Baptist has a counselor's credential. Why pay a lay teacher when a nun can do it for so much less? Dixon can cover her teaching job with part-time teachers, and even if he doesn't, who cares how overworked a nun is?"

"And guess what Father Farley did after he gave out the notices?" added Kelly, leaning forward, lifting his eyebrows and brushing his bushy hair off of his Irish eyes, which twinkled as he suppressed a wide grin. "He wished us a Happy Easter! Can you imagine that? What a farce! Have a happy Easter without a job! Bah!" Kelly, who'd had quite a few beers by then, kept muttering under his breath, "What a hurter! What a hurter!"

"Daddy's home. Daddy's home." This ritual greeted me each time I got home from school. These are the most uplifting words I'd heard all day. Kristi, a blonde, blue-eyed child with a wide smile, led her little brother and sister. John Paul was a bubble of activity and excitement; Wendy, our youngest, relatively quiet and determined.

"Woof, woof." That was the family dog, Broken Doggy. He was called that because John had a toy doggy that looked like him. It broke, and we got him a real Bassett Hound puppy.

"Woof!" The dog always greeted me with four barks, a pause, and then added a final bark like a period to his barking sentence. Dog turned and ran toward the back yard as our three children, ages two, four, and six, followed.

"Guess what Dixon did now?" I asked Muriel.

"Now what happened?" she replied.

"He fired us all: Me, Radisch, Stan, Kelly, and a few others. It's crazy. He won't get away with it."

Muriel looked concerned. We had an old school traditional deal. I was the breadwinner. She took care of our three children. "What's going to happen to us?" she said.

"Don't worry," I replied. "We've got the union behind us. We'll get our jobs back. No big deal."

After dinner, Kristi, John and Wendy returned to the back yard with the dog; Muriel poured me a glass of wine and we began to unwind slightly. "I've never been fired from anything," I said.

The two photos above show the evolution of Muriel Atchinson August from a wide-eyed country girl living in the Sierra foothills to a composed city woman living in the Bay Area. Right, John Paul is holding baby Wendy. On the left, I'm performing to my captive audience as I did most nights. For a while, the children were in the same bedroom and I sang them to sleep with songs from the fifties and sixties, plus my originals. Note our stereo console consisting of painted lumberyard boards and square bricks.

Muriel listened. She knew I needed to vent.

"Ever since I was a kid, my relatives and neighbors hired me to cut lawns, paint their houses or water their garden. I sanded cars for painting at Gordon's auto body repair shop for fifty cents an hour to earn my first salary during high school.

"All I really wanted to do was be a freelance writer and songwriter. I took a cut in pay to teach, as a day job, and I don't regret it. But I didn't expect this." I looked into Muriel's worried eyes. "He can't get away with it."

"But what if you have no job next year?"

"That's a big 'what if.' I'm still trying to absorb it. I'd love to go to work for *Rolling Stone* as a writer but I screwed up my recent assignment. I haven't proven myself to them." I didn't tell Muriel what happened. I was frustrated about an assignment related to a campaign to legalize marijuana. *Rolling Stone* sent me to various prisons in California to interview marijuana convicts. At Folsom, a Mexican inmate was surprisingly candid with me. He was doing 15 years for marijuana, an excessive sentence.

Interviewing Marijuana Prisoners: Paul J Scanlon, *Rolling Stone's* managing editor, gave me a letter introducing me to prison officials as an "authorized representative of *Rolling Stone*." It explained that I was researching "individuals who have been arrested and prosecuted under existing marijuana laws."

"I was robbing a bank when the cops came," he told me. "I had a stolen car and me and the cops got into a chase and a shoot-out. I ditched the car, tossed the money and got rid of the gun. When they found me, all I had was a bag of pot. They busted me but they knew I robbed the bank. They just couldn't prove it. So, I got 15 years to life for possession for sale."

I had the research but I couldn't concentrate on the writing while I was in a fight for my teaching life in the spring of 1972. During this teacher crisis, I sent in a messed up manuscript and it got deservedly rejected by Joe Eszterhas, a Hollywood writer, who is now making a million dollars a script. He went on to create the scripts for 16 movies that pulled in a total of one billion dollars. Such is life.

I looked out to the backyard again to see Kristi on the swing, Wendy chasing Broken Doggy, and John playing with a toy fire engine. "We'll be okay. Don't you worry," I told Muriel, and tried to convince myself.

Chapter 10

"The Pepsi Generation..."

M Y WIFE, MURIEL, AND I PLANNED to take our family on Easter vacation to visit Muriel's family like we did every year for Easter vacation. Just because I might be unemployed was no reason to stay home. We left the next day. Muriel's folks lived in North San Juan, an abandoned gold rush town in the Sierra foothills near the South Fork of the Yuba River. They have a country house with spare bedrooms and a cabin in the rear. Easter vacation means swinging in the hammock, reading novels, and feeding pond fish while watching feathery clouds drift over mountains covered with ponderosa pine trees.

Intellectually, I knew there were worse things than unemployment. Emotionally, I felt bleak anxiety. My mind was stuck on the school crises. Even as I sat in the swing,

PAUL & MURIEL
AUGUST

North San Juan, at 2600 feet, gets little snow. Here's our snow man during spring break of my first teaching year. This is the Sierra Foothills – God's country: "above the fog and below the snow, under the stars, over the gold." Muriel's grandfather is in the background above, left. Despite growing a moustache with longer hair and sideburns, I still favored a long sleeved shirt and paisley tie. Muriel, pictured here with me at one of the school reunions, supported my extra curricula activities.

fingering my guitar, I could only write songs like this:

*The rites of spring are here again so I'll sing
my song my dear.
The board of education's financial catastro-
phe happens every year.
They like to form committees. They like a lot
of names.
So, whenever things go wrong, no one gets
the blame.*

I hiked out back but my tensions went with
me, like a little blustery Sierra storm hover-
ing above my head. I surrendered myself to
my uncertainties about the future, my
memories of the past, and my anxieties of
the moment. The voice in my head kept asking, "Why are they doing this to me? Do I
belong in teaching? "I always knew too
much about students—and too little about
teaching. Too much about their personal
lives and too little about how most of the
school authorities feared adolescents who
smoked dope or marched in anti-war activities.

I sat in the porch swing near the pond as
I continued to reflect on when I started
teaching. I was young enough to remember
teenage growing pains and old enough to
give advice about boyfriends and girl-
friends, unlike parents and elder teachers
who didn't remember their own teenage
years. At age 24, I had more in common
with the Pepsi Generation than 60-year-old
Father Edward and his 2,000 year-old

church. I liked helping students. It was a refreshing counterpoint to faculty room small talk where 50-year-old Herman Grey yapped about Saturday suburban barbecues, Sunday contributions to the second collection, [18] and daily commutes with his gun by his side for self-defense.

I tried to get my mind off the crisis but it stuck like an obsession. I tried to think back to my youth as a student at St. Liz to think happy thoughts. Even those were tempered with disappointment. I remembered this: She was sixteen. I just turned seventeen, which was a little late for an American teenager but not for an Irish Catholic. The new girl in school is always an unknown. She had an abrupt air, detached and aloof, and a carelessly independent attitude for a Catholic girl: missing too many school days, arriving late to assemblies and cutting classes she didn't like. I was in my junior year as a St. Liz student.

Her long thin blonde hair flowed down half the length of her full body. Her lips formed a natural pout below her high cheekbones and wide blue eyes. In my post-puberty vision, she was beautiful.

At the Friday night dance, I saw her standing there, staring at me. She refused to dance with the other guys. I thought she would turn me down too, but she didn't. We danced frantically to the rock 'n roll of Elvis. We danced closely to the warm slow songs of the Everly Brothers. Our palms sweated into each other. Her mother lived in the suburbs but paid the rent for her daughter to live alone in an old brick apartment on East 12th Street just a few blocks from St. Liz. Teen guys always dream of, but seldom find this type of sexy situation. That night, after the dance, was my first time. It wasn't hers.

The next Monday I saw her at school. "Did you go to confession, yet?" she asked.[19] When I said I didn't, she acted horrified. If we sinned on Friday night we should confess on Saturday. She missed school several more times, then never showed up again. My calls went unanswered until I reached the apartment manager who said she got married and left town. I felt stunned. She just disappeared from my life, leaving an empty, intense, horny yearning.

For a while after that, I walked over to the old brick apartment building as if there might be something I could do to find her. Later, whenever I went by there, I thought of her. As the years rolled by, the city of Oakland demolished that old brick apartment building to extend East 12th Street to Fruitvale Avenue. The location of my cherished memory became merely a section of asphalt.

I think of my first time whenever I drive over that sacred spot. It's enshrined in asphalt and sanctified by a yellow dotted line on East 12th Street at Fruitvale Ave. in Oakland. To this day, whenever I drive over that spot, I think of her.

In retrospect, here I was sitting in the middle of God's country, just 50 miles from Tahoe, surrounded by tall pines, but oblivious to the beauty of Mother Nature. My thoughts, however, were still about my St. Liz high school years as an escape from the obsession about being fired.

Chapter 11

"You guys are in this for..."

WE RETURNED FROM EASTER vacation in the Sierras, April 1972. We drove down through the sweltering Sacramento Valley, across the chilly Benicia Bridge, passing suburban Pleasant Hill. The Caldecott Tunnel[20] opens on a view of little white boxes, surrounding a sprawling basin where sails sprinkle the bay and a thin layer of brown smog obscures the blue water like an oil slick on a rain puddle. Alameda is a little island on the west side of the Oakland estuary where generations live in the same Victorian homes. This quaint Bay Area town exists in a time warp where people protect their peaceful bastion with three drawbridges and one tunnel that connects to the mainland of Oakland.

Coach Bob Howard was a little like Alameda himself—provincial and buoyant, inflated by a rah-rah mentality. He taught driver's education before classes, P.E. during classes, coached basketball after school and drove the school bus in his spare time. We sprawled around his living room, slouching in chairs, sitting on the floor. Rowe tapped the tobacco in his pipe. Kelly fired up a long stinky cigar. The room echoed with the noise of clinking wine jugs against glasses and the snap-pop-fizz from beer cans. We sat silently gathering our thoughts about how to save our jobs and, perhaps, the school.

Coach Howard unbuttoned his red windbreaker to accommodate his growing paunch and stood up to address us. His curly blond hair and red cherubic face made him look like a beardless Santa. "Listen. This is Tuesday night," said Howard. "Let's blitz this thing. They're gonna try to wear us down. Don't let 'em." He spoke in staccato bursts, running words together, holding his shoulders and palms up with a why-can't-this-work gesture. "We've got to get the students, the parents, the faculty, and the priests and the nuns on our side. Dixon is the real problem. Here's what we should do. Let's meet with the nuns to win them over. If that doesn't work, let's go down to the union hall and prepare to picket."

"I do believe that Coach Howard is right," said Tom Rowe, pausing as his lips fumbled for phrases. "It is incumbent upon us to move forward, one might say, while moving laterally." Rowe became flustered with his own words. "That is to say, we should proceed individually, and collectively, to demonstrate that, to reveal that..." He blushed and blurted, "Goddamn it! Dixon's an asshole and that's all there is to it."

"Ah, ha!" laughed Kelly. "Sputtering old Rowe here is trying to say that it's better to hang together than hang separately. Okay. I'm for that. If Dixon won't wise up, then we'll picket the parents when they pick up report cards this Thursday night. I'll handle that."

Stan Cardinet, seated in the lotus position on the hardwood floor, opened his eyes. "I feel it would be an error not to get support from the good sisters. Our picket line needs people like Sister Clem out there with a sign. We have scheduled a meeting with the nuns tomorrow night at August's house."

"Ha, good!" said Kelly. "Augie's got a house in St. Liz parish with the wife and three young 'uns. That ought to grab the nuns."

This was the first time I had heard about the meeting but it seemed like a good idea so I went along with it. The following night we met with the nuns at my house. The good sisters piled out of their hand-me-down station wagon and did their penguin walk up the stairs to my house. George livened the tone, plunking ragtime tune on our upright piano, tinkering with an airy melody to my lighthearted lyrics: *You only have one time being a child one time, one time.*

The nuns smiled happily. We unwrapped the steaming potluck, passed around cheap white wine, and mingled in my front room where a bay window looked out over the homes of East Oakland.

George stood in the middle of the room, the light reflecting off his bald head, a beer can in one hand, a cigar in the other. "Heck sisters, we're good teachers. We're not like the cross-eyed teacher who couldn't control her pupils."

We groaned and chuckled.

"Well," George said, "I'm like the guy who fell into the lens grinding machine. I want to make a spectacle out of myself, so..." George's jokes were terrible, but they made him laugh so hard that we couldn't stop ourselves from joining him. George raised his hands above his head to surrender. "Okay, no more jokes. Seriously folks...." His smile faded and a frown captured his long forehead. "The heart has been cut out of St Liz," he said, lowering his head. "Ever since Dixon became principal, the leadership has been cold and distant. Gates are locked. Doors are chained. There is no more warmth here. The principal is killing the school."

Sister Marie slipped her right hand under her robes and reached out to George with her left hand. "George, I'm not here to defend the principal. He has his faults. It's not Dixon who is responsible for your layoffs. According to his records, there is simply no money to rehire you and the other teachers. The school could go bankrupt. There is no money. This is a financial fact."

Kelly responded, "Sisters, Dixon is firing us for political reasons. It's not the money. He's just out to get us. He doesn't like us and he wants to get rid of us and that's all there is to it." He wound up his speech with a twist of his wrist in the air.

Sister Saint Francis looked at him blankly. She was a nun of true simplicity with a sweet melodious voice who seemed to sing her words, like a mother cooing to her infant. Students thought that she was feeble-minded or emotionally childish, but students tend to exaggerate the weaknesses of authority figures. We thought of her as an innocuous nun who worked best with slow learners. She had been assigned to Saint Liz so that she could visit her mother who lived in a nearby Catholic rest home. When her duties allowed, she visited daily. In her musical voice, she said simply, "But, Mr. Kelly, the advisory board must know things we don't know."

Stan brought both hands up to cover his hairy face. "My God, Sister. You are such a stereotype. Your blind faith in authority is truly disgusting," he said.

"Hey, Stan," Sister Clem came to the rescue. "Come off it. You guys are in this for the money. You get paid. Our money goes to the convent."

Radisch shook his head and pointed his finger at her. "Sister, when it comes to money, you religious types are pathetically naive. You nuns lead sheltered lives paid for by the church. I only have my paycheck to support my family, and Dixon wants to cut it off."

"I don't see any reason why you should not be terminated," interrupted Sister Saint John the Baptist in a cold, lethal voice. "You spend your money drinking beer at The Master's. You act like Godless atheists and radicals. It's our school, not yours. It belongs to us—not to you."

"That does it," yelled Kelly, jumping up, trembling. "That just plain gosh darn does it, Sister! I'm going to the union hall to make our picket signs."

Kelly grabbed a jug of wine and huffed out. Stan picked up his potluck pans and followed. Radisch collected his legal papers and left. The nuns mingled for a moment, in a collective bewilderment. They slowly untangled themselves to thank Muriel and me for the evening. Then they did their penguin walk down the stairs and drove back to their convent.

Chapter 12

"Everything's just fine..."

APRIL 1972. THE NEXT AFTERNOON, as parents arrived to pick up their youngsters' report cards, a line of tired teachers began an informational picket line in front of St. Liz. It swelled into a thick parade when students and union teachers from some public schools joined us.

I strummed my guitar and sang:

Grab your picket sticks. To the streets we're bound.
We'll keep our dignity. They can't push us around.[21]

We shuffled slowly up the street, along the school's front stairs, gazing up to the greening Oakland foothills. Our line looped back, gliding toward the bay, stringing out past the priests' monastery across from the nuns' convent. We hooked back and circled again. For all of us at this Catholic school, this was our first picket line.

Stan stroked his beard and pretended to mourn. "The Cardinet family has always been on management's side. My appearance on this picket line is against family precedent. No doubt I shall be castigated and proclaimed the black sheep of the family."[22]

"My dad always paid his union dues," I said. "He's been through strikes and honored boycotts. He once told me that teaching is a white-collar profession where I would never have to walk a picket line. Hah!"

"Whoa, was he ever wrong," said Kelly. "My daddy, a teacher in New Mexico, told me, 'Be anything you want, but don't ever be a teacher.' If Dixon gets his way, I guess I won't be a teacher anymore," he laughed, sardonically. Kelly pulled out of the picket line and called out, "Mad dog Radisch. How does it feel to hit the bricks'?"

"My feet hurt from walking. My voice is hoarse from chanting. My shoulder is sore from holding this picket sign. Everything's just fine," said Jack.

"Actually," added Stan, huddling with Kelly, "the mere act of walking around in circles gives one an existential sense of accomplishment, as if we were physically getting somewhere. This replaces the emotional feeling of getting nowhere."

Students joined us. "They can't do this," yelled Lisa Politeo, a feisty senior with a short-fuse temper. "Who the hell do they think they are? Gods? Are you on strike now?" she asked us.

"No" said Kelly. "This is just an informational picket line. We'll be in school tomorrow. They don't want us back here next September. We are picketing to keep our jobs next year."

Lisa loved causes—anti-war, pro-choice, women's rights, United Farm Workers. Her eyes gleamed. "You guys are all that's holding this shitty school together. Why don't they get rid of the nuns and priests instead?"

As the students gathered, they joined the line chanting: "We want Cardinet! We want Kelly! We want Radisch! We want George! We want August! We want Thomas! We want Williams! We want Johnson!"

A lone voice yelled, "Hell. Who's left?"

"Where's Bud Johnson?" asked Lisa. "He's not on the picket line. Why?"

"'Cause he's a real turkey," said Kelly. "That's why."

Radisch told Lisa, "Mr. Johnson is not a member of the teacher's union. He believes his chances of being rehired are better if he doesn't rock the boat."

"And he's right," said Kelly. "The last person they'll hire back is the St. Liz rep to the teacher's union, the guy they think is going to organize all the Catholic schools in the Oakland Diocese."

"Who's that'?" asked Lisa.

"Me," said Kelly, with a wide grin. He jutted his chin, tossed the hair out of his

Irish eyes and stepped back into our picket line. Lisa followed him. And in came new reinforcements: Muriel, with a backpack full of baby clothes, pushed the baby carriage with two-year-old Wendy riding in it. John, age four, toddled along to her left and Kristi followed on her right side holding a "Re-hire" sign—one big happy family on the picket line.

As we taught classes the next day, our bodies throbbed with sore muscles and sunburned noses. After school, we crowded into the library for our faculty meeting. Radisch planted his feet behind a rear table as a vantage point for cross-examination. He stood sideways, like a cat pulling back its ears, about to hiss.

After the prayer, Dixon recognized Radisch who began innocently. "I have a few questions, Gil. How did you make the decision to lay off these teachers?"

Dixon sat upright. In a strained attempt to look relaxed, he folded his hands on his lap and stared straight ahead, his eyes glazed but slowly twitching. "We divided the lay faculty into unique and non-unique," said Dixon. "Unique teachers were those who could not be replaced by religious teachers. Non-unique teachers had courses that could be taught by nuns or priests. So, given our budget limitations, non-unique teachers were replaced by the religious."

"Non-unique?" blurted George. "Just look at Stan. You guppies think that long-haired genius isn't unique? You've got to be kidding."

The faculty room tension eased slightly. Radisch suppressed a smile. "Is it a coincidence, Gil, that seven out of the eight teachers you laid off are all members of the teachers' union?"

Dixon lowered his head, raised his eyebrows and shot his thin white arms out from his suit jacket's sleeves. "Jack, the question of union membership is irrelevant. I feel that you are raising this issue as a smokescreen to obfuscate the basic fiscal realities of the situation. If we had enough students for next year to pay all of our expenses, the laid-off teachers would return — union or no union."

As Dixon replied, Radisch looked away from him. When Dixon finished, Radisch glared his one-eyed stare directly at him. It must have been disconcerting. "Why doesn't your budget show bingo income, Gil? Surely that $90,000 is enough to hire back most of the teachers."

Father Farley raised his finger, glancing at Dixon for a nod of approval so he could begin an apology. "I'm sorry," said Father Farley. "The Bishop won't allow us to include tenuous income in our budget. Bingo could be closed tomorrow. It might not be legal. Our parish school board and our pastor agree with the Bishop and support the principal. I'm sorry, but we cannot include bingo in our budget."

Father Farley smiled and sat back. It was not a smile of humor or satisfaction. It was a smile of appeasement and reconciliation. Sister St. Francis of Assisi smiled vacantly in response to Father Farley.

Nobody else smiled.

"Gil," Radisch continued, "These non-unique teachers have over five years of experience at St. Liz. George's been here ten years. Johnson, Stan and I have been here seven years. August and Kelly, six years. These teachers are also highest on the salary scale. Tell me this, Gil: Which lay teachers, with over five years' experience, have contracts for next year?"

Dixon blinked his eyes rapidly and threw up his hands. "What do you want me to do, research this?"

"No Gil, that's not necessary," said Radisch. "I'll tell you. It's Tom Rowe and Martha Dunwell, the same members of the advisory board who made the decision. That's called conflict of interest."

Martha Dunwell, girls' P.E. coach, shoved her large frame forward. She wore tennis shoes, sweat pants, a colorful short-sleeved shirt and a sports wrist watch. She carried a clipboard and wore a cop's whistle on a chain around her neck. "Well, as long as we have faculty elections to the administrative board, we will have this apparent conflict," said Martha. "The faculty elected me and Father Geno. I was classified in the unique category because no one else here teaches girls' P.E." Martha finished in a dull monotone.

Father Geno, the other elected rep, acted as the school's peacemaker. He stated the problem, offered his observation, then suggested a solution that fit into place like a long division math answer with no remainder. Geno would wait until things were sufficiently floundering, then begin by saying, "Why don't we...?" Here he said, "Why don't we take another look at the budget? Let's include bingo so we can rehire everyone."

"And what if bingo is closed down?" Sister Saint John the Baptist said, icicles dangling from her words.

"Sister, the Bishop has an obligation," replied Father Geno. "He won't let St. Liz go down the tubes. If this inner-city school folds, it won't be good public relations for the Bishop's reputation or the church's image. We should not need to lay off these men, some with families, who have given years of service to Saint Liz."

Sister Marie said, "I agree. I would be willing to consider a revised budget."

"I have a new budget," Bob Howard bubbled. "We can do it. This budget includes bingo. It has a lower tuition and an increased enrollment. We cut out computers.

It's balanced, with all teachers returning. All you have to do is accept it."

"Well," said Dixon, sitting straight, stern-faced, his glassy eyes still slowly twitching, "we will vote in a secret ballot. Should we, or should we not, submit this new budget? I'll announce the results to the parish school board next week."

After passing out slips of paper and collecting the votes, Dixon stood solemnly. "Are there any other announcements before I make a statement?"

Sister Marie said, "I have an announcement. Gum-chewing has reached epidemic proportions. We must stop students from chewing gum in school."

Father Farley agreed with her and added, "I'm sorry, but teachers are not to allow students to throw Frisbees in the halls."

Dixon waited. He stood expressionless, like a sphinx with a thin double chin. His eyes skipped around the room before he spoke. "I've heard that there might be a student walkout. Let's try to discourage this. If you get wind of something, put a stop to it immediately. Tell an administrator. Also, make no statements to newspapers, radio, TV, or any type of media— especially if there is a walkout. This is not anyone else's business."

The only unanimous agreement at that meeting came when it was moved that the meeting be adjourned.

As the meeting ended, Father Farley scurried up to me as chairs screeched across the floor and weary teachers shuffled out. "Oh, Paul," he said. "Forgive me, but Mr. Dixon wants me to remind you, it's your turn to help at bingo tonight."

"I know, Father," I replied. "I remember. But tonight we have a TGIF social at the union hall to raise funds for the John Thomas case. I'll be back to help at bingo."

But all the tensions of the past week caught up with me that night at the union hall: our Alameda huddle, the nuns' denial, the sad feet from the picket line, restless nights and 8:30 a.m. classes—all mixed into my drinks: bourbon on the rocks, a twist of fatigue, a squeeze of hunger, in a glass without sleep. My head went numb. My stomach shrieked. The ceiling light became a triplicate fuzzy revolving blur. I never made it to bingo.

Chapter 13

"This man is accused..."

WEEKENDS DURING THIS CRISIS were like two days of cease fire in a war of attrition. Fighting stops, tension builds. By Sunday evening, the mental anguish expands. Who wants us fired? What budget cuts can we save? Will the school board listen to us? Why did I miss bingo last Friday night? I mulled this over in my mind all weekend.

By Monday morning, it almost felt like the middle of the week. Teachers scurry to classes, fumbling with keys before the tardy bell rings. At 10:30 a.m., we untangled ourselves from chalk dust and cranky classes for an overdue coffee break in the faculty sanctuary: caffeine, comfort, and camaraderie. At my mailbox, I rummaged through late homework papers and found a white envelope from the principal. The letter read:

MINDWORKER: MAYBECK

Office of the Principal

Paul August:

You did not show up for Bingo last Friday. Before considering what action to take against you, I would like to ask you for whatever reasons you have for not showing up. Present these reasons in writing to me prior to next Monday.

(signed) Gil Dixon, Principal

I tossed the note to Radisch, who read it with a thin smile. He then read it aloud through the steam from the Styrofoam coffee cups held by Kelly, Stan and George. They laughed. A wide grin brightened Radisch's face. I stapled the note to the faculty bulletin board for all to see. Radisch slid behind the long mahogany faculty table, like a pompous attorney ready for trial.

"OK, Augie," Radisch said. "You stand accused. Kelly, George, Stan—you're the witnesses." Radisch leaned on the cluttered table and pointed at me. "This man is accused of neglecting his responsibilities to God, country and bingo. Kelly, what say ye?"

Kelly jutted his thick chin, scratched his mutton chops, extended his cigar-holding hand and leaned forward in a mock eye-to-eye confrontation with Radisch. "Guilty, of course," he said, jerking his head upward with a smile. "August is crazy. Everyone knows that. He spent every Friday night running dances for our teens. The strobe lights and incense affected his brain. He missed one night at bingo, a Catholic sin. He should be chastised. Where's your sense of Christian values? What's more important, children or money? What a farce."

"George? How do you judge August?" asked Radisch.

"Ha! Augie's guilty on five counts. Are you ready? Now count 'em," George replied as he stroked his bald head. "First, August organized the chocolate drive last year that left cocoa stains on the nun's underwear. Second, he was moderator of the junior class during the newspaper drive when they stole *Chronicles* from the seniors' bin and won by a ton. Third, I know for a fact that he sold day-old donated donuts during Lent for the ski club. Fourth, he's guilty of shivering in the dunking booth, the easiest target at the parish festival. My dead-eye baseball students hit the bull's eye, and sent Augie splashing into a tub of ice cold water on a foggy day. St. Liz only made a lousy 25¢ a throw, peanuts compared to the $1,000 a night bingo operation. Fifth, he took a busload of kids to the Altamont Rolling Stones concert to sell soft drinks as a work program. The nuns thought they all got stoned on music. Everyone knows how much the nuns and the priests and Dixon like August—and if you believe that, I've got land on the mudflats of Emeryville to sell you when the tide goes out."

"Stan, what say you?" asked Radisch.

Stan folded his arms to his frayed corduroy jacket, wrinkling his plaid tie. Then he slowly withdrew a smoldering pipe from his mouth. "Quite frankly, I suspect that bingo is not the issue. August has alienated selective elements of this school with his unconventional attitudes. It's perfectly legal to circulate a petition to legalize marijuana, but this upsets the more uptight parents and clergy."

"And he's not even a pothead—just a liberal," laughed Kelly. "He doesn't smoke a pipe or a cigar because he never even learned how to smoke cigarettes."

Stan continued: "The willingness of August to confront sexual topics in marriage class is a threat to the asexual nuns and priests around here. August is still somehow implicated in the contrived John Thomas 'sex class' incident.

"August's freelance writing, in counterculture magazines like Rolling Stone, casts doubt on his academic involvement and draws criticism from tradition-bound priests. August also sings protest songs in so-called hippie coffee houses. He is all too unconventional for the more conventional members of the staff."

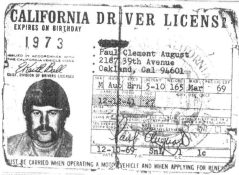

Mr. August
Psychology
Marriage

Early members of the American Federation of Teachers (AFT), above, included Tom Rowe, dean of boys, me, Stan Cardinet, Bob Trost, an English teacher, and Jim Kelly, our union rep. In 1966, I had a clean-cut image. Three years later, in 1969, I renewed my license but not my image.

"Stan," I said. "Look at you: hiking boots, blue jeans, long hair, tweed cap—and you say I'm unconventional?"

"Of course," Radisch interrupted. "Compared to Stan, August is merely unconventional. Stan is called a freak, a weirdo, a hippie."

"Well, then," said George, "why isn't Dixon dumping on Stan instead of Augie?"

Stan replied, "Because August made a serious blunder in the present anti-teacher atmosphere. He went to a union meeting instead of a bingo party."

In my analysis of the situation," Stan went on, "it appears that Dixon is trying to do to August what he failed to do to Santos. He laid off August for budget reasons. Now, he's using this absurd bingo letter to justify keeping him out. Dixon doesn't want to re-hire August, or any of us, if the enrollment rises again."

The bell rang, shattering our faculty room melodrama. "Don't forget," said Radisch, "tomorrow in the boiler room, we prepare for the school board meeting."

Chapter 14

"The most important crisis…"

TUESDAY, AFTER SCHOOL. Our classrooms have two-way intercoms. These PA systems in the wall, however, can electronically eavesdrop on any classroom conversation. So, we decided to meet in the boiler room.

Coach Bob Howard called this meeting. We shuffled down the cracked cement stairs and gathered in a circle under a bare light bulb dangling from wire strung across dusty overhead pipes. George sat on an empty metal drum. Stan took over the janitor's lounge chair near the barely hidden TV. The rest of us sat on boxes, crates and storage bins. "Okay," said Howard. "We've got Mrs. Presho here from the parents who support the teachers. She'll let us all know how much parent support we can count on."

Mrs. Presho carefully stood. She wore wide glasses with her short, black hair. Her dark suit made her look more like a business executive than a nurse. "Most parents will be at the school board to support you guys tomorrow. But the parent-athletic group supports the principal. They want their money to go to football, not salaries. They feel that since they run the bingo games, they control that money. Frankly, I've been involved enough to see clearly what your problem is here. It's the principal."

Jim Kelly placed one foot on a mop pail and raised his index finger. "She's right. I say we polarize the community, isolate Dixon and go to the Bishop. Also, who has the power here? Is it the board, the pastor or the Bishop? Who's really pulling the wires?"

"Okay," Howard said as the gentle hiss of steam eased from rusted pipes in the dim unlit regions of the boiler room. "I have a new budget with higher enrollment and bingo income. It makes sense. Any reasonable board will buy it."

"Ha!" blurted Kelly. "I really wouldn't count on any of them being reasonable, but I have us scheduled on the agenda for tomorrow night's meeting."

Radisch said, "I'm sending a telegram to the Bishop demanding an immediate meeting."

Howard took a breath of stale air, kicked at a sweat stained jock strap on the crusty basement floor and leaned on a rusted valve protruding from a mammoth black boiler that looked ready to explode at any second. "Listen you guys. We'll get your jobs back," he said. "Don't lose the faith."

Wednesday night. The parish school board meeting. As usual, the most important crisis ended up last on the agenda. We sat through a report from a Sunday school teacher, an account of the parish bake sale and presentation from a promoter organizing a country and western benefit concert for the parish.

Finally, Betty Board, a large graying woman with bifocals, called on the high school principal for a report.

"The faculty voted 18-17 to submit a new budget," said Dixon. "The administrative board of the school, however, voted not to submit a new budget. Therefore, I have no new budget to submit tonight."

"Wait a minute," yelled Howard, jumping to his feet, flushing red with frustration. "This is our new budget, not yours."

Young Lisa Politeo stood up. "We want our teachers back. You have to listen to the students. If you refuse to listen in an ethical way then you'll listen in an unethical way." Her words cracked through the still room. "If this school is supposed to be for students then you'd better start to listen or we will go to the streets and you won't have any school."

A board member replied, "Young lady, these pressure tactics only work against you. However, I'll overlook those remarks and make a motion in spite of it. I move we look at the teachers' new budget."

Father Orville, pastor of Saint Liz parish, arrived late. His body bent as he moved through the crowd. As he joined the board members, his stark white hair reflected yellowish in the neon lights of the meeting hall. Thick black frame glasses magnified his eyes and blocked a few wrinkles.

As Howard began, Father Orville listened intensely. His dark eyebrows nervously danced up and down as Howard outlined a new budget.

The Power Structure: The pastor is responsible for the entire parish: St. Liz church, elementary school, and high school. He supervises the school board who makes policy decisions and hires the principals. All pastors of all East Bay parishes are accountable to the Bishop who reports to the regional Cardinal who votes to elect the Pope in Rome.

When Howard finished, Father Orville replied. "The only problem here is that a few teachers are being laid off. We are going through changes." When Father Orville talked, his eyebrows came under control, settling above his magnified eyes. He raised them to make a point and underline his raspy voice. "We have to trust each other and work together."

"Ah, Father Orville..." Kelly stood. "As a union rep here at St. Liz, I cannot understand why you support the Farm Workers' Union in the Central Valley but you refuse to allow teachers in your own parish to organize. Why?"

Orville's eyebrows wiggled out of control as he replied, "We're a Christian apostolate. We don't need unions."

The audience groaned. Betty Board rapped her gavel. Gil Dixon asked for the floor.

"We operate under certain constraints," said Dixon, sitting with his legs crossed at the thighs and one foot nervously kicking the air. His ankle-length socks sagged to reveal a pale skin line. "The Bishop says that I cannot count tenuous income such as bingo and I cannot make contracts with teachers unless I can pay. Let me show you..." Dixon flicked on an overhead projector and filled the room with blue neon statistical figures crisscrossed by red zigzag lines. His monologue lapsed into technical jargon. "Projected enrollment...pupil to teacher ratio...percent of decrease...discrepancy figure...data graph chart...clear pattern of decline."

Betty Board asked Howard, "If the Bishop won't help us, Mr. Howard, how can we take the risk on your budget?"

Howard: "We don't know how much the Bishop has. It's a secret. We take a risk every year on an assumed enrollment. Why is the board here if the Bishop is giving directives to the principal?" Applause.

One board member responded: "If we go down the drain, I say we go down the drain together." Applause.

Another said, "These teachers have years of service. You don't just let them go." Applause.

"The Bishop is like any other employer. Do the best with the least money. That's the bait. We don't know his subsidy to the suburban schools. The reasonable and the honorable course is to support these teachers." Applause.

Betty Board called for a vote. "Will the board accept the new budget and rehire teachers?"

"Yes."

"Yes."

"No."

"Yes."

"No."

"No."

"No."

"The vote is 4 to 3 not to rehire." Silence.

"Meeting adjourned."

We joined up after the meeting at Mary's Pizza Shop, a funky picnic table spot near school that always has an "open" sign even when they're not. Howard's cherubic face twisted with loathing. "That son of a bitch Dixon smiled after the vote. He actually enjoyed that."

Stan became analytical. "School principals such as Dixon have an advantage over teachers. They spend days preparing stats and lobbying board members. No one spoke against us but they voted against us. Teachers are at an obvious disadvantage. After a full day in the classroom, our energy is low and our opportunity for preparation is limited."

"I feel sick," said Kelly as he slouched outside for air.

"The stress is beginning to get us." Stan looked tired. "I feel fatigued. Sometimes I feel dizzy. It's the pressures of classroom lessons, students' demands, correcting tests, union meetings and financial uncertainty. We are under a heavy tension."

"We can't let them win," said Radisch. "If we can begin negotiations, we can end this mess."

I said, "If we are not rehired, we'll be unemployed. I'll have time to work on my song, 'The American Federation of Unemployed Citizens.'"

"You gotta be kidding," said Kelly as he tottered back to the table.

Stan took a bite of cheese pizza then washed it down with a swig of beer, leaving a slight fringe of foam on his moustache. "August has a point. Colleges produce too many teachers while mothers produce too few babies. By the end of the decade there will be one unemployed teacher for every two working."

"Well don't you fret, Stan old boy," said Kelly. "We'll get your job back or there won't be any St. Liz."

That evening, I came in through the basement entrance, grabbed my guitar and continued working on my song:

I ain't a socialist, a Maoist or an anarchist.
I'm not a Democrat, Republican or Inde-
    pendent.
I'm no reactionary, no revolutionary.
I don't shout no cause, no platform, no
    propaganda.

I'm not a capitalist or a philanthropist, but
    I'll tell you this.
All I want's my name on some job list.
Don't give me your philosophy, that's not
    what I need.
Don't give me your rhetoric. I can't get a job
    from it.

'Cause I'm automatically a member of the
    biggest group the USA has ever seen.

I'm in the A. F. U. C. That's the American Federation of Unemployed Citizens. AFUC![23]

Chapter 15

"The man is not normal..."

THE MEN'S ROOM DEBATE. THURSDAY, noon. Priests have a terrible time in the toilet. They wear these long, Franciscan robes with wooden sandals and black slacks underneath. St. Liz's faculty men's room has only one stall. When that's occupied, the poor padres have to struggle up to one of the urinals and grapple with their bulky attire as they steadfastly pee.

Father Farley had just begun this ritual as I entered. The stall was taken. He fumbled with his robes as I stepped beside him and unzipped. "Hi Father," I said, looking over at him.

"Oh? I'm sorry. Hello, Paul." he said as he stared vacantly at the monotonous green wall ahead of him. The men's room is often the scene of private conversations. No phones or students to interrupt.

As I zipped up, Father Farley struggled to put himself back together and said, "Er, Paul, could I ask you, I'm sorry, but please refrain from Xeroxing Mr. Dixon's bingo letter to you and putting it up on the faculty bulletin board. It creates problems."

"I'll keep putting it up as long as you keep tearing it down," I said, hitting the Borax dispenser. "It shows how reactionary Dixon is. Besides, bingo is technically illegal. I'm supposed to be a chaperone at a 'student art show' or a 'spaghetti dinner,' not an illegal gambling activity."

"Well, er, ah..." Father Farley stared hard into that dull green wall while he fumbled with his garments and tugged at his zipper. "I really think you should speak to Mr. Dixon about that letter."

"Bullshit," I said. "He knows why I wasn't at bingo. I told you. I'll be there tomorrow night. I'm not going to Dixon. You tell him to see me."

"Oh, no," replied Farley, shaking his head. "I'm sorry, but I can't tell the principal what to do."

"Dixon's dishonest," I said.

Farley started washing his hands. "I'm sorry, Paul. I don't think you should say that."

I stared at him. "Father Edward gave me tenure. He said I had a job here as long as St. Liz existed. Then ten days before our contracts are due, Dixon changes the tenure policy so he can fire us. Dishonest!"

Farley replied, "I'm sorry, Paul, but the state code does not apply to private schools. We only adopted it. How can we have tenured teachers without students?"

"Oh, come on," I said. "We've had this policy for five years. Dixon changes it in one day to get rid of us. That's dishonest."

"Well, Paul," said Farley, shaking his head again, I'm sorry but...."

"And stop feeling sorry for yourself," I said.

"I think we should try to get you a job, Paul."

"Don't do me any favors."

"But the tenure policy had to be clarified."

"Clarified my ass. Your 29-year-old boy principal did a fine job. Changing tenure in mid-contract is underhanded."

"If Mr. Dixon didn't balance the budget, he wouldn't have a job," said Farley.

"Educational Darwinism," I said. "Survival of the fittest. The Bishop pulls the purse strings. Either the teachers' jobs or the principal's head. The Christians versus the lions, right Father?"

Radisch came out of the stall, shouldered his way through the men's room and said, "Our union lawyer just met with the school's lawyer. Dixon and Orville kept insisting that the union got in the way of negotiations. So, we said, 'Okay, The union won't be there. Now the school can negotiate with the teachers in good faith.' They had to agree."

"Well, I guess that's good news," said Farley as he backed out the door and left.

"When?" I asked.

"Tuesday," said Radisch. "They insist that the John Thomas case is separate. They laid him off for next year. Now they want to fire him for this year. They'll decide that on Monday."

"Oh, Paul." Father Farley peeked back in. "Don't forget bingo tomorrow night. Also, Mr. Dixon wanted you to have this letter."

Dixon's letter began:

You are directed to appear before the administrative board on Monday. Please bring a written statement about your involvement in and knowledge of John Thomas' remarks in your class on sex.

Radisch looked over the letter. "Screw him. Don't write anything. Let me file this piece of shit." He threw the letter in the toilet and flushed it. We left the faculty men's room.

Friday night. St. Liz bingo games grow to $1,000 jackpots every Tuesday and Friday. Since gambling is illegal, the game operates under the façade of a spaghetti dinner: pay three dollars and get a paper plate full of spaghetti. Collect six bingo cards and win

$15 to $20 a game. St. Liz's faculty is required to help as part of our extra duty time.

After arriving I reported to the president of the athletic parents who was a local department store executive. He was upset because he needed helpers an hour earlier. "We donate our time, twice a week for bingo," he said bitterly. "Why do we few parents have to do it all? Where is the faculty? Why don't they help more? During my two-week vacation I spent 12 hours a day installing the snack bar. We don't want to see the money we raise go to teachers. Our money goes to the athletic program first, then to extras, like closed circuit TV for the school."

I shrugged and went over to join Bud Johnson stamping this evening's bingo cards. "I think there's something unhealthy about those obsessive parents," Johnson told me. "They spend all their time helping the school. Why aren't they home with their own kids?"

"I'd rather have over-involved parents than none at all," I replied.

"But I'm more concerned about the mental health of our principal," Johnson continued, smoothing back his graying hair. "I believe Dixon's a sociopath. I remember the case of a black girl who said 'shit' in class. He wanted to kick her out of school. I explained that the doctor had her under psychiatric care. Then Dixon wanted to go to her 5th period class and explain to the students that the reason she has not been expelled was because of her psychiatric condition. It all felt incredibly tense for three days. Sister Marie hid the girl. I stood in the halls ready to pull the fire alarm if I saw him go to her classroom. The man is not normal, whatever that means in this insane place. Dixon simply never considers the possible consequences of actions. He is under the delusion that what he intends to accomplish is the only outcome of the act—like firing all of us. He thinks he is simply going to get rid of us. He doesn't consider that he might just destroy this whole school in the process."

We sat together stamping bingo cards as parents and parishioners streamed through. Stamp. Slam. "Is it my imagination, or did Sister Saint John the Baptist walk in the opposite direction to avoid us?" asked Johnson.

"These athletic parents show a strained smile when they greet us shit disturbers," I replied. The bingo game became more crowded, more hectic. Four hundred hopefuls bumped each other.

"We're out of seesaw tables. No more folding chairs."

"Move to the balcony. Bring out the school desks."

"Open the classrooms. Closed circuit TV can transmit the bingo numbers."

"Watch it! Don't spill the spaghetti. Where's the cart pushers with the peanuts, pretzels and pickles?"

An electronic bingo board flashes, B-7. The caller reaches for the ping pong blower, which the good fathers imported from Las Vegas. Another number. Bingo cards slide tiny black shutters over bold digits. Cash money prizes look for lucky winners. Here it comes...BING-OOOOOOOOOOO!

Chapter 16

"What about the orgies?"

THE JOHN THOMAS SEX CASE. Monday after school. St. Liz advisory board meeting. I entered the principal's conference room with John Thomas and Jorge Stokes. Dixon sat at the end of a grey Formica-top table. "Mr. Stokes," said Dixon in stone-face, "I'd like you to meet my school site board. To my right is Sister Saint John the Baptist, Father Farley and Sister Marie. To my left, Father Geno, and I'm sure you know Mr. Tom Rowe, our elected faculty rep and member of your union."

Dixon continued, "I interviewed several students about this case, including the two who originally complained. We will review the charges, then members of this team will have questions, I'm sure." Dixon licked his lip, glanced up from his file, then passed out a single sheet of paper from which he read:

MINDWORKER: MAYBECK

1. *John Thomas asked the boys and girls separately, "How many of you are virgins?" When one girl raised her hand he said, "far-out," as if to approve of such a loose class. He definitely implied he was not a virgin.*

2. *He thought it was silly for a girl to remain a virgin until she gets out of college since she is capable of reproduction at age 14. "By abstaining, she lives eight years in frustration." He said, "It's unnatural to constantly deny your sexual desires. I don't see how they can hold back the urge."*

3. *He said that sexual intercourse—although he used a word beginning in "f" and ending in "k", four letters in length—is boring if done in the same position all the time. Unfortunately, the law prohibits certain sexual acts.*

4. *When asked if he favored premarital sex, he said that living with your girlfriend was a good idea since you find out some of her personal habits. He said he lived with one girl for three years but never married her.*

5. *He said he was having too much fun 'playing around' to get married. This was referring to playing around sexually.*

6. *He said he once had a male roommate who kept "pissing and shitting on the toilet seat." He used the words "bullshit" and "shit" repeatedly in his talk.*

7. *He said he gets a "great deal of pleasure out of popping a girl's cherry."*

8. *He said, "Seeing two men make love turns me off but seeing two women make love turns me on."*

9. *He said he had been to many orgies and he was known as the "Colt 45 kid" in college.*

Dixon slumped in his armchair and invited questions. Stokes said, "Mr. Dixon, I think these statements are greatly exaggerated and badly distorted."

"I would like to hear Mr. Thomas tell his side of this," said Sister Marie.

"Thank you, Sister," said Thomas. "You know, I have never said things like 'popping a girl's cherry.' I said I like girls who are cherry, meaning fine, beautiful, and classy. This reference to seeing two men making love: I responded to a question from a student who had a Playboy Magazine in class. It had photos of lesbians. I simply agreed with the statement of the article. Most men are disgusted by male homosexuality but are more tolerant of lesbians. I admit to being indiscreet when I asked, who are the virgins in class. I told the class that they didn't have to reply if they didn't want to. I perceive this to be my only error."

"What about the orgies?" said Sister Saint John the Baptist with a glare.

Thomas replied, "Sister, the word 'orgies' is not to be taken literally. At State, and most west coast campuses, we used the phrase 'drunken orgy' to describe a drinking party. Colt 45 was the fad drink at the time."

"I'm sorry, but what's this about illegal positions of sexual intercourse and using four-letter words in class?" asked Father Farley, a slight blush to his cheeks, his eyes downcast.

I interrupted. "May I answer that? Marriage class deals with sexuality that is different from biological reproduction. Many students are limited to four-letter street words in expressing their questions."

"Oh?" said Sister Saint John the Baptist. "Tell me, Mr. August, how do you handle these words that, according to Mr. Thomas, begin in 'f' and end in 'k'?"

"Just like our former principal, Father Edward, who taught the class before me," I answered. "I tell the class the difference between the German vulgate and the Latin derivatives. Latin words are the formal polysyllabic phrases like intercourse, feces, urine, penis and vagina."

Father Farley lowered his eyes again and started to turn red.

I continued. "The German vulgate has the four-letter words – the 'F' word, shit, piss and so on."

Father Farley closed his eyes and burned crimson.

"Do you tell this to your students in class?" gasped Sister Saint John the Baptist.

"Yes," I said, "But I've never had a student or parent complain, because I depersonalize it. I can answer any student question using formal terms. For example, in class a girl asked, 'What's a blow job?' That required a sensitive explanation."

Father Farley looked puzzled. "A blow job? I don't understand."

The room went quiet. Both nuns held a steel-faced glare. Dixon frowned. Tom Rowe suppressed a smile.

"Oral-genital sex," I said, "I translate from student street talk to clinical terms. I explain that oral is mouth and genital refers to penis or vagina. They get the picture."

"Oh, well, yes..." Farley faded.

John Thomas said, "I wanted to be direct with the kids. That's why I used some street slang and talked about my personal life. I did not make an effort to use clinical terms because the students wanted me to be completely honest, and I was."

"Perhaps too honest," said Dixon. "Are there any more questions?"

Stokes, who had an artificial hand, raised his silver prosthesis. "You don't have a case against Mr. Thomas. The two students who complained were both whites from San Leandro, one of the most racist cities in California. John Thomas is the first black male teacher to be hired at St. Liz. The majority of the class enjoyed his talk. There are simply no grounds for any action against him."

Dixon shrugged his shoulders. No more discussion. Stokes and Thomas left. Dixon asked me to stay.

Rowe raised a finger and an eyebrow. "Ah...I presume we all know that no blame for this incident will be attributed to Mr. August. I feel we owe him a clarification of his status."

Dixon raised his chin in a statuesque priestly pose. "I absolve you, Paul, of any responsibility for the John Thomas incident and no charges will be brought against you."

"What about Thomas?" I asked.

Dixon said that John Thomas would be given a choice: Resign or be fired.

I left in disgust.

Chapter 17

"School starts six hours..."

TUESDAY AFTERNOON. The day dragged on with an ominous lull of expectation for the after school negotiation session that could end it all. It was a grey overcast day, silent and sunless. We unionists gathered in the library after school. Dixon, Father Orville and Sister Saint John the Baptist sat with their backs to the windows. Kelly ambled in and lit a cigar as Radisch flipped through his legal files and Howard passed out purple ditto budget sheets. Stan started doodling, George cracked a joke and Dallas Williams quietly took a seat. Levinson and Bud Johnson came in with Rowe, who puffed gently on his pipe. I sat next to Santos.

Stan said leaned over to me and quietly observed, "Here are the twelve prodigal apostles versus the unholy trinity."

I laughed.

Our first proposed agenda item is to agree on these ground rules.

1. Basic courtesy. Right to caucus.

2. Open financial disclosure. Budget solution determines all other issues.

3. Results of negotiation will be final.

Father Orville twitched his eyebrows and said, "The three of us will caucus now to discuss ground rule number three." They left the library. When they returned, Orville explained, "It's unlikely that we can decide anything here without the approval of our school board. This is a dilemma. A lay principal is now answerable to a lay school board. You are asking me to overrule the very people I supported to make the church more democratic."

"It's like the longshoremen and ship owners," agreed Dixon. "Their representatives meet but they take results back to the owners or union members for final voting."

Radisch replied, "We have foregone our right to union representation to negotiate in good faith with you. You are the owners. We are the teachers. We have all the power to settle everything in this very room."

We agreed to a recess so Dixon could poll board members by phone. When we reconvened we learned that Betty, the board president, refused. The board decided to meet tomorrow night in closed session.

We caucused. Kelly said, "We have to decide to drop our presentation now or go ahead with a meaningless meeting."

"Put it off?" said Howard. "After four hours here just trying to establish the ground rules? Let's battle it out."

We continued. They were intransigent. We were frustrated. We tried other issues. Radisch leaned forward. "Gil, your new tenure policy gives all religious teachers seniority. The most incompetent religious teacher has seniority over the most competent lay teacher."

Sister Saint John the Baptist clenched her fist and snarled through her teeth, "We make less. We work more. We have a right to our jobs."

"That's just plain wrong," replied Radisch. "If we were priests we would have our jobs now. Also, you charge more tuition for non-Catholics. You're penalizing people for their religious preference—clearly discrimination."

"That's not true," said Father Orville. "Catholic parishioners subsidize the school through church donations. That's why outsiders pay more."

The battle raged into the evening.

Radisch: "You lay off Stan, the chairman of the history department, but you keep Santos, who has less seniority."

Dixon: "Santos teaches Math. Stan doesn't."

Howard: "Look. Some of our classes have 42 students. If we have a drop in enrollment—and I don't believe we will—but if we do, we could keep our teachers to a lower class size."

Dixon: "Studies have shown that there is no correlation between class size and learning."[24]

Me: "What about bingo? There must be some way to use that $100,000 a year on teacher salaries."

Orville: "We can't issue contracts on the basis of tenuous money. Bingo could be closed at any time. It may not be legal."

Santos: "The key is enrollment. If we accept more students, we can hire back the teachers."

Dixon: "My calculations show a drop of enrollment from 720 students to 550. We won't have enough income to support all our teachers."

Levinson: "Father Orville, why is it that the Franciscans import wooden panel doors to create the illusion of poverty at your monastery? Can't the church eliminate this pseudo-humility to save money?"

Orville: "My dear Mr. Levinson, my hands are tied by our financial situation. The school has no money. The parish has no money. The Bishop won't help us. Piedmont priests live in mansions and drive Cadillacs.

My doodles became bizarre as the negotiations became inconclusive. My doodling evoked intense anxiety, unsettling frustration, and suppressed anger.

I'm lucky to have a VW bus. The rich Catholic parishes keep their money. They don't share it with us."

Radisch: "There's one other small item here, Gil. Some of the teachers who were given notice asked for letters of recommendation. What you gave us is worthless. Your letters end with this kiss of death statement: 'For more information please call me.'"

Dixon: "I'll rewrite the letters to your satisfaction."

Stan: "It's midnight. The only point we have negotiated is a revised letter of recommendation."

Orville: "Remember that the parish school board will meet tomorrow night to decide whether or not we have the power to make final decisions."

Stan: "Is this a Catholic school? Father Orville, you stand on the pulpit on Sundays preaching faith. Have you no faith in your own faculty? No faith that we can build enrollment? No faith in the future of this school? For seven years I have had the good fortune to help build this unique school. Most of my colleagues are my best friends. This school has evolved into an ideal place, the most rewarding occasion for fulfillment that could be granted a teacher working with beautiful and talented children. Suffice it to say that I am very happy to have lived a meaningful life as one of the teachers here at St. Liz. There must be some way that we can save this school, as we know it."

George: "Stan's right. Receiving a lay-off notice at St. Liz is like getting a rejection slip on 14 years of my life. I went to St. Liz.

So did Bud Johnson and Paul August. St. Liz is special to all of us. We're a Christian school. We have to look at the morality of all this. This is wrong. We have to work together to find a way to save this school."

Me: I spent eight years in Catholic elementary school, four at St. Liz, four at St. Mary's and six teaching here. Twenty-two years in Catholic schools. I'm 30 years old. I feel I deserve better.

Dixon: "Perhaps we have missed the moral side in considering the financial. We are different from a public school. We do have a heart. I want to give this some very deep consideration. I don't want you guys to get jealous but, tomorrow I'm going to sleep late, have a leisurely breakfast, then walk through my garden and meditate."

As we shuffled off into the night, Kelly said to me, "What a farce! This can't be real. It's 2 a.m. A real hurter. We've been here since eight this morning. I just can't believe we put in an eighteen hour day. School starts six hours from now and the principal is going to sleep late before he strolls through his garden to meditate on our fate! What a farce."

Chapter 18

"St. Liz never expelled..."

The next evening, we waited at Kelly's Fox Court apartment for news from the closed session of the St. Liz school board. Would they allow us to bargain without them?

As I entered Kelly's apartment, he greeted me. "I have an excellent burglar alarm system here. I leave the door unlocked. When these rip-off artists find my door open, they figure that I'm either home or I'll be back in a minute. It scares 'em off."

I pulled out my guitar and began singing.

"Betty is the heavy on the school board, she's bored with life...."

George popped a beer and crawled into the chain-held hammock. "School just isn't the way it used to be," he said.

"Uh, oh," said Kelly. "Look out. George's on his soapbox again."

George rocked gently. "Augie and I went to St. Liz as students and returned to teach here. We've seen the change in the way kids act. We had our traditions. You were queer if you wore green on Thursday, although no one knew why. The senior steps were off-limits to lower classmen. God, America, and marriage were right. Atheists, communists and unmarried sex were viewed as wrong. Every decision appeared black or white. No shades of grey.

"We had all the answers about life but we didn't know the questions. Today, the kids have the questions and they know the answers don't fit."

Stan sat on the floor puffing on one of his pipes. He said, "George, you're a reductionist. You simplify everything. School traditions go in cycles. They melt down, go through a metamorphosis, and then the same rituals return in a different form. Your classmates painted the flagpole green on Saint Patrick's Day and went to the Sadie Hawkins dance.[25] Young people today celebrate Martin Luther King Day and Cinco De Mayo."

"No, Stan," said George. "It's not the same. Even the Franciscan priests have changed. Paul, do you remember Father Marlon? As an All-American tackle at Notre Dame, he turned down the pros to join the priesthood. Those old priests were tough. He tossed one kid down the stairs to shape him up."

"Oh come on, George," said Stan.

"He's right," I said. "Physical punishment came swift in our day. After I pulled the fire alarm after school as a prank, Father Emery Tang, our Korean principal, later called me up to the front of class and gave me a choice: body pain then and there or detention until the end of the year. I chose the pain. He said he would beat me until someone in class yelled 'mercy.' I knelt and held out my arm because his fist usually caused a 'frog' when he hit it. As I prepared for the pain in my arm he suddenly rapped me hard on the head with his knuckle. We called it a 'konk' because you could hear my head konk when his knuckle rapped it, hard.

"As I reached for my head, he used his fist on my arm. The skin immediately welted up into a big bump, which is why we called that a 'frog.' He gave me a twist of the wrist, a tweak on the nose, another frog and two quick konks. When my tears began, my Italian friend Gene Dick yelled 'mercy.' I felt relieved. But my classmates playfully jumped Gene for ruining their fun."

"Augie's right," said George. "In our day, the school padres had a macho image. Real men. Nobody messed with them. "

"Ha!" said Kelly. "Look at them now. Farley is a wimp. Boomer is an egomaniac. Father Edward was a wishy-washy Bishop's boot licker. It's really a shame."

Stan said, "August here has always been in trouble with St. Liz, even when he was a student."

"Yeah," I said. "I wrote an editorial against the student court and smuggled it into the school newspaper. The school put me on probation."

"It's ironic, isn't it?" said Stan. "St. Liz's never expelled you when you were a student agitator but now that you're a teacher activist, they're kicking you out."

"What a farce," said Kelly. The phone rang and he answered it. "It's Radisch. He said the secret school board meeting is running late. He's waiting for the results. He wants to meet us at The Master's."

"Sure, why not?" said George. "A pitcher of beer, a game of pool and a toss of liar's dice. Let's go."

Kelly and I made it to The Master's, our local St. Liz neighborhood bar. Radisch was waiting. Stan and George decided to skip it.

"What's up?" asked Kelly.

"No surprises," said Radisch, sipping a beer. "Four negatives. No to our budget. No to reviewing the rehiring. No to letting the unholy trinity negotiate with us and no to John Thomas. They announced his resignation tonight."

"What a hurter," said Kelly. "That's just terrible. I can't believe it."

Gradually, we all got tired and left except for Kelly and Radisch who both stayed for a last round of pool.

The next morning I greeted Radisch and Kelly in the faculty room. Radisch had a bandage above his swollen left eye and looked like he didn't get much sleep. "What happened to you?" I asked.

"I don't feel like talking about it," he replied, without his usual energetic cynical smile. "Ask Kelly. He'll tell you."

"I kind or started it," said Kelly. "After you guys left the Master's last night, we played a last game of pool. Radisch here was cuing in the nine ball when a woman got tossed across the bar and slammed into the wall. Then a guy started slugging her.

"I yelled 'Stop it!' I figured the bartender would break it up, but he didn't."

"Then I stepped in to pull the guy off the woman," added Radisch. "I didn't see his friend, a 200 pound biker gorilla. His fist hit my head before I knew it was coming. He wore a big ring that gouged my forehead."

I couldn't believe what I was hearing first thing in the morning. My two friends got into a bar room brawl. At one point, bodies crashed into a St. Liz trophy case in the back of the bar. Trophies, broken glass and beer spilled across the linoleum floor. No one got cut deeply.

"One of 'em had me on the floor, pummeling me," added Radisch.

"I pulled Jack away from those goons and took him to the restroom," Kelly said to me. "We used paper towels to stop the bleeding. I checked above his eye and told him it was cut bad and we should go to Kaiser emergency for stitches. As we left the Master's, we walked right by the woman-beater, the beaten woman, and the biker guy still drinking together at the Bar."

"Here I was at 3 a.m. getting five stitches in my forehead at Kaiser," said Radisch, managing a weak smile.

Kelly said, "Well you guys, my daddy, a teacher himself, warned me not to go into teaching. Last night we were emotionally put down by the school board, then we were physically wiped out by those thugs. I'm beginning to think that maybe, just maybe, my daddy was right."

Chapter 19

"Did you hear that?"

OG ROLLS THROUGH THE GOLDEN GATE, pushes against Berkeley, and filters into Piedmont, where the Bishop's lives, an elite white city within the city of Oakland. Exotic green and purple plants reach for moisture. Dew clings to tile roofs of mansions dwarfed by giant redwood trees. The fog circles the Oakland hills then creeps down to the flatlands of St. Liz where it mixes with auto exhaust fumes and tomato cannery odors during the summer. The world here is covered with a dull overcast. No trees. Few flowers here. No mansions.

Another St. Liz parish school board meeting. These school board sessions resemble the six o'clock news version of angry parents and frustrated teachers. We all jammed into a small meeting hall.

Shortly after Betty called the meeting to order with a prayer, Kelly spoke up. "Betty?

I wonder if we could get a spot on the agenda to—"

She cut him off. "I'm sorry Mr. Kelly. You have to submit items one week in advance."

Father Bill O'Donnell stood. Father Bill was from the Flatland Fathers, a small group of radical priests who believed more in social justice than Catholic doctrine. His assigned parish was St. Joseph's the Workman in Berkeley, but he claimed the streets as his pews and the curb as his kneeler. He wore the Roman collar with his black priest suit and dirty white tennis shoes. "Members of the board," said Father Bill. "I have prepared a statement—"

Betty raised her gavel and slammed it down. "You are out of order!"

Father Bill ignored her, turned toward the audience and began reading from his notes. "I have come here tonight to—"

"The agenda is set," Betty raised her voice. "We cannot change it." She cleared her throat, glanced at the audience and continued, "Now our first item of business—"

Kelly jumped up and addressed Father Orville. "Father, as pastor of Saint Liz, perhaps you could clarify this. Didn't you tell me to contact Betty for a spot on the agenda? She says she needs a week's notice."

Orville shrugged, "If those are the rules of the chair..."

Father Bill asked, "Why don't you let us speak?"

Orville frowned at his priestly adversary. Anger rose in his voice. "I don't like being given these ultimatums at the last minute and being told to make a decision." He slapped his open palm hard against the table. The sound echoed through the room and left a moment of awkward silence until Kelly stood again.

"Will we be allowed to speak or not? Please give us a yes or no answer," said Kelly.

Betty replied, "The answer is no. Now our first item of business is the Sunday school report..."

Mrs. Presho, Lisa's mom, stood up from the middle of the crowded room. "I beg your pardon. Parents pay tuition. We want to be involved. Surely you are not going to refuse to listen to your own teachers."

Betty replied, "They are not on the agenda."

Father Bill objected. "These are your parents. How can you refuse their request?"

Sister Clem lumbered up out of her seat. "I've had enough. I'm here for the Sunday school report. I reviewed the teachers' case over the weekend and there are no—"

"But Sister," pleaded Father Bill.

"Don't you interrupt me!" bellowed Sister Clem as she lowered her head, stretched out her arm and pointed an index finger at Father Bill, ready to zap him with a jolt of spiritual lightning. "You listen to me," said

PAUL AUGUST

Sister Clem. "There are no new facts. You cannot come here and cause trouble. We won't let you."

Another parent yelled, "How can we hear the teachers?"

Father Orville, obviously annoyed, replied, "If you wish to have your own meeting, there are other rooms in the school. Why don't you rent one?"

"Ah ha!" laughed Kelly. "Rent a nice cozy school meeting room, folks."

Betty pounded her gavel, "Order! Order, please."

The crowd grew louder. School board members squirmed in their seats and looked about wide-eyed. Finally, through the shouting, we could hear a board member yell out, "I move this meeting be adjourned."

Another voice: "I second that."

The crowd became silent as Betty announced, "Meeting adjourned."

From the back of the room came the sound of Jorge Stokes, rolling like union thunder. "They're done with their session. Now we can all stay for a community meeting."

Stokes, the husky union organizer, usually kept one hand in his coat pocket. At this moment, he suddenly flashed his gleaming silver hook, attached to the stump of his right arm, a single metallic claw. The claw opened when his voice lowered and clenched shut when his words reached a crescendo. "Your meeting is over. Now we can have our own meeting."

The board members stirred, looked at each other, perused the wall-to-wall crowd and resumed seats to listen. Dixon's jittery eyes darted about behind his expressionless face. Taking his cue from the board, he reluctantly returned to his seat.

Father Bill smiled and said, "Good. Thank you. I am here because…"

Sister Clem grunted out of her chair again and threw out her palm in a stop motion. "Wait a minute, Father. Just who are you? What parish?"

"I'm Father Bill O'Donnell, St. Joseph's the Workman's Church in Berkeley, and one of the Flatland Fathers."

"Well, Father, I'm going to be just as impolite as you were. I came here for the Sunday school report tonight, not to hear you."

Father Bill turned to the audience. People stood against walls and in the hall and students with their little brothers or sisters pressed their faces against the windows from outside. "How many of you are here for the Sunday school?" he asked.

Three hands went up.

Sister Clem said, "These sisters have waited three months to get on this agenda."

Father Bill sympathetically replied sarcastically, "Well, organize, Sister."

"I'm not organizing," she yelled as she bustled through the crowd towards the door. "I'm leaving."

With that exit, most of the board members scraped back their chairs and followed.

"I just want you to listen," called out Father Bill.

"I won't listen to any more of this bullshit," screamed Sister Clem as she waddled away into the night.

"Did you hear that?" said one of the parents. "That nun actually said 'bullshit'."

Betty paused. "She did not."

But the crowd near the door responded, "Yes, she did."

"I heard her."

"She did."

"You've got to be kidding," blurted Kelly. "Lay teachers, like John Thomas, have to resign if they talk like that."

The meeting deteriorated. Small groups of parents surrounded board members. There was an occasional outburst, followed by a blustery exit. Finally, Kelly got everyone's attention. "Now let's have an orderly meeting."

As Betty made her way out through the crowd, she called out to everyone, "Why don't you go somewhere else for a community meeting with your union friend over there?"

Betty pointed to Stokes, who stepped out of the shadows, raised his silver hook and scowled at her. "I didn't call a community meeting. Your board adjourned. I didn't adjourn your meeting."

As Betty left, she yelled back, "Don't forget to lock the doors, turn off the lights and close the windows when you relinquish the building."

We gathered in a large circle to hear Father Bill speak. "Once we find the problem, we can find the solution. The problem here is the principal, Gil Dixon."

Our top student activist, Lisa, spoke out. "The students are going to picket tomorrow after school. We expected them to give you guys the shaft tonight. So, we're ready to go."

"And the teachers are going up to Piedmont to picket the Bishop's mansion tomorrow," said Kelly.

We broke up into separate groups of parents, teachers and students. Stokes led our group. "I can't believe this. You guys go through daily changes. The last word I had was that you got into a barroom brawl last week."

George had heavy eyes, like iron, steady and unswerving, concealing the thoughts behind them. His hair was unfashionably slicked down and combed back from a weather-beaten face. No one knew how he lost his arm but rumor had it as a war injury or a waterfront accident working with the longshoremen. "Bring me up to date on your inquisition."

Stan removed his glasses and stroked his blond beard as he answered, "One priest resigned from the administrative board. He said he could not, in good conscience, implement Dixon's policies. He's the only priest in the school who barely supported us."

"So, you have an elected opening now, right?" said Stokes.

"Yes," said Stan. "We nominated Santos. They nominated Martha Dunwell."

"Who is she?" asked Stokes.

"Girls' P.E. teacher," said Radisch, rolling his eyes. "She's a former St. Liz alumna who is still working on her BA degree at San Jose State."

"No college degree?" said Stokes. "And no teaching credential?"

"That's right," said Radisch.

"Now, let me get this straight," said Stokes. "They're firing you tenured and experienced guys and keeping a lady with no degrees or credential. And they want to elect her to represent the faculty?"

"Right again," said Radisch. "And it's legal. It's a private school. They can do what they want."

"That's absurd," said Father Bill. "Surely you can beat Dunwell. When is the election?"

Kelly laughed. His beer belly shook. "Would you believe, we had it today? Dixon wants to ramrod this. He'll announce the winner tomorrow."

The meeting melted away and we left, some going to the union hall to make picket signs, some going to The Master's for a drink and some going home, like me, to sleep.

"Not a single nun voted for me... I'm disappointed. I guess I over-estimated my charisma."

The next day at St. Liz High School. The faculty parking lot is limited to cars with permit stickers. Yesterday, Dixon called the police. Most of us on the lay faculty were too busy with our crisis to renew parking permits for April 1972. We received parking tickets.

Dixon usually backs his red Mustang into his official parking space (number one) near the front of school. This morning, Stan backed his blue Ford into the principal's parking place. This set the mood for the day.

In the faculty room, we read the latest memo:

Dear Faculty:

There is the possibility of a student walkout today. Following are instructions for all faculty members:

a) If you get wind of something, nip it in the bud before it happens.

b) Do not use coercion in dealing with students, at least not at this stage. Use persuasion to dissuade students from walking out.

c) Inform an administrator at once in the event of any destructive act.

d) Make no statements to any newspaper, TV, radio or any other type of media.

e) Pray. I mean this.

Thanks,

Gil Dixon

Next to that memo, on another sheet, were the results of the previous day's voting:
   Dunwell—24
   Santos—15

"Not a single nun voted for me," said Santos. "Only union members. I'm disappointed. I guess I overestimated my charisma."

"Forget it," said Kelly. "It's what we expected. This faculty is polarized. We don't have the numbers."

MINDWORKER: MAYBECK

The bell rang. We left the faculty room for first period. In the halls, students replaced protest posters and demonstration flyers as fast as Father Farley tore them down.

> **STUDENT PROTEST**
> **DEMONSTRATION**
> **TODAY AFTER SCHOOL**
> **TV CREWS AT 3 PM**
> **SAVE OUR TEACHERS**

At the end of each year we had a special intersession of four weeks when the school took on mini-courses in camping, dance, travel and other classes we don't offer during the year. By the end of second period, Farley had made the rounds of the classrooms asking a rhetorical question, "Will it interfere with your schedule if we drop sixth period for the intersession registration?" We never stop classes for registration because we do it during homeroom.

"They're just trying to sabotage the protest," said Radisch during our coffee break in the faculty room. "By cutting sixth period, kids will go home at 2:30 instead of 3:30. Dixon won't announce his decision until the last minute."

Radisch was right. At the beginning of sixth period, Farley announced that school was over. But students didn't leave. They stayed for the protest.

After school, we unloaded hand-lettered signs from Radisch's battered VW bus and unwrapped flyers from Kelly's dented red sports car. I strapped on my guitar and started singing and strumming as we slowly circled in front of St. Liz. As we gathered, students left their books, jackets and purses on the lawn while they marched and chanted, "Rehire teachers! Rehire teachers!"

Suddenly, the sprinklers went on.

"Hello?" Lisa yelled to anyone still inside the school. "Our books are getting wet. Turn of the sprinklers!"

But they didn't stop. We scrambled through the water to pull out belongings. Several self-appointed student heroes were soaking wet. Since the front was crowded, I took the wet heads around to the side door but it was bolted. We went to the front.

"No good," yelled Kelly. "Keys don't work. They have the front doors chained and padlocked from inside."

"That's against the fire code," I said.

"We need to get to our lockers to get our homework," yelled the students.

We stood outside. Levinson was still in the faculty room. Radisch yelled to him, "We're locked out. Get my briefcase."

"Dixon has a door over by his office," Levinson shouted. "He'll let us out but he won't let anyone in."

"The hell with him," said Radisch as he waded through the sprinklers to the faculty room windows.

Then the fire alarm went off. Students cheered. Within minutes three long fire trucks rolled up but the firemen couldn't get into the school. The doors were padlocked, but the firemen, friends of St. Liz, issued no citations.

As the firemen left, we continued on our picket line as I strummed my guitar and sang my song: "Betty on the School Board."

Betty took out her mini-computer from her velvet purse.
The calculator rang as she decreed, let's cut the teachers first.

TV crews arrived, panned along the picket line, interviewed a few students, got "fair comment" from Dixon, then moved quickly to the scene of their next show.

"Goddamn media," mumbled Radisch under his breath. "All they care about are the visuals. They can't even begin to scratch the surface of this situation. Damn. Let's get up to the Bishop's mansion."

I threw my guitar in the back of Stan's Ford and we chugged out of the flatlands, twisting through the Oakland hills, up to the bay view of Piedmont.

Another picket line. More picket signs. Students arrived. A white police car drove up, followed quickly by another.

Howard explained to the Piedmont police, "The Bishop lives in this mansion in luxury and splendor. We have teachers who are laid off in the flatlands and we're told that it's because of lack of funds. The Bishop won't listen to us any other way. That's why we're here."

The police checked for parade permits and finally agreed that we had a right to the sidewalks as long as we didn't obstruct anyone. As the police cruised by, we spotted a red Mustang parked a block away. There was a man behind a tree. He was aiming a video camera at us.

"Look at that," cried Kelly. "It's Dixon. He's taking movies of us! Ah ha! He's wearing sunglasses, no coat or tie, like he's a plainclothes detective. What a farce! What an incredible farce."

"I'll get a picture of him taking our picture," said Stan. But every time Stan stopped to aim his 35mm at Dixon, his target turned his back and ducked behind a tree.

"He must be some kind of a nut," said Kelly. Howard went over and confronted Dixon, who quickly left.

Coach Howard came back and told us, "I was hoping you guys wouldn't let that asshole intimidate you. You guys showed a lot of class. I asked him if he was taking movies for our trial. He said he just wanted some films for graduation. The guy is weird."

We marched on. I sang my song about bureaucracy: "The Cardboard Box Brigade."

If anything is simple, they make it complex.
If anything is right, they make it a mess.
In a paper world of carbon triple packs
They rejoice when they find mistakes so they
*   can send 'em back.*

> **At the Bishop's Mansion...**in Piedmont, an elite upper-class city surrounded by Oakland, we strung out our picket line (left to right): Jack Radisch followed Stan Cardinet who used his artistic talents to create picket signs. I'm strummin' my guitar. Peter McDonough, another teacher who attended St. Liz, is supporting his colleagues. Jim Kelly, AFT union rep, led the charge.

We were chanting, singing, and strutting when Radisch's raw swollen eye opened in surprise. "Hey, the Bishop just pulled into his driveway."

The word spread along the picket line. We moved toward the Bishop's mansion. We began chanting: "Bish-op Be-gin, we want our teachers back again!"

The chant grew louder. "Bish-op Be-gin, We Want Our Teachers Back Again!"

The walking stopped. The chant got louder:

"BISH-OP BE-GIN, WE WANT OUR TEACHERS BACK AGAIN!"

The Bishop smiled nervously, climbed out of his shiny new Pontiac, and hurried inside.

Radisch said, "I thought he had a Cadillac. That must be his ghetto car."

When the cops arrived again, we retreated to the sidewalk and continued walking in circles. As we plodded along, Stan said, "This is getting monotonous."

Lisa stepped out of line. "I've got to go to the bathroom."

She went up to the Bishop's porch, tapped on the double doors and a nun peeped out. She listened to the student's request to use the Bishop's bathroom, then told her to go away. It was what we expected.

The picket line moved again. It was a sullen, silent plodding. Our conversations broke us up into separate groups as we shuffled endlessly forward.

"Dixon is a semantic liar," said Stan. "He's like the little kid who gets caught and cries, 'I didn't hit the ball through the window. It was the ball that broke the window.' Dixon says he didn't fire teachers. It was a 'drop in enrollment.'"

Radisch, Kelly, Stan and I clustered together as we slowly moved in line. Stan continued, "These picket line battles make it all the more difficult in the classroom. Teaching isn't easy. We're confined to the four walls of the classroom. We're limited to 45 minutes regulated by bells. We're responsible for the 35 young souls in each class."

"It's work, all right," said Kelly.

"We retreat into these florescent caves they call classrooms," said Stan. "Then they expect us to work on a kid's mind. We should call our union the United Mind Workers, like the Pennsylvania teachers."

"Mindworker! There's a new song for you, Augie," said George.

"Mindworker? Yeah," I said. "Songwriting keeps my sanity. You know, this whole battle is an obsession. When I leave here I'll still be thinking about all this crisis reality. I really didn't know what peace of mind was until I lost it during this mess."

My hands were numb from grappling my guitar. I had a sunburn and sore feet. We stopped in the Bishop's driveway to watch the sun go down between the distant towers of the Golden Gate Bridge. It sank into the incoming fog. I strummed and sang:

I pulled the kid aside.
I tried to make him see.
I'm not the one causin' his hostility.
I'll work his mind 'til I set it free.
Mind ... worker.[26]

We were tired of picketing. Tired of the struggle. Tired. Tired. Tired.

Chapter 20

"Get us to work for free..."

TEACHER'S UNION HALL. A fundraising party for our rehiring expenses. Friday night.

Before we began our serious drinking, Howard called us together in the kitchen between a crusty gas stove and two large aluminum sinks. "Look, you guys. The last couple of days we've been pounding the pavement. We're sore. We're tired. We can't keep this up long without losing momentum. I say, let's call off the picketing Monday and make a new proposal."

"Well, bulldog," said Kelly, arching an eyebrow, "Our numbers go down as each day adds up. So, shall we quit for awhile? Does everyone agree?"

"Yeah, yeah," said Radisch, impatiently. "Now I want to hear Howard's new proposal."

"Okay, okay," replied Howard, talking excitedly. "Look, you might think this is crazy, but hear me out. They said they laid us off for financial reasons and that they don't have the money. We know that Dixon's lying. The money is there."

"So?" said Radisch.

"So," replied Howard. "This is radical. But it will work. If they say the money isn't there, we propose to work for free."

"Free? That's insane," said Stan, slapping his forehead.

"No salary? That's crazy," I agreed.

"Keep talking," said Radisch.

"Look," said Howard. "It's a ploy. They will refuse. We'll prove that it's not financial. Should they accept, we know we can build enrollment and cover our jobs."

"We've been stonewalled by the Bishop and the board. Who will we propose this to?" asked Stan.

"I say go to the Pastor, Father Orville. It's his parish. He hires the principal."

"It is a novel idea," said Radisch. "I'd like to consult with Stokes and our union attorney."

"I still think it's crazy," I said. "Dixon cheated me out of money when I had a contract for summer dances. If there is any way he could get us to work for free, he will. I don't like it. It's nuts."

Howard replied, "The idea might sound nutty, but think about it. How can they refuse this offer and claim that it's a financial problem?"

We broke up our caucus as our friends filtered into the dimly lit union hall and paid their dollar at the door for the party.

I took the mike and began the show. "Here's a new tune I'm kicking around. It was inspired by my co-workers on yesterday's picket line at the Bishop's. Mindworker."

In a shabby school on an asphalt yard
I'm working with the future and man it's
*   hard.*

Mind...worker.

George backed me up on a few songs with the old upright piano we borrowed from Saint Paul's. Then he stepped into an imaginary limelight. "Okay all you guppies. Here's a problem for you. If love is one and sex is two, what is three and four?"

"Marriage and divorce," replied Kelly.

"Naw, come on. Stan? Do you know what three and four are?"

"No," replied Stan. "I'm afraid you have me at a disadvantage on that one, George."

"Three and four is seven, silly. You're not such a Berkeley intellectual as you pretend to be, are you Stan, my good man?

"That Santos. I'm giving my opening day lecture—that's the day I fly in like Superman and jump on the desk—when I hear that Mickey Mouse projector making noise in Santos's classroom. The walls in our basement are prefab.

"I also had guppy row down there. Ah, those wonderful guppies. Are you a guppy? Here's a test. Santos, how do you pronounce the capital of Kentucky? Lou-is-ville or Lou-ee-ville?"

Santos said, "Lou-is-ville."

George laughed, "No. It's Frankfort, stupid."

George moved to another topic. "People in the Bay Area are the friendliest in the world. Just drive down the freeway and find out. When I took my driver's test the guy asked me, 'What do you do if you see a car coming at you with high beams?' I said, 'I close my eyes.' He said, 'You flunk.'"

George brushed his fingers down the piano keys as I hit a chord on my guitar. He said, "Augie finally wrote a song we can all sing. Later on tonight I'll do my latest song for you, 'I Left My Heart at the Stanford Medical Center.' Now here's August."

You only have one time being a child, one
   time.
One time.
You only have one time being a child,
One time.

As the party ended, George and I pushed the piano down the street to Saint Paul's. It was 1 a.m. We knew the others were cleaning up but for some reason we stopped in front of Saint Paul's, pulled a bottle out of the upright and poured ourselves more white wine. George ran his fingers down the keys. We sat under the street lights singing:

Children are the parents of grownups.
Child is father to the man.[27]
You were the child of yesterday.
That's how life began.

You only have one time being a child, one
*   time.*

An Oakland policeman arrived to suggest we not use the streets as our stage. We pushed the piano into Saint Paul's and returned to the union hall where George told corny jokes until sunrise. We felt as if we wanted to cling to the party atmosphere, to our friendship, to our camaraderie. Monday would return all too soon.

Chapter 21

"The diocese yanked old..."

SUNDAY AFTERNOON AT POINT REYES, Drake's Beach. Pacific Ocean. We wanted to escape our stuffy, smoke-filled meetings and get away from the city and relax. As Stan said, "If we really have to meet, let's do it in the sand and the sunshine."

George, Radisch, Rowe and Howard pulled together a poker game. Dallas Williams and others gathered around the driftwood fire. Kelly and Stan played chess. Kelly, the mathematician, played with all the textbook moves, calculations and tricks. Stan, the humanist, played with his heart, his intuition and his feelings. Kelly won again.

As the sun set, we gathered in a circle, on the beach, around the glowing embers of the dying campfire. Stan said, "This might be our last time to meet until graduation. Next week is the last week of regular classes. After that, we begin our two-week, end of school, intersession. We could lose our momentum when we all split up to do different activities."

"Well, maybe," said Kelly. "So let's get on with it now. Howard – you old bulldog – what about your crazy work-for-free plan? Does everyone agree to let 'er rip?"

"I don't like it," said Radisch, tipping a jug of wine to fill his paper cup. "The issues are sacrificed to get jobs back."

"But if they accept, we can return in force to get Dixon," replied Howard, rubbing white cream on his sunburned nose. "If they refuse this offer of volunteer labor, it will prove this is not a financial problem."

Kelly asked, "Everybody for it?"

We all nodded, although I knew, privately, I wouldn't do it. I thought of Muriel and our three kids. No way would I work for free next year. I remained silent because I had no alternative.

"Well," said Kelly, "Nobody's dead set against it, so go get 'em, bulldog."

"I will," said Howard. "I'll take the plan to the press and the pastor on Monday."

"Okay," said Kelly, "What about the WASC letter?"

"We're asking WASC to investigate this situation," said Stan. "The improvements made by St. Liz no longer exist. They've taken away tenure and security. Our internal problems are worse than ever."

"Well," said Rowe, removing his corncob pipe to speak, "I dare say this is a severe move. We're really asking that the school be discredited. It smacks of desperation tactics. Is that wise?"

"Ha!" laughed Kelly. "It's obvious that we're getting screwed. I don't see why we have to prove it to WASC. But if we once showed them how we improved, we can also show them how Dixon destroyed everything. August, you're the writer. You put together the WASC letter, OK?"

"Yes," I said. "I'm the writer. I'll do it."

"What about a strike vote?" said Radisch. "Let's decide."

"Yes, please." Dallas Williams, sniffling, with watery eyes, pulled a blanket over herself as the sun set below the Pacific horizon. "Listen you guys, we have to get this resolved. My health went from good to bad. I really shouldn't be here, but I want to see this ended."

Kelly took a swig of beer. "I'm sure not opposed to a strike but we're simply not in a position of power to strike from. It's a real hurter."

"Kelly's right," said Stan. "When the New York Catholic teachers went on strike, the diocese yanked old nuns from rest homes and drafted grumpy Irish priests from surrounding parishes. They had no teaching experience."

"They were just warm spiritual bodies," said George.

"Yes," said Rowe. "They did the same thing in New York and they'll do the same thing here if we go out."

"Why bother to strike? We're more of a pain to them while we're still around," laughed Kelly.

"If we don't strike, do we have a legal case?" Howard looked over to Radisch, our schoolhouse lawyer, for his answer.

"We have a yellow dog contract," replied Radisch. "They can change it anyway they want. My advice to you guys is to cover your options and look for jobs for next year. I've applied to several areas to be a public defender."

"Bah," shouted Kelly. "We'll all be back at St. Liz in the fall."

"I fully expect to return to St. Liz next year," echoed Stan. The rest of us said nothing.

The following week, Stan and I found ourselves waiting for bingo duty after school. There was a lull in the battle of union teachers versus the nuns, priests, and Bishop. "Paul, let's take a run over to Berkeley for the demonstration against the War and the blockade of North Vietnam. A new battle scene. A change of atmosphere."

In Berkeley, we walked down Telegraph Avenue, past the shambles of People's Park where the wire fences were bent over and police were guarding work crews as they made repairs. We walked by broken windows and asphalt ripped from the street in sections. I reflected on my draft status. In the draft lottery of 1970, my birth date (12/12) came up as the 19th guy to be drafted by my local draft board. At the time, however, I was age 28 and too old to be drafted. I didn't complain. I no longer needed to carry a draft card everywhere.

"This is worse than the Cambodian invasion protests," I said. "I remember seeing National Guardsmen on the street corners of Berkeley holding rifles with fixed bayonets and live ammunition. Scary."

"Uh, oh," said Stan. "Up ahead about a half block. A can of tear gas just went off." The wisps of gas drifted down in our direction.

Within seconds, I got a breath of gas that made me gag and choke. "Damn," I said. "My eyes are burning. I feel like a super pepper shaker emptied itself into my nose." We stopped in a doorway and it took me about three minutes to recover.

"Stay away from the crowds," said Stan. "They're targets for Billy clubs and gas. Let's go up near the cops and the University." Stan was a Berkeley veteran of various protests, most of them anti-war.

We walked up near the cops and stood on a corner. A policeman chased one guy past us, stopped, faced us, raised his club and yelled, "I said clear this area!"

It was hard to believe. I'd seen it on TV, in newspaper photos, and heard radio reports, but reality was jarring. This cop almost went berserk simply because we were standing on a corner. Stan and I, and a couple of others, walked by the cop as we headed up to the University.

The Cal Student Union was the protestors' staging area. The crowd held up fists, shouting: "Hey, hey, LBJ. How many kids did you kill today?"[28] Telegraph ran into Bancroft there, making a "T." The cops told us to go up (east) or down (west) on Bancroft, not forward to the student union. A rock flew over my shoulder, skimming the ground past the police. I nervously looked back, indicating that I didn't throw it.

We turned west, down Bancroft where we immediately encountered the Sheriff's Department deputies. They were wearing blue vests over bright blue coveralls and blue helmets.

"Uh, oh." Said Stan. "It's the Blue Meanies. They're from southern Alameda County. Redneck territory. The cops in khaki outfits are Berkeley police. They're comparatively friendly to the students."

We were surrounded by a battle zone of overturned garbage cans, smashed and toppled bus stop benches and newspaper racks strewn around the streets. As we walked down Bancroft, a bottle with a rag stuffed in it came from a crowd ten yards to my left. It skidded across the street toward a Blue Meanie and came to a stop without breaking. I couldn't tell if it was a real or fake Molotov cocktail.

A Blue Meanie leveled his shotgun and aimed directly at the crowd next to me. "Stan," I yelled. "What's going on with those weapons?"

"Their guns are loaded with clay or wood pellets. They can hurt but usually don't draw blood." Stan motioned toward the Student Union. "Let's go up those stairs to the second floor balcony."

As we climbed the stairs, a student above yelled down at us. "Behind you. Behind you!"

A Berkeley khaki cop began clattering his club along the stair railing, charging up the stairs and yelling: "Clear this balcony. Now!"

We retreated down the stairs and over to the front stairs. "They're using classical counter-revolutionary crowd control methods," said Stan. "They yell, 'clear this area,' and then they herd folks into another area where another cop echoes: 'clear this area.'"

As we walked across the front stairs, a Blue Meanie waved his club and bellowed out in a fierce authoritarian tone: "CLEAR THIS AREA, I SAID."

We moved. I became nervous. I had no control over my own actions. I was perceived to be part of a mob where I had no identity. The cops were my herders. I told Stan, "Let's get out of here."

As we walked across the lawn toward Bancroft to leave, someone on the street threw three pieces of tile at the police behind us. They retaliated by leveling their shotguns and giving the crowd a little time to scatter, which they did. No shots were fired.

Suddenly, a Blue Meanie came up behind me and shoved me in the left shoulder while clubbing me in the leg. "Get moving," he shouted. "Get down there."

He reached out and repeatedly clubbed Stan on his thigh while he loudly ordered, "Get down there." Stan later told me that the trauma probably caused the bone death that resulted in his partial hip replacement.

The police tried to herd parts of the crowd together but there was nowhere to go except in the direction of more police. We got across Bancroft with our backs to the cops as a kid kicked over a garbage can and began rolling it back toward the law enforcement lines.

We finally freed ourselves from the main conflict and walked back along Telegraph, "The protestors clap and stomp until someone does something," said Stan. "Totally unstructured. Most of the troublemakers are junior high types who came to do some mischief. They broke the windows in Sproul Hall. About once every 15 minutes, the cops make a sweep in the direction of the crowd to keep it moving. They try to confine protestors, isolate troublemakers and maintain a façade of control."

As we walked by an outdoor restaurant on Telegraph, the Blue Meanies were taking a break, sipping milk shakes through straws under their riot helmet shields and holding the cup in one hand with their baton in the other. As we returned to St. Liz for bingo, my eyes were still hurting from the teargas attack. My leg felt bruised. "The eyes of the world are on the Vietnam War, the battles, the bombs, the dead and dying," said Stan. "The protestors versus the cops in Berkeley are merely a sideshow. It may not even make national news. Our little Catholic conflict, by comparison, just doesn't matter."

"And bingo matters even less," I said. "But we gotta do it anyway. Oh well."

Chapter 22

"My energetic spark..."

HOME. CORRECTING PAPERS. Early May. Thursday evening. School was winding down. Turmoil has exhausted all of us. I taught five classes this semester: one period of creative writing; two periods of ninth grade English; and two periods of marriage. This was the last week of regular school. Next week we began our intersession.

I had a headache, a cold, and the end of school is always a letdown. At the end of the year, we still had to go through senior ball, graduation and all those separation rituals. My teaching had suffered from this fight. Students knew what was happening. When my mind was on job survival instead of school, it affected my classes. My energetic spark was missing; the tone of the classroom shifted from vibrant to static. Students sensed the mood shifts. A poem by one of my perceptive creative writing students, Tony Lopez, reflected my mood:

Captain Paul's Fifth Period Brigade

Capt. Paul. How proudly he stood
In the breeze of gentle voices. Yet boarded by
*   the man in 4 walls.*
He spoke gentle words of the past. Today we
*   wrote of*
Dostoevsky and London.

Around the room
Boredom grew with such intensity I fell
*   asleep.*
Ted was goofing off. Wanda read her fan
*   mail. Beverly laughed.*
The 5th period brigade began to chatter.

Paul yelled, giving orders.
Ju Ju Bedes dropped on the floor. Did I
*   smell burnt licorice?*
Who dropped coffee cubes?
The brigade listened.

Paul faded again into gentle voices.

Tony's poem was voluntary. No need to grade it. I rolled out of bed, popped an aspirin and returned to correcting papers. During the last few weeks, classes suffered from our conflict. I was often late in reading and returning student assignments. I curled up with a batch of essays and final exams. These papers included student evaluations of my teaching and their thoughts about classes at St. Liz. These were their comments:

"The school is good and the only teacher I want to see rehired is Mr. Stanley Cardinet (pop de do)"

"I think it is wrong to let the teachers go if the school can pay for the t.v.s. and other junk that they use (and don't need) then why can't they rehire the teachers!?"

"The class was good, you were good, the school was O.K., the teachers are pretty good, the principal and deans stunk (if you will pardon the expersion), but for an overall opinion of the place—it's a pretty dumb school because they are firing the best teachers we got!"

"The school is bogged down by bureaucracy and because of it, human beings are sacrificed for the rules. This I can see just by being involved in student government. Lack of understanding and communication—a lot of passing the buck. I enjoyed the class and you as a teacher."

"I liked the course, although I didn't especially like your choice of books. As for the administration, I think you know the extent of my disgust. If I had my way, I would be

smirking at a few funerals right now. I know this is VICARIOUS?? but I have passed the point of being rational with those imbeciles!"[29]

"The teacher, well he has the potential of being a great writer and song composer. He should work on the singing though (ha! just kidding Elvis).

"English Dept—not enough courses offered for college preparing students. Administration—a big joke!"

"I'm glad I won't be here next year. The teachers they'll have really won't be able to give that well rounded of an education. Who'll be a better teacher in American Legal Systems than Radisch? We're losing our best and most creative teachers because of the money problem. Fine. But whoever comes here next year as a student better not expect an education."

"I admire the administration (Mr. Dixon, Fr. Farley, etc.) for putting up with junk about the teachers. I think the "fired" teachers are acting in such a way to get the students against the administration. Well, I suppose you'll flunk me for the above stuff, but you asked for my opinion and that's it."

"Marriage and Psychology are the only two courses, and you are the only teacher holding this shoddy department together. The other courses are old idea courses taught by

old idea nuns. The administration is holding everything up and pushing the whole school backward into the 30's in which everything was taught by closed-minded religious people. As far as the administration goes I think they're a lot of bull. And when they learn to treat you teachers as people instead of contracts that they can change when they please, the better off we'll all be. The most important component of a good school are good teachers and when everyone realizes this the better."

I finished the papers, popped another aspirin, and then buried my head in my pillows to escape into the sweet oblivion of sleep.

Chapter 23

"The pastor closed down..."

THE PARTY FOR MARGE HARDY. Friday night. Marge Hardy, a statuesque middle-aged brunette, resigned as bookkeeper of St. Liz. She had a smile that warmed the room, but not the principal. She did people-work during school time and paperwork after hours. Her son, Kevin Hardy, an athletic all-star, graduated from St. Liz with scholarships everywhere. He went on to become the first athlete to letter in all three major sports at Notre Dame: football, baseball and basketball. He was the first round draft choice of New Orleans and briefly played defensive lineman for the 49ers and other pro football teams until an injury ended his career.

Everyone loved Marge, but Dixon was uncomfortable with her popularity. He didn't trust her because he didn't trust anyone. So, when this crisis exploded, the school atmosphere became unbearable and she resigned. This was her going-away party.

The night sparkled with an unusual clarity. We shared a sense of relief as we exchanged social pleasantries in the cafeteria. "This is like the First World War," said Father Bart, nervously tugging at his Roman collar and stretching his neck. "This is a truce, like when the Italians and Austrians exchanged gifts of turkeys and geese at Christmas during WWI."

Betty Board smiled her greetings to Kelly. Father Orville shook hands with Radisch. Dixon joked with George, "Skillful role playing," Stan said. "We all compartmentalize our anger. Tonight we socialize. Tomorrow we battle in the school board arena."

We took our places at a cafeteria table covered with butcher paper. "Hey Radisch, pass the bread," said George. The nuns, priests, and conservatives all sat at one end of the long tables. We all sat at the other end.

"Sure," Radisch replied. He spoke directly to our group. "Well, you guys should be the first to know. I got a job for next year."

"Oh, really?" said Stan. "Public defender?"

"No," Radisch replied. "I'll be a deputy district attorney for Alameda County."

"Deputy DA.?" said Stan. "But that's a prosecutor. You're more humanitarian. I don't understand."

"Simple," said Radisch. "It's called survival. Jobs as public defenders are as rare as teaching jobs. Actually, I'll come back here if we get rehired but after all the shit that's hit the fan, I doubt that they would take us back under any conditions."

"What about teaching somewhere else?" asked George.

Radisch replied, "I've already reached the end of the salary schedule. I can't see spending another twenty years in the classroom."

George said, "You don't see many old high school teachers. They're like motorcycle riders. They either wear out or crash before they get old."

"You guys should be looking for jobs, too," said Radisch.

"I say we start our own school," said Stan. "I've been meeting with people from Berkeley alternative schools. If they can do it, we can do it."

"I'm with Stanley," said Kelly. "We got a core of kids here at St. Liz who will follow us anywhere."

"If you two guys do the groundwork," I said, "I'll help get it started in September, if we're not back here."

The conversation switched focus for me. Curt Levinson, seated to my right, toyed with his spaghetti. Levinson was a bachelor living with his wealthy Marin family. He was also chairman of the St. Liz English department. "Paul, suppose I don't come back next year? They would have to rehire you, wouldn't they?"

"Forget it," I said. "They won't rehire me because I'm fighting this. They'd only say that Bud Johnson has seniority."

"Yes, I guess," said Levinson, "Didn't Dixon mess you up like that before, when he hired his brother?"

"Oh, yeah." I remembered the incident. "When I first came to St. Liz, I was in the history department. The next year, when they had an opening in English, Dixon hired his brother instead of moving me into English."

"Nepotism," laughed Levinson.

Dixon, seated at the head table, tapped a water glass for attention. "Well, Doris, I'm not very good at making speeches, so here's a little gift from all of us."

Father Farley brought in a set of red luggage. Marge Hardy smiled. Her warm heart and sympathetic ear made her the informal hostess of the school. She helped teachers find lost paychecks and gave students advice about life and young love. She cherished her role at St. Liz.

After the formalities, we moved about in clusters. Stan debated Father Orville about the future of Catholic schools. "It looks bleak," admitted Orville. "In Pueblo, Colorado they closed every school in the diocese. Church attendance is down. We have fewer baptisms."

"But Father," said Stan, stroking his untrimmed beard, "Surely the Catholic Church is not hurting for money."

Orville said, "Catholic assets are invested in real estate like churches, schools and convents. They're not easy to sell."

"Father," George pulled a long cigar out of his mouth to speak. "the survival of a Catholic school depends on what I call, if you will pardon the expression, the give-a-shit theory."

We all laughed.

"Really," insisted George. "My friend taught at Saint Bridget's grammar school. The pastor closed down the school because the nuns were leaving and school problems interfered with his golf game. That pastor just didn't give-a-shit."

"I can assure you," said Orville, "I don't plan to close St. Liz."

"Of course not, Padre," said George. "You're out there with flea markets, pancake breakfasts, and taking up second collections at mass on Sunday. But if the Bishop won't help you and the nuns leave, what will you do?"

"The sisters have a more serious problem," said Orville. "There are few young girls entering their system. As these sisters grow older, they wonder who will take care of them in old age at the Catholics old folks' home. They need young sisters, but most of the new faces leave the order. The sisters have a great fear: what will happen to them if their community dies out?"

Our party dynamics shifted and Martha Dunwell, newly elected faculty rep to the school management team, came up to me. "Paul, I'm sorry that you're involved in this, but I think this enrollment drop is good for St. Liz." She took a swig from her beer can. "We're not really a Christian school any more. All the other schools get the good kids. We get the leftovers."

"Leftovers?" I said. "You think our minorities are leftovers?"

She replied with a sigh. "The minorities beat up the whites. The white parents take their offspring out of school and move to the suburbs. We're keeping the scum and losing the best. If I had any children, I wouldn't send them to this school."

"Oh, come on." I said. "When two whites scuffle, it's called a schoolyard fight. But when it's mixed, you say it's the blacks beating up the whites."

Martha shook her head. "Look Paul, you might label me as racist, but I'm not. I'm discriminating against thugs. We have too many fights, too much abusive language. There's no more respect. Maybe we can give

St. Liz a new start and make it a Catholic school again."

"Again?" I really couldn't believe what she was saying. "You and I went to St. Liz. Sister Marie taught us. You're calling for a return to days that never existed. Don't you remember the gang fights under the freeway? It was mostly white boys when we went to school here. Now the school is mostly black. St. Liz has always had a reputation as a rowdy school."

Sister Marie came up to us and held out an article from the *Oakland Tribune*. She pointed to it and spoke to me. "Paul, this has got to stop. I was very hurt by this article."

An article... by Bev Mitchell, in the *Tribune* gave a good account of the principal's side of the story: that enrollment would drop from 930 (three years before) to 550 (projected next year), that there was a surplus but it was already spent, that all religious teachers had first rights to any teaching jobs, and that several lay teachers had to be laid off because there were no jobs for them.

"*You* were hurt?" I said. "What about us? We've been fired. You've got a job for next year. We don't."

The newspaper article quoted me as saying that, "The most under qualified religious teacher has seniority over the most qualified lay teacher."

"Well, it's true," I said.

"Paul," said Sister Marie, "You know there are financial reasons."

"Yes, Sister," I replied. "The religious seniority is just a subterfuge for hiring the religious as cheap labor."

Sister Marie closed her eyes and shook her head. It reminded me of the time when I was her student. She had been my U.S. History teacher when I attended St. Liz in the 11th grade. When I launched paper airplanes in her class, she would gently chastise me by not calling me Paul. Instead, she'd say, "Saul, this is not a paper airport. Saul, retrieve your inventions, please."

One day after school I asked her why she called me Saul. She replied by quizzing me. "Who was Saul?"

"It was Saint Paul's name before he converted to Christianity," I said.

"And what did Saul do?" said Sister Marie.

"He persecuted the Christians."

Sister Marie looked directly at me and said, "I am a Christian. You are persecuting me, Saul."

Now, Sister Marie was my colleague and St. Liz's Mother Superior. That night, I was persecuting her again, but this time she showed no sense of humor.

"Sister," I said. "As far as I am concerned, this is religious discrimination. If I were a priest, I'd still have a job. Dixon's running a business now, not a Christian community."

Stan joined us. "Sister, you know that Dixon is getting rid of us for political reasons. Howard even presented a proposal that we work for free. No one accepted it. That proves it's not financial."[30]

Sister Marie stood her ground. "It's illogical. Last year you were complaining about losing the Oakland salary schedule and now you're asking to work for free. We can't ask family men to work for free. It's immoral. Frankly, I think the whole suggestion is bizarre."

I didn't say anything, but I reluctantly agreed with her.

"It sounds like we're playing ring-around-the-issues," said Stan. "You say we want money to teach but there is no money so we can't teach. Now we want to teach without money and you say we can't because it's immoral. I think your position is the illogical one, Sister."

Radisch grinned and stepped into the cluster. "You sisters think that your monthly salary is charity to your community. You make about one third of my salary but I have to support a family of five. You might have a low per capita salary but the income to your convent is much higher than any of us bring to our homes."

Sister Clem lumbered up to me, slapped me hard on the back with one hand and held out her wine glass. "Augusshh," she said, pulling me aside. "Augusshh, you are being used. There are two men who set out to maliciously destroy this school and you are being used by them." She peered at me through her rimless glasses. "You probably would have been rehired. But now, after all this, it is going to be very hard to rehire you."

"I know," I replied. "Fired for financial reasons, not rehired for political reasons."

"You guys have hurt our sisters. I never wanted them to go to that meeting at your house last month. They came back crushed. They can't take it. They're just too feminine."

"Too feminine?"

"I can tell you to shove it, and Sister John the Baptist doesn't give a damn, but some sisters were very hurt by your remarks about unqualified religious and qualified lay teachers. Some sisters are just too feminine." Sister Clem grouped her fingers, sneered, and accentuated each of her words with a strong finger thrust to my chest. "Just too feminine to tell you to SHOVE IT." She paused, then lowered her head again to peer at me directly over her glasses. "You're not a good teacher, Augusshh. Get out of teaching. Get into public relations."

"Public relations? What makes you say I'm a bad teacher?"

"Because you have too much sympathy for the kids. This is not the structure for you. Maybe a private school in a less-structured environment where you can use your candle."

"My candle?"

"You have a class where kids sit around and stare at a candle all day."

"No I don't," I said. "The candle class is a special event, only once a year. It's an exercise in—"[31]

"August, it's a joke whatever it is. I'll talk to you about it but I won't talk to Cardinet or Radisch. Those two men are evil." Sister Clem swaggered away.

I went over to Stan and said, "You and Radisch are on the nuns' hit list."

"Paul," Stan replied as Radisch joined us. "I treat the nuns as normal women."

Radisch said, "That's why they don't like us. They expect charity and deference. We treat them like we would any women. They made an adult choice to live the way they do. No marriage. No children. I really think those nuns have their life served to them on a plastic platter. They get room and board and go to church. They live like sheltered adolescents."

"I can see why they don't like you guys," I said.

Father Boomer interrupted everyone as he began to sing solo. He played with the rope belt that hung from his friar robes: *"Oh Danny Boy, the pipes the pipes are calling..."* Boomer belted the song with a vengeance, building volume into his voice and abruptly ending stanzas. He sang in French, then pirouetted like a coquettish clown, earning laughter and applause from the nuns. "Everybody sing. Everybody sing." Soon the cafeteria vibrated with artificial merriment.

Farley, Boomer, Dixon, Sister Clem and Father Bart all flung their arms around each other and wailed: *"When Irish eyeees are smiiiiling..."*

At our end of the room, George and I took up the challenge and sang our song: *"You only have one time being a child, one time..."*

Levinson, Santos, Howard, Rowe, and Radisch all joined in: *"One time..."*

As the religious sang louder, the song duel was under way. Music echoed through the flatlands of East Oakland until we all began to lose our voices and regain our senses. The music stopped. The truce ended.

Chapter 24

"Tomorrow you will be..."

MONDAY. ST. LIZ AUDITORIUM. Student assembly. First day of the intersession. Students and teachers listened as Dixon gave an overview.

"As you know, this is our experimental session, which last semester was very successful. Mr. August came up with the idea and he deserves the recognition." The students applauded.

I thought to myself: *he didn't like my idea, at first.* Saint Mary's College introduced the concept on the West Coast. I adapted it for high school and proposed it to Dixon who resisted until I told him this could get national publicity at no extra expense to the school. We'd be the first to try this with high school kids. The teachers were already on salary and paid for. It's simply a re-allocation of time. Once he understood that, then he really liked it and took it to the faculty who approved.

> **Intersession:** I got the idea from Saint Mary's college who got it from an East Coast Catholic university. As far as I know, we were the first high school in California to try it. Some schools now do a version of this every year. Most never do it. Wikipedia credits mostly East Coast colleges for having intersessions.

Dixon continued. "After our special program, we return for graduation. After graduation, teachers will stay three extra days for department meetings. Now I'll turn things over to our dean of boys, Mr. Rowe."

Rowe took the microphone, adjusted it down to his rotund level and began flipping through notes on his clipboard. "Thank you, Mr. Dixon. I will simply call on teachers to explain their programs so that we all know who is doing what, when and where, so forth and so on. First, Mr. Kelly and Mr. Cardinet, our camping team teachers."

Stan stood, folded his arms and lifted his chin. "Mr. Kelly and I are taking 25 students to Yosemite for our cultural expedition at six tomorrow morning."

Kelly stood up. "We're taking the SCUFO telescope. For all you rookies who don't know, SCUFO is our local Society for Communication with Unidentified Flying Objects. The Yosemite nights have no smog or city lights. You just won't believe how good it is to gaze at the stars from Yosemite. Don't forget your astronomy books."

"Drama class will begin auditions." Father Boomer nervously twirled the white rope dangling from his brown robe. "Sister Saint John the Baptist and I will hold rehearsals in the afternoon."

"American Legal Systems will meet in the morning in room 101," said Jack Radisch. "We'll take the public bus to the county courthouse every afternoon to visit trials."

"I have assigned my students to the police department," said Bud Johnson. "Career exploration, we call it. You will ride in police cars, do volunteer work at the City Hall and find this very exciting."

"The Black Culture class will have their first field trip tomorrow evening," said Dallas Williams. "Please meet the bus in front of the school at seven o'clock for the African Ballet."

"Our individual study class meets every morning in my classroom," announced Sister Clem. "This is all tutorial work. So if any of you get bored with fun and games, see me for some real learning."

Students groaned. Rowe observed, "It certainly is considerate of you to provide that option for us Sister. Now then, let's go to Sister Marie."

"I have already discussed the independent study class with each of my students. Please remember to keep your appointments to meet with me about your poetry, short stories, articles and reports. Thank you."

"George and I are holding the basketball clinic in the gym," stated Bob Howard. "Hey, you guys, be there at 8:30 on the dot tomorrow morning, okay?"

"Mr. August?"

"Record workshop begins auditions in Room 105 tomorrow at 8:45," I said. "Bring your instruments and equipment. We have studio time donated next week for recording. We'll publish two songs on a 45-rpm record."

"I'm driving a busload of my Spanish students down to Ensenada, Mexico," declared Mike Santos. "My bus leaves at five tomorrow morning. If you are sleeping in the gym tonight, I'll be here. Lights out at ten. Remember, in Mexico we stop speaking English and only speak Spanish."

"Tennis class. Bring your rackets," said Curt Levinson. "We meet at Dimond Park tomorrow morning around nine."

"I'd like my woodshop students to meet tomorrow morning at nine over on the veranda of the monastery," proclaimed Father Bart. "Since we have no vocational shops on campus, we will use the woodshop behind the monastery."

"Girls' volleyball will use the schoolyard courts," said Martha Dunwell. "Be there at 8:30."

"I am taking some lovely boys and girls to help out at the old folks' home," said Sister Saint Francis. Bring your lunch, boys and girls, because we begin by helping out at lunch tomorrow."

Rowe stepped back up in front of the microphone. "Please check your schedules for other classes. Before we break into groups, here are a few more announcements. The Biological Seashore Expedition scheduled by Mr. Thomas has been canceled." Rowe didn't bother to explain that John Thomas had been suspended and was forced to resign after speaking to my marriage class. "My backpacking class will leave for Tahoe tomorrow morning at nine. I have volunteer parents who will drive us in their cars, drop us off and pick us up several days later. Remember, this is a wilderness trip. You are advised to indulge yourselves with hamburgers and French fries today because tomorrow you will be living on a healthy diet of raisins, peanut butter, and sunflower seeds. Parent volunteers will drive buses and generally coordinate our transportation here and there. Oh, I see I forgot Father Farley. Did you have a few words?"

"I'm sorry," replied Farley. "As you students know, this early end of school means that those of you who want summer jobs have a big start on the market. I will gladly help you find jobs."

"Any questions?" asked Rowe. And before anyone could respond, he said, "Good. Now meet with your teachers in groups and good luck with your first intersession."

Chapter 25

"Your wife just called..."

RECORD WORKSHOP. TUESDAY. Room 105. When I attended St. Liz as a student, one of my English teachers had a banner across the front of her classroom: "Well begun is half done." This special session was not well begun. Only half of my students showed up. "Where's our lead guitar player?" I asked.

"Dixon gave him detention. He's pulling weeds."

"Where's the bass player?"

"He's been suspended a week for cutting classes."

The drummer showed up without his drums. In came the rhythm guitar player with his electric guitar but without an amp. The tape recorders were locked up. Our piano player came in late with a long thin scratch, bleeding slightly from his eyebrow to his chin.

"What happened to you?" I asked.

"Some dudes jumped me. They're hitting on everybody. Even Miss Williams got pushed on her butt when she tried to stop 'em."

"Let me get class started before I take you down to the office for first aid," I said. "Class, you all have the lead sheets. Look over your parts."

A freshman girl came to the door with a message from the office. Another class interruption. "Mr. August? Your wife just called. She said to come home and take her to the hospital because she's having a baby."

"What?" I was motionless. "My wife isn't pregnant. It can't be my wife. Maybe another teacher."

"She said it was Mrs. August."

"There must be some mistake." Students don't always deliver accurate messages, I thought.

"No. It was Mrs. August. She's going to have a baby." The student smiled a big smile, as if she were bringing happy news.

"I have to get class under way. I'll call her," I said.

After the students started working, I took the victim to the office, then started toward the faculty room to phone home. A few clusters of young males in the halls ran

when they saw me. With most of the man-
power away from school (Rowe, Kelly, Santos, Radisch, Stan) some students were
cutting Boomer's drama class and starting
fights.

As I entered the faculty room and the
phone, I passed Father Bart who peeked out
the window and yelled, "Look at that." Two
students ran across the street. One threw a
bottle into the gutter. The glass shattered
across the sidewalk as they ran away. Father Bart's eyes bulged. His face turned
crimson with rage. "Why those—! Send all
of 'em back to—! No good sons of— Bart
stormed out of the room.

"Christ," I said to Bud Johnson, who sat
reading a paper. "Did you hear that?"

"He's been hospitalized before," Johnson
said nonchalantly. "He has to go back in the
hospital next week. He's really not himself."

"Either not himself or he's his real self," I
said.

I called my home: no answer. The baby
mystery would have to wait. Out in the
halls, I helped Dixon and Sister Marie es-
cort class-cutters back to class. After the
halls were under control, I returned to my
classroom and spent most of the afternoon
searching for the key to the cabinet with the
tape recorders. Before the end of the day,
my class rehearsed two extremely rough
songs.

MINDWORKER: MAYBECK

I had received two days of donated recording studio time from Joe, the brother of
Leo's Music, the major source of rock and
roll equipment in the East Bay. I couldn't
get the time or the money to go through
publishing and royalty copyrights to legally
use any popular music so we practiced two
of my original songs. The lyrics of "Black
Man, White Man," a rock tune, were about
integration:

Black man, white man, white man, black.
Get yourself together before there's no turn-
    ing back.
White man, black man, black man, white.
Get yourself together everything will be all
    right.

Black and white got to blend together into a
    different color called brotherhood.
White and black got to blend together into a
    different color called brotherhood.

"Mrs. Abraham's Jesus," using acoustical
guitars, offered a mild rebuke to religious
beliefs. During the 60s, questioning authority was popular, even within the church.
These would never be top-ten hit records.

Mrs. Abraham wanted to name her baby Je-
    sus, and she did.
Her baby Jesus died when he was three and
    free from life.

PAUL AUGUST

*Now Mrs. Abraham goes to her church every
   morning and prays.
She prays to her own baby Jesus every day.*

Vocals were done by Derrick Youman (Black Man) and Tony Perez
(White Man). John Ferguson sang the Jesus song. The 45 rpm
(revolutions per minute) was the music recording system of the time. It
evolved into the cassette tape, the 8 track tape, CDs, MP3s and so on..

Tuesday evening. Home.

Home is on 39th Avenue in East Oakland, just a few blocks from St. Liz. Neighborhood houses are separated by driveways with an old garage in back. The lots had small backyards, which showcased each family's culture.

Our backyard was lush with pine and fruit trees, sunflowers, and a thick lawn. It reflected the country girl influence of Muriel, who grew up in the Sierra foothills.

Next to us, a Chinese family cultivated small flowers surrounded by bricks, which were precisely slanted at the same angle. Their yard was crisscrossed by a concrete path under neatly trimmed trees.

One backyard over, a Navajo family piled wood near an unpainted shed. Their ground was dusty and barren, and dog was chained up from their back porch. It once bit my daughter, Wendy, on her leg.

On the corner, the home of a Mexican family was painted orange and surrounded by tall brick walls. When they have a party, a Mariachi band blares from their back patio. The sound echoes through the streets. Black youth stop riding their dirt bikes, turn off their portable radios and listen in wonder to this foreign brass music. Then most of them ride back to their apartments, which have no backyards.

Levinson came home with me for dinner. "Muriel," I said, "one of the new girls in the office said she got a call that you wanted me to take you to the hospital to have a baby."

"No," she said. "I called and wanted you to take me to the hospital *with* the baby."

"Oh, no! What happened?"

"The baby pulled the cord to the coffeepot and was scalded with hot coffee. It's all right, though. A burned arm. I got a ride to the hospital with a neighbor."

"Oh, great," I said. "I'm sorry. We really do need a second car for our family." Two weeks later, despite our tenuous income situation, I bought a used station wagon.

We sat down to dinner. "Well, Muriel," said Levinson, "how are you holding up under all this? It looks like Paul might not have a job for next year."

"I'm angry," she said. "Father Orville baptized our daughter Kristi at St. Liz church and baptized our son in the Sister's new convent. Now this." Muriel had tears in her deep blue eyes, which sparkled below her brunette hair. She swept a finger across her high cheekbones. She usually had an easy-going manner, but not tonight. "I don't think I better tell you what Dixon told me at the party last week."

"Come on Muriel, don't bait us," said Levinson.

Muriel said, "After I told him how worried I was about our security, Dixon had the nerve to tell me that if Paul—well, he told me not to tell you guys this..."

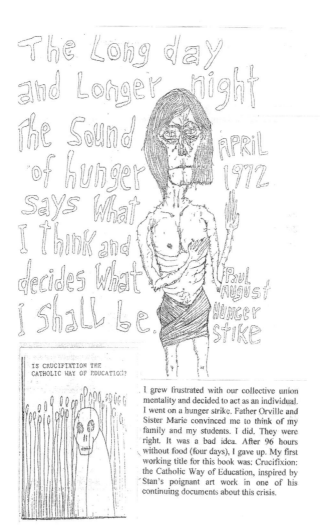

The Long day
and Longer night
The Sound
of hunger
Says What
I think and
decides What
I Shall be.

APRIL
1972

Paul
August
Hunger
Strike

IS CRUCIFIXTION THE
CATHOLIC WAY OF EDUCATION?

I grew frustrated with our collective union mentality and decided to act as an individual. I went on a hunger strike. Father Orville and Sister Marie convinced me to think of my family and my students. I did. They were right. It was a bad idea. After 96 hours without food (four days), I gave up. My first working title for this book was: Crucifixion: the Catholic Way of Education, inspired by Stan's poignant art work in one of his continuing documents about this crisis.

"So, tell us," we pleaded.

"He said that if you couldn't get a job by September that you could probably be a janitor."

Levinson and I looked at each other and broke out laughing.

"A janitor?" I said. "What's he going to do, fire the janitors and replace them with teachers?"

"Paul," said Levinson, tongue in cheek, "Here's your big chance. Remember when the janitors spilled the popcorn butter on the floor after school one day, then swept it right back into the can? We could eat popcorn again because we could trust you as janitor. Don't pass it up."

"Hell," I said. "As a songwriter, it's a great job. I could work with my hands and free my mind."

"Really, Paul," said Levinson. "Have you applied for other jobs?"

"Yeah," I said, "but no luck. The teacher market is full. No jobs for unemployed English teachers. They only want teachers in math or science. When Stan gets back from Yosemite, we're meeting about his plans for an alternative school.[32] If I'm not at St. Liz as a teacher, I won't bump the janitor out of a job. I'll probably help Stan start his school."

"Sounds like educational Utopia," said Levinson. "A school you guys can run without any principal or school board to mess it up."

"But you can't run a school without money," said Muriel.

"Details," I joked.

Nobody laughed.

Chapter 26

"They lost $10,000..."

A WEEK LATER AT THE BLIND LEMON, San Pablo Avenue in Berkeley. Stan and Kelly returned from Yosemite. The Blind Lemon is a dark bar with peanut shells on the floor, candles on the table, and dart boards on the walls. Both of these returning campers had a healthy Yosemite glow despite the dim surroundings. Radisch and I joined them.

"Yosemite was absolutely beautiful," said Stan. "I had a chance to put together my plans for our own school. It was as if the mountains were an inspiration to this dream."

"It's a dream that may not materialize if we get rehired, which is almost impossible," I said. I didn't want to risk starting a new school but I had decided to fight this injustice and help my friends rather than try an even more dubious career in music or writing, where I had no full-time experience. Our new school would be my way of continuing our struggle. Besides, there were no teaching jobs out there.

"But we've been out of touch with the St. Liz reality. Not that I missed it, mind you," said Kelly. He twisted his wrist, raised an eyebrow and said, "What's been going on?"

"You're just in time for the senior ball. It's tomorrow night," I said with a smile.

"Oh come on now, August. You know what we're talking about," said Stan.

"Yeah," I replied, "The issues remain the same."

"Figures," said Kelly. "Before we left I heard that the parish planned to make big bucks on a country music concert. What happened?"

Radisch said, "The parish hired an outside promoter to hold a fundraiser. He put on a country and western show at the Oakland auditorium."

"Country and western?" choked Kelly. "In the middle of Oakland—soul city?"

"They lost $10,000," said Radisch.

"You got to be kidding," said Kelly. "They could have hired back a teacher for that amount."

"Honest to God. Instead of making money to rehire us, they are throwing money away," said Stan. He leaned forward as he raised his eyebrows. "By the way, has anyone found a job for next year?"

"Bud Johnson," said Radisch. "He landed a counseling job in a small Northern California town in the Sierras."

"Up in the boondocks," said Kelly. "That's the only place they have school jobs now a days."

Radisch reached for the pretzels and said, "There were several hundred applications for that job. Bud's got almost 20 years' experience."

"What about the others?" asked Stan.

"Nothing," replied Radisch. "There are practically no teaching jobs."

"That brings us to the point of making our own way." Stan hunched over his files, put on his thick black rimmed glasses and opened a legal size folder. "Tonight is officially the first meeting of our new school. We are the board of directors. Radisch is handling our legal work."

Radisch said, "To become a school in California, we simply incorporate and declare ourselves nonprofit."

"Is that all?" asked Kelly. "Don't we need teachers or accreditation?"

"No. All we need to do is submit school names. The state will let us know which name is available."

"I've got an idea for a name," I said. "Alinsky High School. The battles that Saul Alinsky fought as a community organizer were like the battles we're fighting at St. Liz. Remember when the Oakland city council actually voted to ban Alinsky from the city limits? He rode across the Bay Bridge in a caravan waving his passport as an American citizen."

"I'd like it to be Einstein High," said Kelly. "Top-notch all the way."

"I'd like to suggest Maybeck High," said Stan. "Bernard Maybeck was a local architect who used ordinary materials in an innovative style. Maybeck is synonymous with quality."

"I also like Jack London High School," I said.

"I wouldn't put Jack London in a class with Maybeck or even Alinsky," said Stan, with a touch of arrogance.

> **Establishing a Nonprofit Private School:** It's true. All that was needed to start a private school in California was to become incorporated, receive a name, and declare ourselves nonprofit by publishing an ad in the newspaper saying we didn't discriminate. California, at the time, didn't require credentials, degrees, background checks, or fingerprints.

"I know," I said. "It's just that Jack London lived in Oakland. He's more appreciated in other countries. There isn't even a single school in Oakland named after him."

"But there might be a Jack London private school else-where in California," said Radisch.

"So, the state will review these names and notify us as to which one we can use."

"I think it's an absolute disgrace," said Stan, "that to become a private school, all we have to do is submit names and pay our fees."

"That's it," said Radisch. "You'll have your school on paper before the end of summer, but what about the reality?"

"The reality is that alternative schools are growing," said Stan. "Public and Catholic schools are down. It's those nuns and priests and tyrants like Dixon. There's tremendous unity in the face of adversity."

"Some of these little schools don't last long," I said.

"Truism," Stan replied, removing his glasses. "When a small school depends on one key figure who burns out, that's the end of it. The four of us, however, have worked together for several years. We have an excellent rapport.

"We all have diverse fields of expertise," Stan continued. He knew us well enough to organize our talents. "August, you can handle PR, proposal writing, and English classes. Radisch is our legal advisor and he'll teach a legal systems class at night. Kelly will handle finances and teach science. I'll plan the curriculum and teach social studies. All we need is a teacher for math and foreign languages."

"Most of the dedication is going to fall on you two guys," said Radisch, nodding to Kelly and Stan. "I'll be in the DA's office. August has his music and writing. But to you two guys St. Liz was your life. School is your life. Now this school will be your life."

"You ain't just woofin'," laughed Kelly.

"What about a location?" I said. "This is only a school on paper. We need an actual physical place to teach our classes. There's a vacant church and Sunday school just a few blocks from St Liz. It's a real beauty, like a Maybeck building."

"Paul," said Stan. "Location is a mere detail. The legalities and the curriculum are top priorities. Students and parents from St. Liz will go where we go."

We passed a carafe of wine around the table. A short candle flickered in a squat bottle covered with dusty layers of melted wax. Darts smacked the wall. A muffled jukebox droned in a distant corner. We sat there, for a moment, mulling over the uncertainty of the future.

"I think it can work," said Stan.

"I know it will work," said Kelly.

Chapter 27

"Historically speaking..."

THE SENIOR BALL ON FRIDAY NIGHT. The Royal Inn in San Mateo was a distant second choice to the usual San Francisco venues, which were sold out on that night.

The senior ball was the annual metamorphosis of girls into women and boys into men. Before the ball, girls wore Catholic school uniforms with pleated skirts to school, little make-up and no jewelry. This evening they were dressed up in strapless gowns, done-up hair, and sparkling red lipstick. The guys evolved from Levis, sneakers, and T-shirts into velvet-collared tuxedos, ruffled shirts, and patent leather shoes. I didn't even recognize some of my own students.

Stan couldn't resist a clothing counterpoint. He wore faded blue jeans, hiking boots and a polka dot tie under his wrinkled tweed coat, frayed at the cuffs. "I'm going to have a little fun this evening."

As Santos and I watched, Stan made the rounds of the tables. He shook hands with Dixon. "Good evening, Gil. Certainly a pleasant evening for the ball, eh?"

"He's doing his British accent routine," said Santos.

Stan wandered over to Sister Saint John the Baptist. "How Are you this fine evening, my dear Sister?"

She didn't acknowledge him. She stared straight ahead at the empty stage. The band was late. Stan lit up his pipe and strolled over to Martha Dunwell, who was standing near the entrance. "Why, hello there Martha, my dear. You will reserve a dance for me this evening, will you not?"

Martha rolled her eyes, checked her wristwatch, then stepped to the other side of the door. We laughed at the scene.

George came over to our table. "August, they've got a problem with the band."

"What's that?"

"The band was supposed to show up here at eight o'clock. They arrived exactly at eight over in Oakland in the middle of the St. Liz bingo game."

Santos said, "I can just picture all those overweight bingo players doing a boogie."

"Come on, August," said George. "Let's get up on stage and do our stall routine. We can fake it like Dixon thinks we fake it in class."

George and I got on stage. "Look at that," George whispered to me and glanced into the audience. "As soon as we got on stage, Dixon and his wife walked out. There goes Sister Clem. I don't think they're our biggest fans."

With George on piano and me on guitar, we traded blues vocals and stretched our 12-bar blues into 16-bar blues. George did his comic routine between songs for the audience. "Hi there, folks, and if you're going to the boy's john this evening, you'll really get high there."

George's humor just didn't fit. It felt so contrived, so strained in front of unsmiling nuns, priests, and administrators. We were glad when the band finally arrived and the music started blaring. We returned to our seats where the sparse dinner consisted of the usual assembly-line prime rib. Sister Saint Francis came to our table and gave her dessert to Stan. "Her act of charity for tonight," Stan snickered.

Sister Clem took to the dance floor, a little tipsy, and bopped with a senior guy who wore a black tuxedo and top hat, carried a cane, and romped about in oily motorcycle boots.

During the slow dances, the guys and girls wrapped their arms around each other and curled their bodies closely together.

"If Father Edward were here tonight," said George, "he'd be out there with his

flashlight insisting on a six-inch dancing distance." George continued. "Ah, these senior balls are all alike. The food is lousy—warmed over prime fat. They always locate it as far from Oakland as possible, here on the beautiful mudflats of San Mateo. And there is always some last minute mini disaster. The band didn't show up and, what's even worse, Augie and I went on and bombed. That's a maxi disaster. Anyway, we will have to wait nine months before we get the final results on this fine night."

"How's that?" asked Radisch, preoccupied, as he passed a flask of Jack Daniel's whiskey around underneath the table.

"Historically speaking," said George, "there's always at least one Catholic girl who, as a result of the activities after the senior ball, ends up pregnant."

Sunday afternoon, a couple of weeks later. Graduation.

"What a way to spend a Sunday afternoon," groaned Radisch. "We could have a good poker game going."

The faculty sat together waiting for the graduates.

"Sunday has always been a church day for me," I said. "When I was in grammar school, we would rise and shine for the 9 a.m. Mass. We had to fast before communion in those days. After church, my mom bought a big Sunday newspaper, my sister and I bought a comic book and we came home to a sumptuous Sunday brunch. What an appetite I had after starving all morning."

"You can plan to go to Mass tomorrow," Radisch said. "The last faculty meeting of the year begins with Mass in the sisters' convent."

Stan leaned over the folding chairs and said, "The convent? That's unusual. I must admit, I am looking forward to giving my parting shots. Those last three days of school without students is such an absurd waste of time."

"That's the way they meet the requirements for the legal minimum number of school days," said Radisch.

The graduates arrived. They took several slow steps in time to the music, then broke from the procession and skipped to their seats. The solemnity of the ritual shifted into a light mood, irreverent and gleeful.

"Look at the seniors' protest," said Santos who leaned forward from his seat in back of me. Most graduates wore a black armband with the word 'rehire.' They carried bags of peanuts.

"Why the peanuts?" I asked Santos.

"To create a little confusion during the ceremony. Watch," said Santos.

Tom Rowe took the stage in his capacity as dean of students to MC the event. He also wore a black armband. "Quite an act of defiance for an administrator," said Stan, "even if he is a known sympathizer to our cause."

"Rowe has nothing to worry about," said Radisch. "Nobody else around here wants his job because no one wants to be the heavy with student discipline."

Rowe stood behind the podium and began a brief announcement to parents who wanted to take pictures. "The graduates on the left –your left, which is my right – will exit with their diplomas on your right, to the left of me."

Peanut shells began cracking and dropping to the floor. Rowe became flustered. "On the other hand, graduates on the left...on my left that is...your right. Graduates on your right will exit on the left. My left. No, I mean your, er, ah, left. Er, ah..."

Feet smashed and crunched shells into the plastic covering on the gym floor. "Ah, I do believe it will facilitate matters somewhat if I simply pointed." Rowe pointed. The audience laughed. The graduates cheered. The senior class president then led the audience in the Pledge of Allegiance. There was no American flag on the wall: only a crucifix.

When Father Orville took the podium to deliver his speech, the solemnity of the ritual was again dissolved by cracking and munching of peanuts. Orville's basic message to the class was, "There is nothing more permanent than change. We have to accept change as a continuing part of life."

The graduates stood to receive their diplomas. The first girl to receive her scroll stepped up to Orville, accepted the diploma with the wrong hand, shook the wrong hand, winked at the audience, and generally tangled things up. Orville smiled at the confusion. The girl leaned forward to say a hearty "Thank you." Orville winced at the peanut breath. Many graduates followed this ritual of confusion.

The graduates crushed their way through a layer of shells to return to their seats. At the end of the ceremony, when they were excused, peanut shells flew into the air and showered down like brown confetti. The exit procession broke into a mad run for the door.

"Well, that certainly was an unorthodox graduation," observed Stan, looking at Santos. "I'm not sure I understand the significance of the peanut protest."

"Hell, man," Santos threw up his hands, apparently feeling unappreciated for organizing this symbolic protest. "We had to do something."

"Oh? Curious," said Stan. "This whole thing is very curious."

Chapter 28

"Those nuns are a little..."

OUTSIDE THE NUNS' NEW CONVENT. Monday morning. St. Liz.

"This is it," said Stan, walking across the street to join several of us in front of the nuns' convent. "This is the last faculty meeting of the year and perhaps the last time we will ever come together here at St. Liz."

Tom Rowe lifted his double chin and gazed toward the stained glass window of the nuns' new convent. "There is, of course, the traditional year-end Mass before the faculty meeting. Even I, a non-Catholic, an avowed Presbyterian, I am required to, and I shall, attend Mass with my Catholic brethren."

The end-of-the-year Mass was always held in the cavernous St. Liz church with 30 staff members and hundreds of empty pews.

It was followed by a farewell faculty meeting in the school library. But not this time. Mass would be in the nun's convent, in their chapel, with a faculty meeting afterward.

Radisch skimmed a purple ditto sheet he held. "This memo from Dixon says that the Mass and faculty meeting is for 'teachers contracted to return next year.' It sounds like he doesn't want us in there."

"That's just the usual administrative mumbo jumbo," said Kelly, tossing back his shaggy hair. "What's he going to do, ban us from Mass? Hah. Let's go in."

We moved toward the huge wood door of the nun's porch. I rang the bell. Sister Saint John the Baptist peeked through the peephole and then we waited.

"Hey you guys. I didn't get an agenda. What's going on?" asked George as he arrived.

"Dixon gave the returning faculty an agenda," Rowe said, "but he ignored the guys who were laid off. I rather doubt that he wants to encourage you to attend."

"That's ridiculous," said Stan.

Sister Saint John the Baptist finally cracked opened the door. She glanced past most of us and looked at Tom Rowe. "Mr. Rowe...?" Her voice lifted with the tone of an invitation. She gestured with her upturned hand for Rowe to come forward.

Rowe acknowledged the gesture with a slight nod of his bald head, then stood to the side. "After you, gentlemen."

Kelly raised an eyebrow, glanced at Rowe and stepped forward. Suddenly, the nun at the door flung her arm across the entrance and stared beyond us, into nowhere, and stoically announced, "I'm sorry. Teachers only."

Kelly stopped. His mouth dropped open. He blinked his eyes and shook his head. "Sister, you've got to be kidding."

"Only Mr. Rowe is a teacher for next year," the nun said.

Kelly slapped his forehead in disbelief and walked away.

Stan stepped forward and said, "But sister, I am a tenured teacher this year."

"This Mass is for the planning session, for next year's teachers," Sister replied.

"I am on temporary layoff," Stan argued. "I could be here next year."

Sister Saint John the Baptist clenched her teeth and glowered at Stan. "You are not needed here. Planning session only."

Stan turned back.

Rowe stepped forward. "Sister, these men are members of this faculty this year and part of this meeting. Surely, you cannot, in good conscience, deny them access to fulfill their contractual obligation as faculty members of this school."

"Planning session only," the nun repeated.

Rowe rolled his eyes, tossed up his arms, turned on his heels and left. The nun slammed the door.

George and I exchanged shrill, wordless sounds. "Ooooo eeeeeee..."

George said, "Those nuns are a little confused. She invited Rowe, the Protestant, into Mass and actually banned all us fired Catholics."

As a Catholic from birth, I was astonished. We're all told to attend Mass and worship God or be guilty of a mortal sin if we didn't. I've never known anyone, for any reason, to be banned from Mass.[33]

"Surrealistic," said Stan. "To use Kelly's words: this is, indeed, mind-boggling. It's like they're turning away evil from their door."

Dixon meandered down the front stairs of the school and crossed the street. We signaled him over to our group. "Gil," said Stan, "I've been here for seven years and I wanted to be thanked by the faculty for all my work at this school." This was not sarcasm. He was serious.

"Don't you think that's a little unrealistic, Stan, in light of all that's happened since March?" replied Dixon.

Kelly stepped forward. "What possible reason could you have for not allowing us to attend the faculty meeting?"

"Well, you're not obligated to attend." Dixon spoke slowly. He appeared outwardly calm, but his eyes were glassy. "This is only for next year's teachers."

Kelly said, "We don't *have* to attend? Does that mean we can attend if we want?"

"No," said Dixon. "You *cannot* attend. There are just too many bad feelings."

Kelly rolled his eyes, then curled his fingers at Dixon. "Are you suspending us for the last two days of school? You won't allow us to attend the meeting?"

"I am not suspending you."

Howard arrived and joined the debate. "It seems to me that this is not legal. How could you hire teachers to attend a meeting and then tell them they can't attend? What possible reason do you have?"

Dixon shrugged his shoulders and made no reply.

Radisch spoke up. "This isn't even consistent with your own rules."

Dixon said, "Well, you're entitled to your opinion."

"You're the principal," I said. "You have an obligation to bring the school together instead of splitting it up into more frustration."

Dixon replied, "This is one of those situations where you're damned if you do, and you're damned if you don't."

Radisch sneered, "The real reason we're being barred from the convent is because those nuns are so pissed off they don't want to see our faces."

"Some sisters are very upset," said Dixon. "They don't want to hear this all over again."

"Very well," said Rowe, with a conciliatory tone to his voice. "Let's go in and stick strictly to the agenda."

"Okay," Dixon replied. "Our first item of business will be whether or not to let you guys come in and stick to agenda items only. I can't promise anything."

Kelly raised his index finger toward Dixon. "But you have to let the entire faculty decide that. We're part of the faculty. We have a right to participate in the discussion of whether or not we stay."

"Sorry. I just can't do that."

"This is a real mind-boggler," said Kelly.

"I'll bring it up, first item," said Dixon.

As Dixon entered the convent, Kelly looked to the heavens and said, "What a farce. Can you believe this? It's a real hurter."

We retreated to St. Liz and waited in the faculty room for the decision we knew they'd make. Father Farley came over with the news we expected. "I'm sorry, but you will not be allowed to attend the Mass or meeting."

"This is just terrible," yelled Kelly. "How can you possible justify this terrible rejection?"

Farley shrugged lamely, "I'm sorry."

I sat down at the faculty typewriter and began a letter to the nuns.

Stan approached Farley. "Father, you are the messenger who brings the bad news. We do the same. If we talk to the newspapers, the nuns become angry with us. We are seen as the culprits because we are the messengers of facts that the sisters don't want to hear."

"But some of your facts, Stan, are misleading and placed together as if there was a cause and effect when there really isn't," said Farley. "You guys give facts but not reasons or explanations."

"Father, that is absurd," replied Stan. "The nuns locked us out of Mass and say it is a planning session only. Dixon says the nuns are upset with us. Each person has a different reason or explanation. Who can say? But everyone will agree to the naked fact that those nuns refused to let us in their convent to attend Mass."

"Well, I believe, er..." Farley stuttered, "...er, perhaps these lay-offs will be settled in the courts."

Stan took one step back and feigned disbelief. "What? Bring in the paid legal mercenaries who tell us to act like a mummies? Don't say, do or write anything to weaken their case. No. I don't want this to wilt under dry legalities in stale courtrooms. The jury decides the legal issue." Farley was about to leave when I finished my letter. "Wait a minute, Father. Take this letter with you."

St. Liz High School

Oakland, California

Dear Sisters,

Your refusal to allow me and my colleagues to go to Mass is an unforgivable insult.[34] Let's not pretend that there was any reason other than your unwillingness to have us physically present. Such vain motivations are unbecoming members of any religious order.

Sincerely,

Paul August

Farley left with my letter. We exiles spent most of the morning in the faculty room with the end-of-school paperwork.

Just before lunch, Levinson came back from the faculty meeting. "Those nuns are steaming. Sister Clem said that if you guys return, she's leaving. Then Sister St. Francis said that when any of you talk to her, all she says is that she doesn't know anything. Sister St. John the Baptist said that if she goes into the faculty room, and you guys are there, she turns around and leaves. Not very charitable."

Levinson turned to me and opened his hands, palms up. "Paul, Sister Marie is...shall we say...What's a good euphemism for 'very pissed off?'"

"Perturbed?" I ventured.

"Yes. Our dear sister is perturbed about your letter. She was so upset she couldn't read it. After Dixon read it to the faculty, Father Farley rose to your defense, announcing that you wrote it in a moment of passion."

"Bless me Father, for I have sinned," I hissed. "I wrote your nuns a letter. Thank you, Father, for your unsolicited absolution."

"It gets better," said Levinson with a twinkle in his eye. "I saw Dixon taking down the names of faculty members who did not attend Mass like Rowe and Father Bart. This is, of course, in contrast with the mythical list of those to keep out of Mass like Kelly, Radisch, August, and all you guys."

Santos came in, gritted his teeth, and howled, "That meeting in the nun's convent was unreal. Dixon was close to freaking out. Sister Marie became real flippant and sarcastic over the least little issue, like the school calendar for next year. The nuns are turning on Dixon. It could be a power struggle."

"The religious are morally-retarded people. You can't be real with them," said Levinson. "You should see the self-consumption. They get rid of their scape-goats and now they're turning on each other."

"I agree with the self-consumptive theory," said Stan. "They won't have us to kick around anymore."

"The faculty meeting in the nun's convent was all so medieval," Levinson continued. "It was like the meeting of a secret society. We retreated to the stained-glass cavern, voted not to admit the Godless heathens from the outside world and then took the secret oath."

"An oath?" said Stan.

"Not literally," said Levinson as he reached in his briefcase and pulled out a purple ditto paper. "Here. Check this out. After they voted not to let you guys attend Mass, they had us all recite this creed together."

CREED

I believe that God is goodness.
I believe in honesty and open discussion, for there we shall find God.
I believe in the basic human dignity of every man, white, black, yellow communist, capitalist, rich, poor, retarded, deformed, ignorant, dirty, dishonest, good and bad together.

I believe that morality should be legislated and preached, and be lived by young and old alike.

I believe many people in this world cannot see God except in the form of bread and medicine.

I believe all of us have some growing to do.

Stan read it and fumed, "Open discussion? Dignity of yellow communists? Bread and medicine? What is this, a ruthless charade?"

"...You, a priest, say that no moral standards exist to judge human behavior?"

"What a bunch of crap," I said. "Kelly, did you see this?

Kelly read it and wailed. "Oh, you've got to be kidding. I just plain don't believe it."

Father Farley entered the faculty room and we pounced on him. "Father," I said. "This creed is nonsense. The nuns don't care about us. You don't care about me."

"Oh, but I do care, Paul," said Farley, wringing his hands as if to mollify me.

"No, Father," I said. "You believe you care but that's all. You don't act on your beliefs."

Stan stepped up to Farley. "Why don't you apply this creed to yourself, Father, or better yet, apply it to Dixon. If a man says one thing and does another, wouldn't you call that man a liar or a cheat?"

"Well, Stan, that would depend."

"What?" Stan placed his hands on his lapels and said, in his most pompous tone, "You, a priest, say that no moral standards exist to judge human behavior?"

"No, oh no," said Farley. "I'm not saying that. I'm saying that you have to start with specific events to apply to moral standards."

"Isn't it conventional Catholic philosophy that the ends do not justify the means?" said Stan.

"That's correct. The ends do not justify the means."

"Then how do you justify taking our jobs to balance your budget?"

"Well, you see, er, ah..." Farley stammered. "The drop in enrollment. We don't need so many teachers."

"Even if that were true, you don't get rid of veteran teachers just because they oppose the principal. I simply cannot understand how you priests and sisters can close your eyes to this blatant injustice."

"Well, I'm sorry," said Farley, weakly.

"We've come a long way since you helped Dixon give out those layoff notices last March, Father." Radisch spoke up from across the room. "You're not as cheerful now as you were then, when you wished us a happy Easter."

Farley left, silently.

George looked out the faculty room windows toward the nun's convent. "The nuns are still cloistered in their oyster. Will they ever come out again?"

I felt a headache and I sneezed several times. My nose itched. My eyes watered. Allergies. "I've got an attack of hay fever. Damn it. I'm going home."

On my way out, I pulled all my books, files, and papers from my faculty room shelf, stuffed them in a cardboard box and left. I would return tomorrow for the last official day of school.

"Take it easy, Augie," laughed George. "Don't get held up by the nuns' blockade."

Chapter 29

"I think it's time..."

MEETING WITH JORGE STOKES, union rep. After school, Tuesday, St. Liz. Room 105. We squeezed into student desks. Stokes stood near the chalkboard and led the group. "Looks like our last meeting. Where do we stand?"

"It's a solid stone wall," said Radisch, squinting in thought and pausing to formulate his words. "Two months ago I believed that Dixon was the only villain. Then, in a split vote, 17 members of the faculty, including all the nuns and priests, 17 of our colleagues, voted against us. The Bishop refused to see us. The school board walked out on us. The nuns banned us from Mass. Almost the entire Catholic hierarchy is opposed to us. Only the Flatland Fathers spoke in our favor."

Stan raised his head. "Dixon is doomed. The school is doomed. We won. I'm trying to think of a historical comparison, perhaps the Charge of the Light Brigade. They fought, were destroyed, and they were vindicated.

"Can I say something?" Santos caught our attention. "Last year, when Dixon tried to fire me, you guys organized and got my job back. Now, he's fired you guys and given me a contract. I feel terrible."

"Well you should, you young whipper-snapper," laughed Kelly.

Howard shuffled documents and brought back a serious tone. "I think that all is not lost. I swear to God that the enrollment will be up, but Dixon isn't helping. You know what he told me? He said, 'Why should I help get enrollment up? Then I would have to hire those guys back.' Can you imagine that? He doesn't even care about the school."

"Then why should we?" said Santos. "The school is down the drain without you guys. What's the use? Let it die."

"I am into the alternative school reality," said Stan, as he looked out the window at the cloudless sky. "Perhaps we should have Howard recruit for our new school instead of St. Liz."

"Now you're thinking, Stanley, my man," said Kelly.

"One other thing," said Radisch. "Although we get paid through the summer, Dixon is cutting off our health benefits at the end of June."

"He's really a sweet guy, isn't he?" Stokes cleared his throat. He had a deep frown on his face. He adjusted his coat with his silver hook. "I think it's time to face facts," Stokes said. "You had to get a numerical majority and assert your economic will over his but you didn't. You lost." "I don't want to hear this," said Kelly, rising from his student desk, trembling. He moved toward the door. "It's just so obvious we're being screwed. Why do we have to go through this? It's just so depressing. I'm leaving. I'm going down to The Master's."

"I feel like Kelly does," said Radisch. "It's not over. I can't resolve all this until Dixon gets what's coming to him. Lyndon B. Johnson had a sign on his desk when he was Speaker of the House. It said, 'Don't get mad, get even.' I'm going to get even with that guy if it's the last thing I do."

"Well, I think Kelly was right in one direction," said Stokes. "Let's adjourn to the local pub."

At The Master's, we moved chairs around two small tables barely big enough to hold drinks and beer nuts. Stan leaned back as if he were holding court. "A few years ago, people back east would watch the Rose Bowl on TV and see California as the land of sunshine, short sleeves, and college pom-pom girls wiggling in short skirts in the middle of winter. Folks everywhere fled the ice and flocked to California. Now, fewer people buy that myth. The reality of California includes smog, earthquakes, fires, mudslides, militants, murder, and unemployment. Less population, fewer teachers. That's why we won't find teaching jobs. That's why I am looking forward to starting our own school. What about you, Paul?"

"I really don't know, Stan," I said. "I can't resist fighting to keep a job I really don't want anymore. If I help start the new school it will partly be vindictive, to hijack students from St. Liz. Not a good motivation."

"You wouldn't go back to St. Liz?" Stan asked.

"Not after all this. Not without you guys. They will never rehire me. I've been working as a freelance writer, doing work for *Rolling Stone* magazine, but my present assignment just isn't coming together. I can't concentrate. My future is at *Rolling Stone* or a local newspaper but I feel like I'm obsessed with this injustice. I can't give up this fight. "

"It's your Irish background," said Stan. "Fighting for a lost cause."

"That too," I said. "Part of the reason why I'll help your school is because it's my way to keep on fighting."

"You seem upset with the way the nuns acted in all this," said Stan.

"Stan," I said. "When I was a kid my dad inherited a small farm on an acre of land in San Leandro. We brought the nuns the fruits of our labor: corn in the summer, pumpkins in the fall, lilacs at Easter, and roses to crown the Blessed Virgin Mary, Queen of May. Those Dominican sisters were always so grateful. I grew up believing that the good sisters sacrificed everything, including their sexuality, for the greater good."

"Whatever that is," said Stan.

"It's almost like I inherited this sister obsequiousness, this be-good-to-the-sisters persona. My mother, a devout Catholic, went to Mass every morning. My Godmother, Goody, paid my tuition for Catholic school."

"And now?" asked Stan.

"Now?" I took a drink of Jack Daniels bourbon. "I can't believe I'm being kicked in the teeth by a bunch of nuns."

Kelly interrupted us. "August. Stan. Let me buy us all another round of drinks. We're on the way to somewhere. We just don't know where."

Chapter 30

"The key to the men's room..."

THE LAST DAY OF SCHOOL FOR FACULTY members. I walked ten blocks to school. We bought our old English row house in the St. Liz parish because I didn't want to commute. It's a good walk. I enjoy the exercise. At St. Liz, Stan stood in the hall next to a colorful mural his class painted on the wall across from the Dean's office. A yellow and orange smiling Mr. Sun, puffing rainbow bubbles from a long ivory pipe, brightened the otherwise dim green halls. Stan simply stood there, admiring his students' art.

"You know, Paul, this was one of our finest paintings," said Stan. "It's amazing. We had to fight so hard to get permission to do this. There were all the usual reasons why we couldn't paint murals. 'The union won't let you paint the halls.' 'It's too expensive.'

'It has never been done before.' But we did it and there it is."

"You're in a pensive mood," I said.

"Intellectually, I know I will never return to St. Liz, but emotionally I am still not ready to accept this," said Stan. "I feel like Bartleby, Melville's character who haunted a law office and preferred not to leave even after they fired him. Finally, they moved the office. Yesterday I went to the history department meeting. After six years as department chairman, I told them I wanted to listen, offer suggestions. Marie got uptight. Sister Saint John the Baptist started yelling at me. Dixon almost called the police. When I refused to leave, they left. Our ghosts will haunt these halls. Ghosts like Mr. Sun here. I wonder if they will paint over our mural after we go?"

"Oh, Stan," I said, and sighed. "In a more practical vein...are the paychecks in?"

"Yes," he said. "But they're not in the faculty room mailbox. You have to go to the principal's office. Martha Dunwell is temporarily covering Marge Hardy's old job."

"Great," I said. As I sauntered down the hall I passed by the wall photos of graduates from each year. My young face was up there somewhere, looking down on me now.

In the principal's office, Martha sat behind a clean desk.

"Do you have the paychecks?" I asked her.

"No," she frowned. "You have to see Mr. Dixon. I'm only the acting bookkeeper."

"Say," I said, lightheartedly. "Which word in the English language has three double letters together?" She looked at me as if I were crazy.

"Bookkeeper," I said with a grin. She frowned again. I shrugged my shoulders and entered Dixon's office.

"Hi, Paul."

"Hi, Gil."

We both played calm, restrained roles.

"Have you found a job yet, Paul?" Dixon asked. "I haven't had any requests from you yet for letters of recommendation."

My first urge was to tell him that I'd never ask him for a recommendation. Instead I said, "There aren't many teaching jobs out there, Gil. The Oakland Public Schools cut over 100 teachers. There are thousands of unemployed teachers in the Bay Area alone."

"I certainly hope you find something. Our enrollment is less than expected." Dixon opened a file and read. "500 is very low compared to 700 for this year. Bingo has leveled off to barely a thousand dollars a week. We're not getting the big crowds. This school is in real trouble."

"Survival of the fittest," I said. "The weakest Catholic schools are closing. More religious are leaving. Eventually, the remaining Catholic schools will be staffed by lay teachers."

"That may well be." Dixon lifted an eyebrow in thought. "If the religious took over the school and lowered the tuition, then maybe they could make it."

"Perhaps," I replied. "The financial problems placed you in a terrible position. The Bishop used you as a hatchet man to balance the budget and make the school self-sufficient."

"Well, you're entitled to your opinion," said Dixon. "I told the Bishop I was holding down expenses. The alternative to balancing the budget was my job."

"Instead, you got rid of us," I said. "Your main purpose here is financial, not educational. You hurt a lot of people. You fired men who have dedicated some of the best years of their lives to this school."

"I know there are some religious teachers staying who are inferior to teachers we released," Dixon said. "Ideally, we should get rid of the inferior teachers and keep only the best. But this is a Catholic school and we have to keep the religious. Personally, I do not believe in the seniority system."

"If you don't use some kind of seniority, then teachers are simply judged by who sets the standards," I said.

Dixon perked up in his swivel seat. "I'll bet you, Paul that if we both sat down to make a list of the best teachers in the school we would come up with approximately the same teachers. You can tell what kind of a teacher you have by just looking at the floor of his classroom after school. Some rooms are terrible: papers, chalk, candy wrappers, sunflower seeds. Other rooms have clean floors, spotless. Those teachers have real control.

Dixon went on. "Radisch has a job in law where I think his real ability lies. I think you would be best in music." He swung around in his chair and pointed to the record we produced in the music workshop. "I listened to those two songs. I like them. You have real talent. I think you can find your pot of gold in music."

"Music, eh," I said. "Well, that's not as bad as Sister Clem. She thinks I should go into public relations. I think I'll help Stan with his school."

Dixon frowned. "If Stan's school is successful, we will probably lose another 40 or 50 students." He reached in his desk, handed me a paycheck, and called to Martha, "Where's the other check?"

Other check? What? A bonus for six years of service? Trying to buy a clear conscience, is that it? That wasn't it.

"Here's the rest of your salary for the summer," said Dixon. "We want to clear our books." Dixon self-consciously glanced down at his desktop. "Ah, do you have your keys?"

I pulled out two keys. "I have the class-room key and the key to the faculty men's room—the only place we shared a common purpose." Both keys were on a strand of rawhide, slicked by years of wear, with a knot of each end. I fumbled absentmindedly with the keys, trying to untie the melted rawhide lump.

"Didn't you have more keys—keys to the entire school?" asked Dixon.

"Yeah, I did," I said. "When I ran school dances I had the key to just about every-thing and just about everyone wanted me to unlock just about every door—fuse boxes, padlocks, bookroom, kitchenette, janitor's closet. I turned them in last year. All 28 keys."

"Oh," said Dixon. "We can't be too careful about keys."

"Remember when Martha lost her keys?" I said as I continued to tug at the rawhide knot. "Her purse disappeared from the girls' PE room with all her school keys. Father Edward immediately ordered every lock in the school changed."

"Yes," said Dixon. "And I called a special faculty meeting and announced that any teacher who lost or loaned out keys would be subject to reprimands and fines."

"Then a week later," I continued, "a jani-tor turned in the purse, keys, and all. He found it the day it was lost, but he didn't get around to turning it in until a week later.

Edward kicked himself for spending hundreds of dollars to change the locks."

"Yes, I remember," said Dixon, looking down at my keys.

I tugged again at the knot. "What the hell am I doing?" I said. "Here. Take the whole thing." I tossed the keys on his desk complete with a worn strand of rawhide.

Dixon accompanied me to the waist-high swinging door near the office counter. "This place will never be the same without you guys."

I turned and left with no handshake. I hurried past Stan's fiery and feathery wall murals, through the scarred lobby and the brick stairs to the street. It was a warm day, very warm. Maybe the enrollment will rise, I thought. Maybe they will rehire us. Amazing how I could possibly cling to a dying cinder of hope in a pile of cold ashes. I walked home.

Chapter 31

"Parents will trust us..."

S UMMER CREATES THE ILLUSION of freedom. Students celebrate their liberation from stagnant teachers, musty books and scarred buildings. As summer settles in, teenagers find no jobs available. Their beach roller coaster days are a rarity. Teens sleep late, watch TV game shows and hang out around the neighborhood. Although they won't admit it, students are happy to return to school, to friends and to a sense of purpose.

Teachers are seasonal workers. If we stretch out our thin paychecks, we can make it through summer. Some of us took summer jobs to make ends meet. Rowe chopped wood in the Sierras and trucked it home for winter sales. Howard drove a sightseeing bus in San Francisco. George sponsored a sports camp and weight-reduction clinic. Kelly helped his brother in a paper distribution company. I did free-lance writing. Other summers I worked as a rent-a-cop, a clerk in a five-and-dime store, a dance promoter for school fundraising, or a teacher in summer school. Of course, there was always the exception. Stan packed up and roamed through Europe all summer, but not this year.

We usually returned to school feeling re-freshed. There's a sense of relief from the comparative inactivity of the summer. But this was the summer of anxiety. September was the future of uncertainty.

The big decision. A Wednesday afternoon during the third week of August. My house.

"Kelly! Look at you. You're thin. I ha-ven't seen you guys all summer. You've lost weight," I said in amazement as I invited him in with Stan.

"Oh, just a little. Maybe thirty pounds or so," Kelly smiled.

"So, was it a special diet or maximum workouts?" I asked, knowing that long hours writing had expanded, not thinned, my waistline.

"Well," Kelly grinned. "It was a secret formula of four little words." He paused for effect. "Eat less. Exercise more."

I turned to Stan as we entered the rum-pus room in my basement. "Stan, where do we stand? Do we have a legal school?"

"The articles of incorporation were accepted by the state." Stan ran his trembling fingers through his shoulder length hair, then rubbed his temple in thought. "We submitted our school names: Saul Alinsky, our favorite radical community activist. Maybeck, one of our greatest regional architects. Einstein, enough said. And Jack London, a world famous local writer."

"And the winner is ..." interjected Kelly, holding up his right arm.

"We are officially in existence," said Stan, "as Maybeck High School!"

Kelly slouched on the worn green sofa.

Stan sat on the edge of a thick wooden chair. "We are an honest-to-God, legal, lawful school," said Kelly. "Can you believe it? We needed no credentials, qualifications, or clearance. We're a California corporation and we become tax exempt when we publish our existence in the local newspaper. Now all we have to do is decide whether or not we really want to go through with this crazy idea."

"We have to decide today; otherwise it will be too late." said Stan, biting his bottom lip. I could feel his nervousness. "We only have eleven students. We're insane to think that we can support three full-time teachers. We might have to charge more tuition than St. Liz."

"No, don't do that," Kelly waved his hand. "Eleven students is a nice, small school. Let's keep the tuition competitive because those young ladies and gentlemen are following us from St. Liz. We'll get more students later."

Stan blinked his eyes, rapidly. "Actually, over 100 students already left St. Liz when we did but we've waited too long. They're enrolled in other schools. We've lost them. Financially, with eleven students, we might as well put a razor blade to our throats. We simply cannot, in all logic or rationality, justify starting a school with only eleven students. I've done most of the work so far. I cannot continue under this stress. We've been operating on crisis energy since last spring. I can't take much more. We have to make a logical decision. Eleven students for a school is illogical."

"Stan," I said, sitting on my basement bar stool. "I agree with Kelly. With eleven we can move ahead and recruit new students. Our biggest problem is having no location. We're only a paper school. We have no physical identity."

Stan shook his head vehemently. "Paul, we can start school on a college campus, in a park, an old church hall. Anywhere. Christ preached from the beaches. Socrates led seminars under the stars."

"Eleven students," said Kelly. "Shucks. We can have classes in the back of Radisch's van."

School	Number of Students
ACTUALIZING RELATIONSHIP INSTITUTE, Pleasant Hills	16
EAST BAY JR. HIGH SCHOOL Oakland	20
HOLDEN SCHOOL Orinda	25
LAKESIDE HIGH SCHOOL Oakland	55
OASIS SCHOOL Lafayette	20
ODYSSEY SCHOOL Concord	20
OUR SCHOOL Berkeley	30
RURBAN SCHOOL Berkeley	20
CONCORDIA HIGH SCHOOL[*] Oakland	100
MAYBECK HIGH SCHOOL Oakland	50

This is a list of ten alternative schools existing in the East Bay in 1973. One school evolved into a personal growth program for adults. Another became a special program for use within other schools. One moved to San Francisco, another moved to Southern California and more than one simply vanished. All were nonpublic predecessors to the charter schools of the 2000s. Only Maybeck survived in its present form but with twice as many students. Clip art such as this frequently embellished Stan's documents, flyers and various communications.

"But we cannot exist without an income," said Stan.

"Let's project a budget based on 25 students for September and 50 students by next semester," said Kelly. "We're bound to pick up students in September. I've already received calls from parents who want to know when this new school is going to open. People are learning about us, just by word-of-mouth. I say we get Maybeck rollin'."

"Let's pull away from the decision for a minute," I said. "Where do we stand? How do we compare with other alternative schools?"

Stan said, "Other schools like this have materialized in ways similar to ours: disgruntled parents, disenchanted teachers, visionaries who seek a new life style and educators who want freedom from the big school's classroom regimentation. "

"There are rip-offs out there, too," said Kelly. "One mother yanked her son out of a school because all they do is play pool all day. Her son attended no classes The parents were paying five times the normal amount of tuition for a do-nothing school. The school owner got busted when the cops discovered he also owned massage parlors in Jack London Square where they offered more than just a massage.

"And others are flaky operations," Kelly continued. "Totally unstructured. No classes. One automotive school in Richmond was supported by the car repairs. The auto shop became so important to the school's survival that they stopped being a school.

They became a car repair shop staffed by high school dropouts."

"There are problem schools," said Stan, "But there are also excellent programs. The New Neighborhood School operates out of an old warehouse in Berkeley. They recently bought land in the Sierra. They have sliding scale tuition and a grant from the San Francisco Foundation. Those teachers are honest, energetic and completely dedicated."

"And broke," said Kelly.

"Truism," said Stan.

"There's a price to pay if we want to do our own thing," continued Stan. "I expect to have a college schedule, classes at different times, day and night, with free time between classes so students can develop their own potential. Staggered classes on Monday, Wednesday, and Friday plus Tuesday and Thursday. We should give grades so we can send our graduates to college."

"Can we expect any help from the public schools?" I asked.

"Are you kidding?" said Kelly. "Stan and I met with the director of a million dollar federally-funded school in Oakland. They call it career education. An experimental school called Near East. Know what they spend millions of dollars on? Research. Bah! A whole, entire floor of typists, clerks, and paper shufflers. If we get tangled up with that bunch, we'd drown in a sea of red tape.

Hell, we want to teach, not fill out forms for the rest of our lives."

"We did, however, meet with Percy Moore, director of a federally-funded, anti-poverty program," said Stan. "We also met with Marcus Foster, the dynamic superintendent of the Oakland Public Schools. He encouraged us, saying that public schools need competition and that he would help us all he could, short of outright financial aid.

"When I was in England earlier this summer," said Kelly, "I went to Summerhill School and met with A. S. Neil. They believe the school should fit the child. The running of the school is done in the school meetings. Students can do as they please as long as they don't harm others. They may or may not attend class. I visited the classrooms and they were empty. Neil told me his experiment was a failure. But I like the idea of a weekly school meeting."

"What is our financial picture now?" I asked.

"Worse than bleak," Stan replied.

We discussed our dismal financial future. We decided on a sliding tuition scale to accept students who couldn't pay. We'd have expenses for rent, heat, electricity, postage, phones, equipment and supplies. Even if we projected an enrollment of 25, we could only expect to pay ourselves 10 percent of our regular teaching salaries. That would be a salary of only $1,000 instead of $10,000 a year. Almost impossible.[35]

"That really is insane," I said. "We subsidize the school by not getting paid."

"August, it's a hurter," said Kelly. "But you're going to write proposals. You can get us funded."

"It's a gamble," I said. "I have to support a family."

"That's your choice," said Stan. "Paul, you made the decision to bring children into the world. I believe in zero population growth and—"

"Oh, damn it, Stan," I shouted. "I'm not in the mood for your intellectualizations. I have a family, but I could survive for one year with Maybeck."

"How?" Kelly asked.

"Cash in my life insurance, take out loans, use credit cards, sell one of my cars and refinance my house. As the Bishop said, I can't eat steak on a hamburger budget."

"I have no family to support," said Stan, "I will, however, have to face a major adjustment in my lifestyle. I like rare books, good music, foreign films and fine wine."

"In my case, cheap wine," said Kelly. "Stan, you're the guy who collects paychecks and forgets that you have them in your briefcase."

"That will change," said Stan. "I have a sunny apartment with a southern exposure and a beautiful garden. If we start this school, I'll have to move to less expensive quarters."

"Obviously we are not businessmen," I said. "We could have floated a loan, set up a school and paid ourselves a decent salary."

"We are moving too fast for that," said Stan. "We had a school on our hands before we knew it."

"We certainly couldn't demonstrate a potential profit to a bank with a nonprofit school," said Kelly. He sat up and leaned forward. "Financially, I say we can all survive a year, even without funding. Let's do it."

"What about accreditation?" I asked.

"Bah," said Kelly. "They've got people hoodwinked into thinking there's something wrong with a non-accredited school. Most small non-public schools have arrangements with colleges to accept their students. We'll have no problem at U.C. Berkeley, my alma mater, or with Saint Mary's College where you two guys went. No college will deny our graduates if they meet their requirements."

"And for principal," I said, suppressing a smile. "Stan, will you be the principal of Maybeck?"

"Absolutely not!" said Stan. "It will be shared decision-making. A teacher-run school. We've operated by consensus all through this and we can continue to do so. No principal. Ever."

"Speaking of Dixon," chuckled Kelly, "Stan, tell August what Dixon offered you."

"What now?" I asked.

"Gil called me up this summer," said Stan. "When we met, he offered to hire me back in order to prevent the start of Maybeck. I politely refused to discuss it with him unless, of course, he wanted to hire all of us back. He, in turn, refused to discuss that. It was a stand-off."

"Let's get off this tangent and call the question," said Kelly. "We've got the teachers. We're incorporated as a school. We've got eleven of the best students you could ask for. If we only survive for a year, it will be a fantastic year. I say let's do it."

"It could be a financial disaster but an educational Utopia," said Stan. I cannot ignore the quality of those eleven students. Three of them are near genius potential. They are the reason why I would take this risk, but I still refuse to commit financial hara-kiri."

"I have more to lose than you two bachelors," I said. "I'm willing to take the risk. I can almost guarantee that we can have 25 students by September, 50 by next semester and 100 by next fall. If I can't get federal money or private foundation funds, the parents can be organized into a fundraising group. There are options. We can make it."

"Even bingo," laughed Kelly.

"God, no," said Stan. "We won our freedom from that when we left St. Liz."

"Radisch feels that way, too," said Kelly. "He'll teach as a volunteer at night. He says it's our necks. He's with us."

"Anyway, I say we start Maybeck." I stood up. "Let's do it, damn it."

"I'm with August and Radisch," said Kelly. "Stan? What say ye?"

Stan stared into nowhere. His lips trembled. "It's absolutely insane. We shall be taking on an awesome responsibility. We are the school board. We are the administrators. We are the teachers, the janitors, and the tuition collectors. We'll have no one to blame but ourselves if we fail. It will be a small school with no place to hide. The preparation we do for a class of 30 or 40 students will be done for only a few. Parents will trust us with the lives, the emotions and the future of their most precious possessions."

We were silent for a moment as those last words sank in. Then Stan got out of his chair. "So be it," he said with a mock pomposity, climbing on the old sofa, stretching his hands out like Moses on the mountain. He declared in a loud voice, "Let it be known that from this day forth, Maybeck High School is a reality!"

We withdrew from the St. Liz experience as the summer ended. Stan Cardinet, Jim

Kelly, Jack Radisch and I began to transform Maybeck from an idea into a reality.

George Baljevich, despite his puns and corny jokes, became a teacher and coach in suburban San Ramon, California. Bud Johnson landed a counseling job in a small rural town in Northern California.

Dallas Williams began teaching in the Richmond school district.

Curt Levinson left teaching and became an advertising executive in San Francisco.

John Thomas shrugged off the marriage class/sex talk incident and became the educational director of a San Francisco hospital.

Mike Santos, who motivated our unionization to keep his job, stayed at St. Liz for a year and transferred to a Catholic high school in San Francisco. He eventually became a principal in the Central Valley.

Bob Howard (who suggested we work for free) became a part-time teacher at St. Liz. He continued to manage his own bus tour service.

Tom Rowe resigned from the dean's position and the administration, and returned to the classroom at St. Liz to enjoy teaching.

Sister Marie stayed on as Mother Superior at St. Liz.

Chapter 32

"Methodists accepted us..."

SEPTEMBER. MAYBECK'S REGISTRATION. The first gathering of our students.

On opening day, Maybeck still had no location. Students gathered for registration at the Oakland home of Mrs. Presho, mother of the Politeo girls: Joan, Francis and Celia enrolled at Maybeck. Lisa had led the student protestors back at St. Liz and Anne was the older sister who volunteered her support. This was our mini-version of that archetypal semester event of high school students selecting classes they needed for graduation.

We later met at Kelly's Fox Court apartment in Berkeley. "We were not selective in accepting our 17 students," said Stan. "We didn't deny anyone." I wasn't involved in the interviews because I was appearing on another public affairs TV program to promote Maybeck.

"We have a mixture of Chicano, Black and Native American," Stan continued. "Most city private schools are white enclaves but we have almost half minorities. We were lucky enough to have captured the Politeos, three of the best and brightest out of St. Liz. We accepted the Vasquez's, also two of the best, and Talbot and Carroll, two young men who probably rate closer to college professors in their general intelligence and bizarre, but playful, antics."

"We have a few other average learners and a couple of potential troublemakers," said Kelly, who had joined the conversation. "One of them got expelled from the entire Oakland Public School system because he slugged a teacher at a continuation school. We didn't know that at the time we accepted him."

"We also have two Hispanic sisters from Paul's neighborhood. Their father is unemployed and drives them to school every day. They can't afford tuition," added Stan. "This is a marvelously diverse group."

The next day, for our first classes, we landed on the campus of the University of California, Berkeley. We assembled in the shade of the Campanile tower. After a brief meeting on the lawn, we strolled with our students over to vacant classrooms in Dwinelle Hall. We had no permission to use university classrooms but we did it anyway. We were a school without a building.

Our young pioneers, including the eleven who left St. Liz, made the hour bus trip from

Oakland to Berkeley to our day by day location. I searched for a school site closer to the St. Liz turf. Finally, after a few days, a Presbyterian pastor in Oakland agreed to temporarily take us in, like a Protestant shepherd gathering the castaway Catholic black sheep. The young preacher sympathized with our rebellion against the Roman Catholics and enjoyed his Christian contribution to a struggling nonprofit school. He rearranged church activities and gave us sanctuary for two weeks. His church, not far from St. Liz, had several small classrooms upstairs for Sunday school. This became our first temporary school.

Near the end of our two-week reprieve, we had our first near-disaster, which almost ended our dream school in seconds. Kelly, in his physics class, had a way of enticing students into the mysteries of the universe by surprising students with unusual demonstrations, like transforming soft, fresh flowers into icy solids. He dipped a red rose into a thermos filled with liquid nitrogen, held it in there for a few seconds, and pulled out a brittle replica of itself for everyone to see. Then he smashed the frozen rose into frosty pieces of pink. The students gasped in awe.

Out in the hall, Kelly poured the steaming vapors from the thermos toward the floor when it suddenly exploded. I was there. The thermos acted like a cannon. Glass debris shot out and scattered across the floor.

"Damn," I yelled. "What happened?"

"Whoa. It's a hurter. What a farce," Kelly cried out. "Must have been a defective thermos. We're lucky it was pointed down. If it were facing anyone ..."

After school, we called for a brief faculty meeting: all three of us. Kelly blinked nervously. "Jesus. It could have blinded somebody."

"Kelly," said Stan, "We don't have insurance. A trick like that could sink us. How could you be so careless?"

"Careless?" Kelly looked startled. "Stan, what are you saying? This is common practice in my classes. It was a defective thermos."

"We've got enough problems." Stan raised his hoarse voice, jutted his bearded chin and shook his head nervously. "I'm testy these days. We are responsible for these young lives. We have no school board to blame. No administrators to admonish. We are liable for everything."

Stan turned to me and changed the subject, "August, we've run out of time at this site. Our two weeks are up. Where do we go from here?"

MINDWORKER: MAYBECK

"I've found an ideal site," I said. "A two-story church building, up to code, with classrooms, an office, auditorium, stage, and cafeteria. They have a recreation room with vending machines, ping pong games, and a pool table. Laurel United Methodist Church. It's near the St. Liz neighborhood, about a mile away, perfect for us for the rest of the year."

"Too good to be true," said Kelly. "When? We need a place now."

"Not now, I said. "Not until their board approves it within a week or two."

"Where does that leave us?" asked Stan. "Out in the cold again?"

"No," I replied. "I've lined up yet another Protestant church about twenty blocks from here on Park Boulevard. They have a social hall jammed with tiny tots stuff like teddy bears and small tables. They use it for Sunday school and child care. They'll let us have classes there for two weeks."

Stan looked relieved. "At least we have temporary shelter while we continue our crazy Flying Dutchman journey through the Protestant Churches of Oakland."

"Keep working on it, August," said Kelly. "We're confident that you'll find a nest for Maybeck yet. It's just one of those little problems we encounter when we have a school before we have a school building."

Two weeks later, time ran out again. "A decision on the next Methodist building is near, but not in place," I told the little Maybeck faculty sitting in the middle of the tiny tots' classroom, surrounded by toy cars and scattered wooden blocks. We sat on table tops or the floor.

"Let's use the environmental solution," Suggested Kelly. "Let's just pull out of the city and take the entire school camping in Big Basin. Santa Cruz awaits us." Big Basin is a national monument along the Pacific Coast, about 60 miles northwest of Oakland.

"Good idea," said Stan. We can rationalize this trip as part of our curriculum, and it really is. What better time to get out of the city and back to nature?"

Maybeck students and staff left the tiny tot church social hall and headed for Big Basin to make camp. They used Kelly's army surplus van and volunteer parent drivers. The Maybeckians camped together for a week. We got out of the city and into nature to get to know each other. Then we returned to the classroom for traditional discussions, homework, readings, films, tests, and old-fashioned classes, homework and grades. We used a flexible college schedule: classes on MWF plus TT. Hour classes meet MWF and two hour classes meet TT. Each class met five hours a week on this schedule.

I stayed behind to handle the lease. The Laurel Methodists approved our deal two days later. After Maybeck returned from camping, we began moving into our newest and, we hoped, our last school building.

"Back to reality," said Stan, as he arrived at the latest Maybeck location.

"How was the camping trip?" I asked.

"Excellent," replied Stan. "Kelly used the SCUFO telescope to see the Big Dipper in a smog-free sky. We also had a volunteer from the natural sciences—Dave Kinstle.[36] He teaches science and math. As the result of being a conscientious objector to the Vietnam War, he was ordered to spend two years working as a volunteer helping in the community. Maybeck qualified and we gladly welcomed him."

Dave, bearded with long shoulder length hair, fit the "hippie" visual stereotype but his philosophy aligned with ours: study, learn and do your own thing on your own time. At times, his eyes blinked more than one would expect. Dave was friendly, outgoing and a man of his convictions.

Stan continued his report on the latest Maybeck excursion. "Dave pointed out the types of trees—explaining the difference between sequoia redwoods and coastal redwoods—and we identified rock formations, wildlife and flowers. Much better than any textbook. I held my poetry class in the evening around the campfire. It was all exhilarating but exhausting. I'm glad to see we have our own place to return to."

Students helped us move into their latest version of Maybeck High. Moving wasn't difficult since we didn't even have our own ditto machine. Stan looked over the two-story building and said, "Once again, the Methodists are taking in the forlorn rebel Catholics."

"Catholics rejected us. Methodists accepted us," laughed Kelly.

"There were a few objections from neighbors who thought we were a school for dropouts," I said. "Once they learned who we were—former St. Liz teachers—our stature changed. We were accepted on conditions."

"Uh, oh. Here comes the kicker," said Kelly.

"They can give us a 30-day notice in case our kids screw up their church."

"30 days?" laughed Kelly. "Hell. That's longer than two weeks. Real progress. What about rent?"

Maybeck Headlines

In Oakland: Monday February 5, 1973

A Private School for
Low Income Families

Unique, Flexible School
Makes Learning 'Honest'

BHS – LOVE IT OR LEAVE IT

Students are leaving Berkeley High for smaller schools

New Private High School
Takes a Lab Approach

Volunteer Teachers Support Maybeck Hi

New High School
Opens in Oakland

A Berkeley High School newspaper article, by Lindsey Weil, reported on
a student who left BHS because of receiving not enough attention.
"At Maybeck, there is a smaller, closer, relationship between teachers and
students…things discussed actually get done." The Oakland Tribune gave
Maybeck great PR when ace columnist Bill Fiset praised Jack Radisch,
Deputy D. A. Jack's Maybeck legal class came to court to watch him in
action. By the end of our first year, with this PR, we no longer had to
justify our existence. People knew about Maybeck.

"Cheap," I said. "They use the building
for Sunday school. We can rent it during the
week for $400 a month."

Kelly raised an eyebrow, lowered his head and said, "Not bad. That's less than it's worth but more than we can afford."

"We'll double our enrollment and cover the cost," said Stan as we walked through the upstairs halls and peeked in the empty classrooms. Students swarmed into the recreation room. Ping pong paddles smacked tables. Billiard balls clicked against each other. Pianos began clinking.

"Luxury," said Kelly as we entered the office. "Now would you just look at this? An office with a real honest-to-goodness phone we can use. And a piano in every classroom. Not bad, August."

Downstairs, we sauntered across the polished linoleum floor of the large auditorium. As we wandered, Kelly's Irish eyes gleamed with possibilities. "I'll be darned. This is a real find. There's a cafeteria back here with everything but food."

Stan pompously strutted across the auditorium's stage and took a place behind the podium. "I do believe that we're looking more like a real school every day."

Kelly said, "It has no bells and I'm glad. I don't ever want to hear another bell again. We've got our own ways of starting class."

He said this as a group of students found us and called out, "Hey you guys. When's class gonna start?"

As we headed back upstairs, Kelly flashed a wide smile, "This sure beats camping out all year." Kelly was the picture of contentment. It was the first time I'd seen him happy since we left St. Liz.

In search of funding for Maybeck, I went to the federal government's Office of Nonpublic Education in San Francisco.

After months of phone calls and letters, I finally got an appointment. I did the grant sniffing while the others did the teaching for most of this first semester. Did the Feds really have a department for private schools? Surely that monolithic bureaucracy had red tape we could cut through, I thought to myself. I was determined to get funding.

San Francisco had a small business and financial district, and parking is advertised with small print: PARKING ONE DOLLAR (for every 15 minutes). I knew the back streets, from my record promo days, near Fifth and Mission, where I could park and hike to my contacts. If I didn't get back to my VW Bug by 4 pm, I'd get towed and fined a small fortune to get my Bug back.

The Fed's office in San Francisco consisted of an old guy in charge of—what they called—nonpublic education. My first time there, I felt like I stepped into the pages of a Dickens novel. He had jaundice skin and straggly grey hair. He sat in a corner, at an empty desk, staring into space, explaining he had just been moved here from Washington, D.C. His life was stuffed into cardboard boxes piled behind his desk. He rummaged through the boxes and came up with a copy of a government letter saying that they didn't have much funding for nonpublic schools. He said to come back later.

When I returned the next month, he gave me a copy of the same damn letter. He still had a completely empty desk surrounded by cardboard boxes. The last time I went there, he had moved to a different corner in the same room, but with the same empty desk, and same cardboard boxes. He gave me a copy of the same insipid letter. It was bizarre beyond belief, or, as Kelly would say, "An absolute farce, a real mind-boggler."

A Friday night in November. Home. The great bingo bust.

The phone rang. It was Stan. "Did you hear the news?"

"About what?" I asked.

"The media exposed the bingo games at St. Liz," Stan said. "The Oakland chief of police proclaimed in Seattle that Oakland was so free of crime that there wasn't even an illegal bingo game in the city. Herb Caen ran it as an item in this morning's *Chronicle*, then asked in print: What about all those big $1,000 jackpot games every Friday night at St. Liz, chiefie?"

UNIVERSITY OF CALIFORNIA
OFFICE OF THE PRESIDENT BERKELEY, CA 92720

STANFORD UNIVERSITY
STANFORD, CA 94305   OFFICE OF ADMISSIONS

UNIVERSITY OF SAN FRANCISCO

COLLEGE OF tHE HOLY names

Saint Mary's College of Calif.

The University of Santa Clara

MILLS COLLEGE, OAKLAND, CA

CALIFORNIA STATE
UNIVERSITY, HAYWARD

OAKLAND UNIFIED
SCHOOL DISTRICT

Maybeck didn't want to go through accreditation. So, Stan
contacted individual universities who agreed to accept our
students with conditions: they agreed to accept our qualified
students, based on their academic work, admission test scores, and
letters of recommendation. Oakland public schools accepted our
transfers.

"Whoa," I blurted. "The shit has hit the fan."

"That's not all. The six o'clock news had it all over KGO-TV. Channel seven is sending a crew to bingo tonight."

"Dixon always told us that the police knew about bingo but they just looked the other way," I said.

"Come on over to Radisch's house," said Stan. "We'll have a poker party and wait for developments on the late night news."

As I drove to Berkeley in my rusty old VW bug, the car radio blared, "Big illegal bingo game at a Catholic school, in Oakland, right under the unknowing nose of the chief of police. Other illegal Catholic bingo games have been uncovered in San Francisco, Marin and San Mateo."

We gathered on the redwood deck of Radisch's home in the Berkeley hills. The moonlight shimmered through the arches of the Golden Gate Bridge and across the bay. We played lowball poker as a TV grumbled on a picnic table next to us. A news teaser came on. "Police tonight raided a bingo game in Oakland and arrested the principal of a Catholic school. Details at eleven."

Poker cards flew into the air. Beer spilled. Kelly threw his hands up and bellowed, "I can just see Dixon being hauled to a paddy wagon in handcuffs. I hope they throw him in the clink and give the case to Radisch."

"Hell," said Radisch, with a wide grin, "I'd lock the bastard up and throw away the key."

Radisch then became more serious. "Dixon brought all this down on his own head. He hurt himself with the letter he wrote to you, August, when you missed bingo one night. It was publicly posted on the bulletin board last year in the faculty room. That's proof. Dixon put it in writing, ordering a teacher to work at an illegal bingo game. He should have given you a verbal reprimand."

The 11 o'clock news came on. "The big bingo bust in Oakland tonight could become an international incident. Stay tuned."

"What's this about an international incident?" asked Stan.

"Who knows?" said Radisch. "Dixon is capable of anything. Besides, those TV news clowns love to exaggerate. They'll milk this for all it's worth. If we're lucky, it'll become a local media event."

The anchor man for this ABC Network affiliate, a pudgy fellow with black curly hair and a cherubic face, had a flair for the sensational. His electronic face gawked at us. "The Oakland police raided and closed an illegal bingo game tonight, and arrested a Catholic high school principal. In a surprising move, the principal, Mr. Gilbert Dixon, invoked an obscure treaty related to the separation of church and state. This incident could become an international dispute. We have film of the bingo game before it was shut down. For a report, we go to the little Catholic school with the big bingo games in Oakland."

The video showed hundreds of bingo players hunched over tiny cards in the cavernous auditorium. A TV reporter's voice narrated. "The idea here at St. Liz is that people pay five dollars at the door for a spaghetti dinner and art show and then play bingo for free."

The camera panned over slovenly, husky women who held up paper plates laden with globs of sauce and strands of noodles dangling from the dish. They dug a plastic spoon into the oily clump of food, stuffing it in their mouths, nodding excessively, as if to indicate that they were only interested in the spaghetti.

"But it didn't work," said the reporter. "The police raided the bingo game and closed it down, sending everyone home. Dixon was arrested in the form of a citation."

"Damn," blurted Kelly. "Only a citation?"

The TV news switched back to the spirited anchor man. "If they had a legal loophole there, it didn't work. Police sent an undercover agent to the bingo game. He asked for free bingo cards. When he was refused, the police cited the principal and closed the game. The principal told Channel 7 news that the undercover agent looked and acted like a long haired hippie who just wanted a free meal. Dixon claims he would have given him free cards but he didn't think he was a cop.

"In an extraordinary move, when Dixon was cited, he actually invoked the Treaty of Guadalupe Hidalgo. This is an ancient treaty, which states that property granted to the Catholic Church from the Spanish is immune from the laws of the United States of America. We've been unable to reach the Bishop of Oakland for a comment.

"The Channel 7 news team is calling the Vatican for more information. This little bingo bust in Oakland has ramifications that could extend to the pope himself. In other news..."

"Treaty of what? What's he talking about? That's just plain crazy," said Kelly.

Radisch explained: "The Treaty of Guadalupe Hidalgo granted land from the Spanish to the Catholic Church. This gave Catholic property an independent status, like the Vatican has in Italy. Technically, the treaty is still in effect. Realistically, it just isn't practical for the 20th century. If church property really was independent, the school would get no fire protection, no police protection, no water, and no sewer service—nothing. Like I've always said, these Catholic administrators have been brought kicking and screaming into the 20th Century."

"It's ironic," continued Radisch. "We haven't been able to show everyone that Dixon is a fool. Now he's done the best job of doing that himself."

By the end of that school year, the great bingo bust had reverberated throughout California, bringing grief to hundreds of Catholic bingo games. The California legislature passed a law to legalize bingo for nonprofit organizations. This had the unintended consequence of starting up thousands of "nonprofit" bingo games to draw customers to their games each night. Some bingo operators paid a token amount to little nonprofits and pocketed most of the take. The big churches, including St. Liz, couldn't compete and shut down their big games.

Gil Dixon resigned at the end of the year and moved back to Southern California where he became a lawyer.

Chapter 33

"The Blind Lemon..."

A MAYBECK FACULTY MEETING. One night in January.

The Blind Lemon, the Berkeley pub near the industrial section of town, was usually filled with down-and-out poets, dart-playing intellectuals and self-proclaimed political radicals. We ordered a pitcher of beer and a bowl of Pretzels and began our meeting. I kept the minutes by the light of a single candle in the middle of the table. Kelly, Cardinet and Radisch were the other board members. Our topic, simply, was the future of Maybeck.

Stan hunched his shoulders, took a sip of beer and then stroked his beard. "Decisions are in order. We have a viable school. We've added to our staff: two volunteers and three part-time graduate student teachers. We might reach 40 students next semester and August has lined up a waiting list. We may have 100 by next September. I think it's all too big, too much, too soon."

I disagreed with Stan. "Too big? We can handle 200 in our building. I say we grow. We need the money. We can't survive on skeleton wages. Let's raise tuition and give financial stability to this school."

"Bosh," grumbled Kelly. "A school is not a business. I say let kids attend for free if

MAYBECK HIGH SCHOOL: Catalogue

Stan Cardinet published massive documents which kept the communications clear between Maybeck and the community. In this excerpt, he's quoting from the church newsletter about my interview on KYA radio, San Francisco.

MAYBECK HIGH SCHOOL

A WORD ABOUT MAYBECK: Speaking of graduates, Maybeck High School, which uses our facility, will hold its first graduation this Sunday. Three graduates will be in its first class. Incidentally, every one of these three has received a California State Scholarship which can be used at Cal or Stanford. If you had the impression that Maybeck was for "drop outs," this should be enough to convince you otherwise.

Recently they were on Action Line KYA radio, San Francisco. In reply to one question called in: are you a religious school? Paul August, one of the teachers, replied, "Right now we are a private nonprofit school. We've got nothing to do with any religious group, except that the Methodist Church is letting us use the facility that we're in right now. In other words, they are doing that as part of their mission."

Interviewer: "Then they are donating space for your classrooms?"

Paul's answer, "Yes, basically. We're paying a small amount that barely covers expenses and basically Laurel Methodist Church is doing a tremendous community service in providing us with this building."

Interviewer: "That's wonderful, really."

they can't afford it. We've got the space. I like the idea of a bigger school."

Kelly clenched his fist and twisted it forward. "You know what I don't like about Maybeck? It's too small. There's no escape from people you know. There's no chance to meet new people each day. In a big school, you can avoid some and meet others. But not here. This is more like a family. You have to live with each other."

"Maybeck is tough on our young scholars because they have to deal with the same teacher in more than one course," said Stan. "There isn't much room for personality conflicts. Our small class size of five or ten pupils is absolutely ideal."

"Bah" said Kelly. "I have to prepare as much for a class of ten as I do for a class of 30."

"I've had to adjust," I said. "It's difficult to gear down from big lectures and gear up to small seminars with five to ten kids, but I love the small class sizes."

"I say we hang loose, be flexible and let the school grow," said Kelly, sitting back with a grin of satisfaction.

"No," asserted Stan. "I want a rigorous academic load to balance our camping. I want a careful student selection process. I want a small, non-elitist, highly polished, school of excellence."

"How can we have a school if we go broke?" I asked. "We've got to get some business sense into our structure."

"No," replied Stan. "We are not a business. We make communal decisions. Consensus! We all get the same meager salary because we all do the same work: no seniority, no pay scale. In exchange, we accept real students who want to learn. I want quick expulsion for any troublemakers."

"Come on, Stan." Kelly leaned back and raised his eyebrows in mock astonishment. "Expel kids? Are you serious? St. Liz expelled us. We can't just kick 'em out like they do. Let's work with the rotten apples."

"Kelly," replied Stan, "That's the trouble with you. You're too idealistic. You're too loose."

"Stan, you called me careless when the thermos exploded." Kelly got angry. "I don't want to hear this. I don't have to take this."

"Let's not get personal," Radisch stepped in. He taught a class at Maybeck as a volunteer. His American legal systems class convened one evening a week. Students went to the courthouse during the day to watch their teacher in court. He also acts as our legal advisor and, lately, mediator.

"You guys are getting too upset about this," said Radisch. "What's going on? It's like you're at each other's throats. You never acted like this at St. Liz."

"I don't know," grumbled Kelly. "Maybe it's just growing pains. We're evolving from an idea into a real school."

Stan regained his composure. "I don't know why we take these meetings so seriously. We always worked so well together. Something is different now."

"It reminds me of Fromm's book, *Escape from Freedom*," I said. "We were in bondage at St. Liz. Authority made decisions without our knowledge. We had no say. Together, we fought 'them.' Now, we are 'them.'"

"I think you're right," said Stan. "We are free to make our own decisions, but we are totally responsible for the consequences. We have no one to blame but ourselves if we fail."

Radisch said, "We know where we're coming from. We know what we're capable of. We know we can settle this and keep on helping each other."

"These are all very real survival issues," said Stan. "It's the survival of Maybeck. It's our own survival."

We felt a silence at our table. The candle flickered. Darts hit the wall. We gazed into our beers.

Later that same night. Same meeting.

"August, any results on proposal money?" Stan asked.

"Mythical money," I said. "I've written to every private foundation in the United States that funds private schools."

"Any replies?" asked Stan.

"The usual form letter rejection slips. 'You don't fit our guidelines.' 'Our funds are spent for this year.'"

"I don't understand," said Stan. "They have so much. We need so little. Why does one project get millions—like that career school—and others get nothing?"

"They call it impact," I said. "They have a self-serving philosophy of pouring massive amounts of money into one project to insure success and make themselves look good. I have over a dozen proposals under consideration but it means nothing until we get funding."

"What a farce," laughed Kelly. "They don't want to risk their money on grassroots realities like Maybeck."

"They have their own jargon," I said. "They always want to know 'the problem.' I thought the problem was obvious. We don't have any money. Was I naive? In the world of the grantwriter, 'problem' means the problem in society that you are trying to solve with this proposal!"

"But Paul," asked Stan, "Didn't you recently take a course in grantwriting at Cal?"

"Yeah," I replied. "I thought the teacher was a great grantwriter because he got funded for several million dollars. But after class one night I bought him a beer and got the truth. He had been a campaign manager for The Committee to Re-elect the President (CREEP). It was all a political payoff for Nixon's re-election.

"That's our competition," said Kelly. He shook his fist. "Damn, big time politics. I say, proposals are a waste of time. If we did get funded, we'd only become dependent on that hand out. Right now, we're in great shape. Ha! We got nothin', so we got nothin' to lose."

"I tend to agree," said Stan. "August, the energy you put into a non-funded proposal is lost. It isn't worth it."

"You're right," I said. "The political competition is fierce. There's a group of school lobbyists who meet in Sacramento every Tuesday night. They decide what to support or who to reject. They're also the first ones who know about the money. The pros, the grant-grabbers, get money first. There's nothing left for a genuine grassroots effort."

"Gol darn," Kelly said. "In a proposal, how could we possibly explain what we went through at St. Liz? What a farce."

The Blind Lemon had a small stage where self-appointed songwriters could test their new tunes. Performers sang three songs each. It was my turn now.

"Come on, August," said Kelly as he pushed back the hair over his eyes. "Get up

I contacted over 100 private foundations and almost all responded with rejections but a dozen sent applications. Here are the typical rejections.

Funds are not available.

The program is restricted.

Your request is denied.

It is too late to apply.

Our funds are committed.

We do not support schools.

Maybeck is an excellent school but...

The most pertinent statement came from the Ford Foundation: the trend toward alternative schools has resulted in requests which we are unable to meet. Simply put, we missed the boat for independent schools which expanded during the sixties. Still, every single foundation respected Maybeck's plea for help. I still regard them all with great respect for helping those who meet their guidelines.

AMERICAN OPTICAL CORP.
WILLIAM RANDOLPH HEARST
JOHN SIMON GUGGENHEIM
HENRY J. KAISER FAMILY
NEW WORLD FOUNDATION
DEPT HEALTH, EDUCATION, AND WELFARE
BANK OF AMERICA
Alameda-Contra Costa Counties
MARTHA BAIRD ROCKEFELLER
Rockefeller Brothers Fund
W. K. KELLOGG FOUNDATION
W. Clement & Jessie V. Stone
Southern Pacific
AMPEX FOUNDATION
THE FORD FOUNDATION
National Council on the Arts
National Endowment for the Arts
MARY A. CROCKER TRUST
David and Lucile Packard Foundation
DISNEY FOUNDATION
LEVI STRAUSS FOUNDATION
The Sears-Roebuck Foundation
The San Francisco Foundation
RUSSELL SAGE FOUNDATION
BECHTEL CORPORATION
Rosenberg Foundation
Harrah's **Oakland Tribune**
Motels and Casinos
Reno and Lake Tahoe

there and wail. You didn't get us funded but I know you got some songs out of it."

I climbed on a plywood stage, adjusted the slightly-used microphone, and tuned the metal strings on my acoustic guitar. "Here's a song for all those who have written, are writing or might write a proposal for that mythical money those funders say they have, but never give you. It's called 'Grantwriter.'"

Mr. Grantwriter sits in his cubicle
Cranking out paper, no time to play
Carefully typing, rapidly mailing
Meeting the deadline to get state aid.

Mr. Grantwriter spends your taxes
Using the money for Democracy
Carefully spending every last cent
Funding unemployable PhDs.

He documents illusions, then pretends to
*   solve 'em.*
He's got the solution but he hasn't found the
*   problem.*

Glasses clanked. Feet shuffled. A few hands clapped. Being a saloon singer wasn't my goal in life. "Okay. That's not all. The government has spawned an educational bureaucracy. I ran into a barely living bureaucrat who had his entire career carried around in cardboard boxes. Here's a song called the 'Cardboard Box Brigade.'"

There's a cadre of our comrades, martyrs for
*   our sake,*

Their job has no work. They take no coffee break.
They've been bumped out of one job but they haven't found the next.
Like bureaucratic little birds who fell out of their nest.

If anything is simple, they make it complex,
If anything is right, they make it a mess,
In a paper world of carbon triple packs,
They rejoice when they find mistakes 'cause they can send it back

"Sing that one about the politician in the hot tub," yelled Kelly as I finished.

It was always revitalizing to have audience involvement, even if they were tired of hearing my crazy tunes.

"Okay. Here's another August original. I wish George were here. It's lonely being a solo act. Let's dedicate this next one to all those political big shots who secretly meet in Sacramento every Tuesday night.

Big Max met with the re-election team.
He guzzled the Chablis and slid into the steam.
This is his secret Tuesday evening club
Taking place in the capitol's official hot tub.

Little Melvin said, "I hate moldy bread
And I got a question about the way you guys are fed.

Why do kids get crumbs from cookie sales
While you sit up here drinking wine and eat-
*   ing snails?"*

Big Max wheels and deals for those free
*   lunch meals.*
Big Max gets his kicks from hot tub politics.
*   Big Max.*

I climbed off the stage to the usual sparse courtesy applause and rejoined the Maybeck clan. Usually, we would adjourn to Kelly's Fox Court apartment. However, since we started Maybeck, Kelly fell behind in his rent and they evicted him. He was living with his brother. Stan moved to a smaller apartment. We had no place to continue socializing as a group after our meetings. So, we left each other and went home separately.

Chapter 34

"We dissected frogs..."

ODEGA BAY. FEBRUARY, 1973. A Maybeck excursion to the Pacific Ocean. Bodega Bay is 90 miles northwest of Oakland on the Pacific coast. The entire school went there for ten days, using the U.C. Marine Biology dorms for our winter intersession.

The first day was raining. A volunteer oceanographer, Stuart Haynes, explained the variety of seaweed, starfish and mussels. Stu had become our new full-time Maybeck teacher. He was a tall, thin guy, fresh out of the University of California where he had been a teaching assistant. He taught math and science, enjoyed biology and liked to bring the students into the woods, the ocean, the desert and the natural environment. Fascinated with nature, he preferred outdoor learning over textbooks in classrooms, which we all did. He had a way of seeking consensus in our faculty meetings by looking for a reasonable compromise to avoid conflict or turmoil. After our St. Liz experience, his calm, reassuring manner was a welcome relief.

The wind beat against us. Everyone was soaked. Stan, Kelly, and I hiked up the hill to a slippery cliff overlooking the small Maybeck student body below.

"What a magnificent stormy day," said Stan, as the waves crashed against the rocks below us.

"You've got to be woofin'," said Kelly. "It's wet. It's foggy. It's windy. It's miserable."

"No," said Stan. He had a calm, almost serene look in his Germanic blue eyes as he watched the Maybeck guys and gals digging in the sand and gravel. "It's a beautiful day. This is one of the joys of having your own school. You can do just about anything and find just about any justification for it."

Kelly shrugged his shoulders beneath his rain gear. "I'll say this: it's good to be out of that school building. We do everything there: answer phones, mop floors, empty the trash, stock the restrooms. It's good to get outdoors once in a while."

Stan wiped the salt spray from his beard and managed to light his pipe. "We've done so much with so little. Our friends at other schools have raided supplies, loaned us projectors, hijacked paper and given us discarded typewriters. We've dissected frogs in the cafeteria.

"We've used chalk on the walls when we ran out of chalkboard space. Our classes are small enough to fill a station wagon to visit the San Francisco Maritime Museum then spend the afternoon in Golden Gate Park. We have a dearth of equipment but a wealth of knowledge. All in all, Maybeck is doing quite well."

"Truism," said Kelly, putting his hand on Stan's shoulder. "Congratulations. We did it Stan, my good man. By gum, we did it."

"What now?" Stan asked, pensively. He answered his own question. "Maybeck. It really is a reality. It grew out of the ashes of St. Liz. In a way, we're still haunted by the ghost of St. Liz. It was an adult trauma. I'm still very bitter. We all have deep scars. But I'm not angry anymore. I wouldn't even know who to blame. The school board? The pastor? The Bishop? The principal? It still hurts very deeply."

"Let's keep that ghost behind us," said Kelly. "We got new problems now. The Methodists are perfectionists. We've been called on the carpet for a missing spoon, a broken pool cue and a crushed ping pong ball. They get upset if we accidentally leave a light on or a window open. They said we scratched the floor when we moved the piano. We might need some place where we have more freedom."

"Location is no problem," said Stan. "August, you know where there are other old churches willing to make a dollar off of their unused buildings. Berkeley, especially, is full of educational space."

"I've got the help of the parents," I said. "We're having raffles, pizza parties and bake sales. It's all nickel and dime stuff but it sets up the structure for other parent groups to follow."

"We're self-sufficient," said Kelly. "We might be poor. We might be hurting. But Maybeck is gonna make it."

Stan nodded slowly, looking out to sea." We're creating a sense of perpetuity. One day Maybeck will be an institution. It won't depend on us anymore."

Wind swept the salty waves smashing high against the rocks below. Spray and rain pelted us. We felt the strong storm against us and the ghost of St. Liz between us. We stood together at the edge of the cliff and stared out to sea.

Heading back to Oakland, a Maybeck parent needed a ride back to the East Bay. I had to leave the marine biology labs in Bodega to be at an Oakland TV station to pretape a Sunday morning public service program promoting Maybeck. We were recruiting Maybeck applicants for next year. We had less than 40 youthful pioneers by the end of our first year. Maybeck would be a small school, forever it seemed.

FRANKenstein Never WeNT to A good High SchooL!

Are You LookiNg for A better HIGH SchooL ?

MAYBECK HIGH SCHOOL IS A BETTER SCHOOL.

— MAYBECK HIGH SCHOOL is a small, private, college preparatory school seeking new applicants for a limited number of openings in September.

— MAYBECK HIGH SCHOOL offers the regular college preparatory courses, plus a number of unusual additional classes.

— MAYBECK HIGH SCHOOL conducts special programs throughout the year in such natural locations as Big Sur, Yosemite, Bodega Bay, Big Basin, & Sunol Park.

— MAYBECK HIGH SCHOOL is recognized by universities and colleges alike.

— MAYBECK HIGH SCHOOL offers personal instruction in small classes taught by a qualified and experienced faculty.

— MAYBECK HIGH SCHOOL is located at 3637 Magee Street, just off 35th Ave & Mac Arthur Blvd, on the main bus routes.

— MAYBECK HIGH SCHOOL charges $600 per year in tuition.

→ For further information, a brochure & application telephone 5 3 0 - 9 0 4 3 or write: MAYBECK HIGH SCHOOL, Box 19047, Oakland, California 94619

Stan Cardinet became the catalyst for pushing Maybeck into existence. He'd do the art work and prose for our brochures, documents, reports, flyers and recruitment posters like this classic Frankenstein. But he didn't stop there. He grabbed a staple gun and plastered these posters to telephone poles throughout the streets and neighborhoods of Oakland and Berkeley.

It had been raining hard. Bodega Bay is on the Pacific coast about 30 miles west of Highway 101. We'd have to travel on a two-lane highway to get to the six-lane freeway. No rain, but big puddles covered the road between here and there. As I drove, we talked about Maybeck.

"I understand you're leaving us," she said. "Why? Where could you find a better teaching environment? You've got motivated students, great teachers and amazing resources—such as this Bodega Bay campus the UC let you guys use. Why would you leave all this?"

"Well, it comes down to money," I said. "Maybeck is a luxury I can't afford. It's fun. I love it. But now it's time for me to go get a real job and support Muriel and the kids."

"What about the other teachers?" she asked. "How can Maybeck afford them and not you?"

As we drove, I kept my eye on the road. We'd hit big puddles occasionally and I slowed down where a thin sheet of water covered the road. This was flood territory.

"Most of them are like Berkeley bachelors," I said. "They have no kids. They're far more flexible in their lives than I am." I noticed fewer and fewer cars coming in our direction. There might be a problem coming up. I drove carefully as we talked.

"Couldn't you guys get funding? Write a grant? Raise some money?" asked my passenger.

"We tried that," I said. "I have dozens of rejection slips from foundations. Frankly, I thought I could get this school funded but it never happened. And I'm glad it didn't."

"Why is that?" she asked.

I paused as I noticed a lone car coming toward us. "Because all the other schools that received grants, after five years, lost their funding. All closed or are going under. Maybeck is stronger. We'll never lose our funding because we never had any."

I drove over a small hill and unexpectedly came upon water flowing across the road. It was a gentle stream, from left to right, but I couldn't tell exactly how deep it was. Given the terrain we'd been riding on for the last half-hour, I estimated it was about a foot or two deep.

Sensing my trepidation, she said, "Well, it appears that last car came from here. If they got through we should be able to get through. Will it be a problem?"

"I dunno," I replied. I was looking across 100 feet of water before a little hill, about the size of a big parking space, jutted above the water and quickly dipped back in water for another 200 feet until it reached the highway on the other side. There were no cars across from us and none behind us.

"Let's see what happens," I finally said. I moved my old '60 Chevy six cylinder station wagon forward slowly. If I pushed it, the water could flood the distributor cap, wet the points, and stall the car. I instantly missed my '68 Jeep Wagoneer that had over-sized snow tires, truck brakes and four-wheel drive. It was built like the first

SUV. After being fired from St. Liz, I sold it. I gave up skiing for a less expensive family car.

"Easy does it," I said to myself. We edged into the water until the car was surrounded by a muddy, slow drifting over-flowed creek. I inched the car forward through the water on the road until we finally got to the center dry spot, up on a lump of dry asphalt, still surrounded by water.

Maybeck PR: *Oakland Tribune* columnist Bill Fiset gave Maybeck excellent coverage, although it wasn't always precise. He wrote that I took my "...whole class to Bodega Bay...cut off by flood waters...August and some kids...stranded on Highway One."

No. In all fairness to Bill, I didn't remember the name of the highway, I should have emphasized that the trip included the whole school, and I had no students in my car at the time.

"Halfway there," I laughed, nervously.

"Uh, oh. Look!" She pointed to a car that had been heading toward us. It pulled off on another road, drove over a flat bridge about 100 yards up stream, came in to where we started and went on its way.

We both felt apprehension. "I guess that's what that other solo car did. We assumed he came across the water here, but he didn't," I said.

"He went around. We made it this far. Will we be able to continue on to the other side?"

"Yeah. I guess," I said. I didn't like our situation. We were city folk out in the country. I couldn't think of any other option. "Okay. Let's go."

I eased the Chevy wagon into the muddy, slow drifting water and edged it forward. It was only a couple of feet deep but it felt like it was getting deeper. Then I felt my shoes filling with water. Not good. The water inched upward and my anxiety bubbled up. I nudged the gas pedal. Then the old Chevy chugged, choked, stalled and stopped. We were more than halfway across and stuck there.

"Now what?" asked the parent.

"Not sure," I said in all my wisdom. I could feel my face flush red with embarrassment. "Let me check under the hood."

I got out and stood in the knee high muddy steam. As a signal of distress, I raised the hood and locked it in place.

"Paul. Look. Over there. A truck."

I looked over to the dry road we didn't reach. A farmer wearing overalls, a cowboy hat and a plaid shirt got out of his old pickup truck that had a gun rack in the back, but no gun.

"You folks need some help?" he shouted.

"Yeah, we do. We're stranded. Stalled out."

"You want a tow?"

"Yeah. Please. Could you get us out of this water?"

The country guy waded right in with a tow line, attached it under the front of my Chevy and waded back to his truck. I closed the hood, got in to steer and he pulled us up to dry land. I felt a strong sense of gratitude, liberation from anxiety, and a realization that we'd just been rescued.

"See if it starts," said the farmer. I tried. It didn't start. "Pop the hood" he said. He unclipped the distributor cap, dried off the points, put it all back together and told me again, "See if it starts." I did. It started.

Amazing. Before I had a chance to offer our Good Samaritan some rescue money, he waved me off, hopped in his truck, and took the roundabout way around the flooded creek.

We continued on in silence until we reached the familiarity of the freeway. Then we returned to our conversation as if nothing had interrupted us. "What will you miss most about Maybeck?" She looked more relaxed.

"Well, I love the freedom of a teacher-run school. No school board. No administrators. No principal. No bureaucrats," I said slowly, knowing what I'd miss.

"What will you miss most about the students and the classroom?"

"Class size,' I responded. "The small class size is Utopia. I've got less than ten students in each class. By the end of the first week of school, I knew all my students' names. At St. Liz, I had 35 enrolled in each of five classes for a total of 175 students who get less individual attention."

"But does it make a difference in what you teach, or how?" she asked.

"When I assign an essay on a book, I can read and correct each paper in five minutes. Eight kids. Forty minutes. When I return their papers, I give them one-on-on consultation. Five minutes each. I can do that in one class period. I don't have to spend endless hours correcting 175 papers.

"And when we read drama out loud, each student takes on more than one of the characters. More reading. When I had 35 kids in a class, we didn't have enough drama parts for everyone to even read once. And when my current kids do projects in front of class..."

"What kind of projects?"

"Book reports that are related to our readings. Books we don't have time for during class. If we read Hamlet, someone else gives a report on Macbeth."

"It sounds like you have more time for individuals with fewer students at Maybeck," she said.

"Yes. And small classes help us get out of the classroom. I've got a class of eight students in my psychology class. We're going on a field trip to Napa State Hospital this semester. I can bring all of them, together, in this Chevy wagon. My entire psychology class."

"Napa? Isn't that a mental institution? They let you take high schoolers there?

"Yes. Maybeck also has unique student resources." I said. "One of my psychology kids told me Napa had field trips. I checked it out. They really do allow it."

What I didn't tell her is that I had been there, but not as a patient of course. When I was a kid, about age ten, my dad swallowed a bottle of sleeping pills. Depression. He spent six months getting ECT (electroconvulsive therapy), commonly called shock treatments. My mother spent time in Napa, twice: before I was born, and once in Agnew State Hospital when I was in college. Six months each time. Depression and electroshock therapy. I didn't like to talk about my parents' history of mental illness.

Another thing I didn't say was that Maybeck teachers, within parameters, can "do our own thing." I wanted to teach psychology. But Napa State Hospital was where I remember seeing my dad in loose-fitting institutional green clothes, locked in a big room with bars on the windows. I had mixed feelings about our planned psychological field trip.

We drove the rest of the way back to the East Bay in silence and safety.

Chapter 35

"Is her insanity irreversible?"

NAPA STATE HOSPITAL. Students in my Maybeck psychology class read about mental illness and systems of psychotherapy. We discussed ECT and I gave out information from an organization called NAPA: Network Against Psychiatric Assault.

In preparation for the excursion, I couldn't resist bringing in my guitar and singing one of my crazy originals. This was one of a batch of songs I performed at a fundraiser for Maybeck at Bishop's coffee house in Oakland.

Psychology

Psych–O, psych–E, psychology

Where have all the philosophers gone?

PAUL AUGUST

Whose wisdom gave us morality
Who opened our eyes to humanity.
Have they all gone into psychology?

Where have all the poets gone?
Whose words gave us a world of love.
Who opened the door to insanity
All gone into psychology?

Why can't I find peace of mind?
Will I ever be happy in Psychology?

A bright and sunny day greeted us as we began our Maybeck psychology field trip. I wasn't about to head up north into flood country and have any problems with a car-load of Maybeckians. We had two students in front, four in the back seat and two in the back space of my station wagon. Cozy but functional.

We met with a staff member who explained all that needed to be explained and what to expect on our tour. At one spot, I had a familiar feeling: a big room with depressed folks dressed in institutional green. Was my dad once in here? The patients wandered about with hands by their sides. Normal people, who walk with a gait, let their hands swing freely as they walk along. A depressed subject walks like a zombie. Their hands dangle at their sides, motionless.

MAYbeck High School Presents
File: Maybe
on the evening of Saturday December 2, 1972
At 8 30 At The Bishop's Coffee House
Harrison Near 14ᵀᴴ Street in OAKLAND
PAUL August and the <u>Solo</u> premier of his
psycho-rock musical :

PSYCHOLOGY

A bedlam of such <u>songs</u> as:
Bed-Wetter
Phobia
Hetrosexuality
Self-Negation
Johnny At the University
Fat Lab Rat
Persona
Mental Depression
Oh, Gee, Psychotherapy
It Doesn't Pay to Be
    Paranoid
Penis Envy
Institutionalization
Delusions Of Grandeur
Where Have All The
    Philosopher's gone?

Despite the creativity of Stan's stark posters and my bizarre songs, single event fundraisers absorbed a disproportionate amount of our teacher time and personal energy. They just were not worth the effort. Our only hope for Maybeck's survival was that the teachers would continue to subsidize the school by taking less salary while slowly increasing the tuition.

As we entered the art section of the work rehab I got a cheerful surprise from one of the patients. "Hi Mr. August. What are you doing here?"

I turned to see who it was. Sally Andrews! My former St. Liz student. What a jolt. "Sally! I brought my psychology class. We're on a field trip."

"It's so good to see you. Are these your students?" Sally spoke in a normal conversational tone. She wore the institutional green but, unlike most of the other patients, her hair was combed, her nails done and she had a touch of make-up. She stood in front of a huge painting full of religious imagery, fire, angels, demons and other icons. After a little chitchat, I asked her about her project. I also needed my students to see why such a "normal" person was in here. "Tell us about your painting," I said, with some trepidation, unsure of her response.

"Sure." Sally turned to her painting and began calling out Old Testament names and describing biblical people. She had a story for every fiery icon on her canvas. She ranted on in a psycho-bible-babble that made sense only to her, rapidly and incessantly. At a certain point, when I saw my students getting bored, I had to get closure.

"Sally, we have to go. I want to thank you for talking with us. Class, let's thank Sally." We applauded.

"Good to see you, Mr. August. Give my regards to the St. Liz folks. This is your guys' new school, right?"

"Yes. Maybeck High School."

"Okay Maybeck. Nice seeing all of you," Sally returned to what appeared to be a normal human being.

354

On the way home, the class was full of questions about Sally. Out of respect to her right to privacy, I had to circumvent direct questions and give a more generic answer while I drove through San Rafael back to the Bay Area.

"What's wrong with her, Mr. August? She talked all normal then kinda went crazy with her religious painting. Will she ever get out of there? Is her insanity irreversible?"

"Well, there's no easy answer. I was surprised to see her there. I don't know her diagnosis but I can say this: for folks as young as Sally to be in a place like that could mean a long-term situation. There's always hope, always new drugs, new meds. But this is a long-term place."

"Was she doing drugs?" asked another student.

"Let me finish the first question and include your reference to drugs," I said. "Most of the young folks in places like this are here because of drugs or alcohol."

"Is there a difference in sanity between what drugs do and what alcohol does to the mind? And what drugs?" asked another student.

"Alcohol can result in a 'wet brain.' That's a name for Korsakoff's syndrome. I knew a guy in a light show in San Francisco who worked at the Bill Graham dances. He also worked on my St. Liz dances. He used a lot of LSD and alcohol. When his sister took me to see him recently, he had Korsakoff's syndrome. He had no memory of recent events. He'd ask me a dozen times, 'What have you been doing lately Paul?' I'd tell him. A minute later he'd ask me the same thing."

"So, she probably did too much LSD and she may never get out of there?" a student asked.

"Well," I mused, "She has a right to privacy. I can't talk about her LSD use nor can I predict her release. But, as you can see, she shows no symptoms of Korsakoff's syndrome."

As we headed back to the Bay Area, the students were in an animated discussion about the treatment of the mentally ill in America. Maybeck had just given me a totally new experience in small class size. No more wasted time traveling on field trips. Now I could teach my entire class while driving.

Another day at Maybeck. The small atmosphere at Maybeck made it possible to have informal discussions at any time. Stan and Kelly and I sat down in an empty classroom for morning coffee between classes.

"I believe the strongest part of our school is what we teach," said Stan. "Maybeck offers a range of courses from physics and geometry to Nazi Germany and Biology."

"Those nuns never approved of your Nazi class Stan," said Kelly. "Shucks. Our classes allow electives to meet state required courses as well as college requirements."

"We've got most of the college prep covered," I said. "Stan can do humanities, art, and any of the social studies. I can cover English, writing, U. S. History, psychology and other social studies."

"Oh, and we still need a language teacher," said Stan.

"True," said Kelly. "We'll hire another part-time teacher next year for French and Spanish."

"It's great to have a teacher-run school until it comes to doing the extra work," said Kelly. "We're handling the money, collecting tuition, paying our bills, and ordering materials and supplies. I'm glad we have no principal but I'm not happy about the double duty."

"After I leave, someone will have to do my grant writing, PR, fundraising and finding school sites," I said.

"Our students love the school," said Stan. "Our college schedule is working. These young folks use free time productively. They do extra paintings in art, sit in on poetry readings when a published poet appears in a classroom and they keep the perennial chess game going. Talbot and Carroll are using any available piano to compose their

"Estuary Suite," including a segment entitled, "Crossing the Alameda Bridge."

We all laughed. Maybeck was both exhilarating and exhausting.

MAYBECK HIGH SCHOOL, BERKELEY
SPECIAL PROGRAM MAY-JUNE
"IN SEARCH of CALIFORNIA"

Is California still a land of milk and honey, a garden of
Eden? Following an academic look at California's legend, the
myth that brought so many people here, Maybeck will search
out today's reality in the state on a 1000 mile journey.

Tue   June 3   SACRAMENTO

Walk through Capitol Building: con
Visit with Assemblyman Ken Meade,
Attend various legislative committ
Visit with Mark Pochie, Director o
Visit with Governor Jerry Brown: u
(spend night on Bear River, near C

Stan took a bus load of Maybeck students on an incredible 1,000 mile
journey, "In search of California," for ten days. They began on May 26,
1975 and spent two days in orientation reviewing California history,
painters, issues, and visiting with the mayor of Berkeley.
Wed. Visited Stanford and Cannery Row. Camped in Monterey.
Thurs. Fort Ord. Salinas Valley. Camped at Lake Turlock.
Fri. Modesto. Gallo Winery. Gold Country. Angels Camp.
Sat. Explored the Mother Lode along Highway 49. Jamestown,
Columbia. Jackass Hill. Mark Twain country. San Andres. Plymouth.
Sun. and Mon. Lake Tahoe. Beauty vs. the gaming industry, cars and
real estate. Explored historical sites around Lake Tahoe.
Tues. After attending various legislative committee hearings in
Sacramento, Stan introduced the Maybeck students to his former
classmate: Governor Jerry Brown. Unfortunately, no one took notes.
Wed. After spending the night along the Bear River, they held a round
table discussion and returned to Berkeley by 6 pm.

MINDWORKER: MAYBECK

	8:45 To 9:45	9:45 – 10:00	10:00 To 11:00	11:00 To 12:00	12:00 To 1:00	1:00 To End of Afternoon Class — Field Trips + Labs
MONDAY	Algebra ; Gemoetry	Break	Spanish I ; Spanish II	Biology ; Physics	School meeting and Lunch	AMERICAN GOVERNMENT Cardinet LITERATURE: Fantasy & Science Fiction Kelly COMPOSITION–READING August
TUESDAY	American Govern- ment ; com- reading	Break	Spanish I ; Spanish II	The ARTS ; American writers	LUNCH TO 12:45	MUSIC Cardinet PSYCHOLOGY August
WEDNESDAY	Algebra ; Gemoetry	Break	Spanish I ; Spanish II	Sociology ; Algebra II Trig	LUNCH 12:45 3:45 – 4	BIOLOGY LAB Haynes PHYSICS LAB Kelly
THURSDAY	Algebra II – Trig Biology ; Physics	Break	music ; psych- ology	Break 11:30	Break	THE ARTS Cardinet 20th CENTURY AMERICAN WRITERS August
FRIDAY	Biology ; Physic	Break	Spanish I ; Spanish II	MATH Workshop – All Math classes (2 hour classes)	Lunch	sociology Haynes

359

Chapter 36

"What the hell is that?"

YOSEMITE. WE ENDED OUR CLASSES in the middle of May and transported the entire school to the high Sierras using a couple of army surplus vans and volunteer parents with cars. The Yosemite Valley in spring is cold, damp, and beautiful. The tranquility and sheer peacefulness is marred only by cars and tourists.

The day after we arrived, I hiked up to Yosemite Falls with Talbot and Carroll, the two multi-talented students and musicians. These two 16-year-olds had intelligence that bordered on genius but they shared a whimsical personality, always finding the fun in life. It would take us all day to zigzag 320 feet up the trail, along the steep paths, bordered by granite walls, up to Yosemite Falls.

MINDWORKER: MAYBECK

> **Maybeck's College Schedule:** My psychology class met one hour on Wednesdays and Thursdays, and three hours on Tuesday afternoons totaling five hours a week. The schedule in this book is an earlier (1973) version of four hours a week that didn't work.
>
> The risk of allowing "free" time to students is that they might get into trouble and the school would be responsible. Maybeck students, with their parents' understanding, did not disappoint us.

"Carroll. You look like you lost some weight," I said.

"You're right. Twenty pounds. It was easy to lose. All I did was walk."

"Twenty pounds? Just by walking? How could you possibly do that?" I asked.

"I'm a witness. I walked with him, Mr. August," said Talbot, the more slender one. Students call me "Mr. August" or "Paul." It was up to them.

"Okay, what did you witness?"

"On weekends, we'd walk down to East 14th St. and into downtown Oakland, walk around Lake Merritt, then go up Grand Avenue to Piedmont. We'd go past the Bishop's mansion then walk down Park, past Oakland High and over to Foothill and back to Maybeck."

"Damn. I hike around the lake. It's three miles. How many miles do you guys cover?" I asked.

"About 20 miles on weekends," said Carroll. "During school days, it's only about five or ten miles a day. We do about three miles an hour."

We continued step-by-step up the trail. All we needed was water and enough stamina. A few minutes into the hike those two were on their way, leaving me behind. When I got to the top in late afternoon they playfully greeted me.

"What held you up? We're ready to go back," said Talbot.

"Going up is easy," I said as I watched the water rushing over the edge and crashing to the rocks below. "It's going down where you need to be careful," I added. "All your weight is on your feet and your legs. And your lower back takes a punishment if you bear down with too much strength. Hiking to the top of any mountain is exhilarating. It's a physical challenge and a primitive joy. Either you get to the top or you don't. You guys made it, now don't mess up going down. And enjoy the view. John Muir said that America has only one Yosemite, but there are hundreds in Alaska."

"Mr. August, have you done this before?' asked Talbot. "Hiked to the top of a mountain?"

"Yeah," I replied. "Back at St. Liz, I chaperoned the Spanish club with my friend and fellow teacher Ed Pashote. We all hiked to the top of Mount Junipero Serra near Monterey. That was over 4,000 feet high but it wasn't as steep as this trek."

The hike back down took a matter of minutes. I restrained my temptation to scurry with the flow of gravity because my back wouldn't survive a fall down the trail.

Decision time, again. One night, at a camp-fire, we teachers called a faculty meeting. We made the big decisions together, mostly by consensus but sometimes with a vote. No principal. We actually had a faculty now because we had two new teachers, David Kinstle and Stuart Haynes.

In addition, we no longer had to send a kid out of class to answer the phone when we found clerical help. A volunteer answered the phone, typed up letters, and ran the school office. She was our entire support staff. Kathleen Tillinghast, the wife of the pastor, taught a Latin class, which fulfilled university requirements. Radisch continued to invite Maybeckians to court during the day and then follow up with his American legal systems class one night a week.

"Let's get some of the unpleasant stuff out of the way," said Kelly as we settled in around the campfire flames. "As much as I don't like kicking kids out of Maybeck, I think it's time we do it."

"I wish there were a better way," said Stu.

"Well," said Stan, as he passed out a one page summary, "Here's a kid who only cares about cars and motorcycles. His grades are bad, attendance is weak and he's obnoxious to all the girls."

"He called one girl a 'slut,'" said Kelly. "We should have kicked him out then and there."

"She slapped his face," said Stan, "but he still didn't get the message."

"Who else?" asked Kelly.

"This girl is an intelligent and attractive student. She just never attends class. She doesn't need us so we don't need her," said Stan, passing out another summary sheet.

Stan and Kelly handled most of the discipline. Dave and Stu were still learning and listening.

"We gave her repeated warnings," said Kelly. "It didn't do any good. She's self-centered and she expects to get her own way."

"It makes no sense for her parents to pay money and enroll her in Maybeck if she refuses to attend classes. It deprives another student of a spot in our school," said Stan. "She could go to any school and not attend classes. Why Maybeck?"

"And what about our gypsy?" I asked. She really wasn't a gypsy but she said she wanted to go to a different high school every year for the new experience.

"She's going to Berkeley High, a school with 5,000 students," said Stan. "We have a small staff. We can't provide what a big-time campus can offer. We don't have time for snow trips, dances, football and all those sports. We don't have lockers for book bags or bells to start and end class. No rah-rah cheerleaders."

"They say that Maybeck is Berkeley High's alternative," said Kelly. "Kids at Berkeley High, who want a small school, come here. Kids here, who want a big school, go there."

"We do, however, have a graduating class that will be one hundred percent scholarship winners," said Stan. "All three of them. Even one such award at a school is rare. All young women: one Chicana, one Native American and one white. This shows the strength of our ethnic diversity."

"I'll send a press release to the *Examiner*," I said. "They'll like this."

"I read a previous story about Maybeck in the paper," said Dave as he waved away Kelly's cigar smoke. "The headline said, 'A private school for poverty families.' This story motivated me to contact you guys. I wanted to teach these students to help them get out of poverty."

"Hah," laughed Kelly. "The faculty is in more poverty than the students!"

"Let's decide about next year," said Stan. "This appears to have been a successful year. The parents and students are happy with Maybeck. Are we good to go for another year?"

"Yes," said Dave "I move that Maybeck goes on another year and continues forever."

"I second that motion," said Stu. "This has been a pleasant and productive year for me. This school has a strong positive spirit. I like it."

"Damn," said Kelly, exhaling smoke from his ever present cigar. "These two new teachers are hot to trot. That's good to see."

"So we all agree. Maybeck continues forever. Anyone disagree? August, can you make it another year?"

"No," I said. "I'm almost broke. I have to get a paying job. I can't survive another year. Maybeck will survive without me."

"But Paul, there must be a way to get the money," said Stu. "You're one of our most experienced teachers."

"And one of our teachers and organizers," said Dave. "We need your expertise."

"I admit, I gambled that I could get Maybeck funded so we could all have a living wage. No one funded us. I gambled and lost."

"What are you going to do? Stay in teaching?" asked Stu.

"I'll probably start as a substitute teacher and apply to the public schools," I said.

"The Oakland Public Schools?" asked Stu. "That doesn't sound too appealing."

"I live in Oakland. I've already got six years' experience in a Catholic school and one year from Maybeck. There's a teacher surplus these days, so we'll see."

Our discussion slowly ended. We observed that Maybeck drained us of time and energy. It took all we had to be teachers, counselors, janitors, chaperones, planners, and decision-makers. We closed the meeting, took a roll call of our students and looked forward to a good night's sleep.

Later that evening. Although we had tents for everyone, a few students and teachers decided to throw down our sleeping bags around the campfire. As we lay down, we could look up through the filter of tall evergreen trees and see the bright shimmering Milky Way. Kelly and his SCUFO crew identified the constellations as they found them.

During the night I heard growling and canvas ripping. A bear got into our food tent. Dave and Stu chased him off. He came back, knocked over the entire tent, and then got chased away again.

S. F. Examiner, page 42,

Fri. April 13, 1973

100 Pct.

Placement

By School

<u>Principal Hails The Awards</u>

"Every senior graduating
from Maybeck High...has
earned a scholarship to either
the University of California
or Stanford. Of course, the
school, founded last
September, has only three
seniors in its first graduating
class."

"Don't worry," said Stan. "We only have
canned goods and bottles in the tent. We
hung the meat and fresh food on a branch,
out of reach."

We slowly fell asleep under the clear
starry night as it slowly became obscured

by clouds. I awoke again. This time I felt raindrops splashing on my face. It increased. "Let's get in the tents," someone yelled. Bodies mixed with sleeping bags, boots, hiking gear and blankets. Somehow we got out of the rain and slowly returned to sleep.

Then it happened. We heard a sudden loud cracking noise echoing through the valley, followed by snapping and a loud explosion echoing into a thunderous splash.

"What the hell is that?" I said.

The first hint of a dull mist morning was upon us. We peeked outside. A giant tree, about 50 yards from us, had fallen from its perch on our right and into the river to our left.

"If that thing fell in our direction," said Kelly, "We wouldn't be here to talk about it."

The tree was probably over 100 feet high.

"But look at the river," said Stu. "It's rising. This is a warm rain. It's melting the mountain snow and turning it into those muddy river rapids."

"Let's move the camp back," said Kelly. "And keep an eye out for any flash floods."

The Merced River continued to rise and threatened to cover the low single lane bridge, our only escape. "If the river goes over the bridge, we have no way out. We'd be stuck here," said Kelly. "What say ye?"

We all agreed to leave.

We planned to stay the entire ten-day period but, "Discretion is the better part of valor," according to Stan. We packed up just as the park rangers showed up and told us to evacuate. After only a week, we had to return early to Oakland.

Wesley Hall, United Methodist Church, Maybeck High. Back in Oakland, we got the news. The church might not renew our lease. I discussed it with the pastor and brought the news back to our Maybeck staff meeting.

"Here are their gripes," I said. "We used the gym once without permission. We didn't keep the classrooms as clean as they—the church council—wanted. We're guilty of leaving a light on, a window open, parking in the yellow zone and scratching the floor while moving a piano. The heat was on when the windows were open. A teacher once slept overnight, in a sleeping bag, in the school. We missed a mop up spot after the parent potluck. A student gave the janitor a dirty look."

"I'm not in the mood to be harassed by these petty issues," said Stan. "This stuff reminds me of St. Liz. If we can't be given the grace of a few mistakes, maybe we need to find another location."

"I say, forget the church council," said Kelly. "It's not Pastor Tillinghast who is giving us a hard time or his wife Kathleen.

She works in our office. Some of their board members felt we were taking over and they were right. We need to grow. Forget it. Who needs this?"

"The future of Maybeck will be in your hands," I told them. "I'll stay on the board of directors for another year to keep an eye on you guys."

Maybeck managed to stay with the Laurel Methodists for a second year before moving to Berkeley.

The first Maybeck graduation. We held an informal graduation event in the Eucalyptus Grove of the University of California campus where we began in September. The three members of our graduating class planned the event. No robes. No caps. No speeches. No ceremony. It was simply a picnic with a string quartet and good conversation.

In September, Maybeck began again, but without me.

Chapter 37

"A curious reluctance to..."

MAYBECK'S SECOND YEAR (1973-74). Although I no longer taught at Maybeck, I still held a seat on the board of directors. We met at the Steppenwolf, a bar just down the street from the Blind Lemon in the Berkeley industrial section. Stu Haynes had written a seven page letter of concern about the direction of Maybeck and we were there to address it.

"I feel we're developing a curious reluctance to experiment with the school," said Stu, as he raised his eyebrows, leaned toward the candle in the center of the table and opened his eyes wide. "I heard some remarkable musical improvisation at school by Jackie, Scott, Pat and Sue. It reminded me of the enormous potential our students have and how easily it is lost. This year, I feel we're just trying to survive and the students are secondary."

"Stu," said Stan, removing his glasses to peer across the round table through the flickering flame. "All schools struggle with similar questions. Institutions grow, evolve, progress and even regress at times. We have not yet reached our potential. Consider last year's Bodega Bay program. It was one of our finest events: well-organized, adventurous, educationally invigorating and engaging to the students."

"That's what I mean," said Stu, sitting upright. "That's what we're missing. Why can't we do more of that? Why can't we have more Bodega experiences?"

"Stu, you gotta be woofin'," said Kelly as he twisted a fist in the air. "Do you realize how much time, energy, and organization went into all that? We prepped the students for two days, picking up food, supplies and, equipment, and planning our programs. Then we met at school at 9 a.m. on Sunday morning and took the student body, in cars, to Bodega Bay to stay in the dorms of the U. C. Berkeley Marine biology building. We—including you—worked like dogs to make it happen."

"It really was an excellent program about the ocean," said Dave Kinstle looking over at Stu. "We teamed up on our presentations about marine life and what kind of plants and animals live beneath the surface of the sea. Ocean biology. The tides."

"We engendered some great insights," said Stu. "Like, imagine if the ocean became transparent and humans could see all forms of sea life. We talked about the intertidal zone then walked down to the beach to explore mussels, algae, barnacles and star fish. No need for textbooks there."

"We had a counter-point with our academic lectures, slide shows and films," said Stan, gazing at the candle as if to gather his thoughts. "I talked about the sea in relation to history, music, poetry and art."

"Yeah, but we included play time: sandcastles, flag football in the sand, a hike to shell Beach and volleyball," said Kelly. "August did a weird night ritual."

"Moi?" I feigned surprise. "We had a full moon and a rising tide. I couldn't resist doing my archetypal moon worshipping ritual. 'The sun is but a mere reflection of the moon' and all that mythological stuff. But we also talked about the sea and myth in literature using an old radio program of Melville's Moby Dick."

Stan opened a manila folder. "We had those young Maybeck ladies and gentlemen from 9 a.m. Sunday until we dropped them off in Oakland at 5 p.m. Friday. Six straight days at the ocean. We provided students with food, shelter and a fantastic educational experience. This is the blueprint for the future of Maybeck. We cannot, however, dismantle our two short semesters of traditional schooling: homework, reading, class discussions, grades, and so on." Stan paused for effect and held one finger up. "These students, and their parents, expect to be prepared for college."

"The Bodega experience offers a lot of promise as a way to organize Maybeck for a significant part of the year, not just one week," said Stu as he looked around the table for a response.

I replied, "That was our first year, full of energy, experimentation, adventure, and spontaneity. We spent less time in a school building because we started without one and we moved from place-to-place every two weeks during those early months. No one can duplicate the start-up energy that goes into creating something where nothing previously existed."

"In June of 1972, Maybeck was an idea," added Stan. "In September of 1972, Maybeck became a reality."

"I've got another idea," said Stu. "Since money is a problem and teachers cannot continue to subsidize the school, why don't we simply stop operations for one year to allow teachers to find high paying jobs to then accumulate enough money to return to re-open Maybeck?"

"Start again? Do you realize what it took to start this school?" asked Stan.

"Start again? What a hurter," said Kelly, almost falling out of his chair. "No way. Just ask August about all those high-paying jobs out there just waiting to hire us for a year."

Everyone looked at me. "In high school, on the track team, I ran the mile," I said. "If I stopped to rest it would take me ten times the energy to start up again. We've got to keep our momentum going. As for high-paying jobs for one year, there are none. There's a teacher surplus and I'm lucky to be a substitute teacher, which is low-paying. I had a job offer to be a bureaucrat in Contra Costa County. A good friend of mine and college classmate, Larry Fugazi, set up an interview for me but I couldn't go through with it. I'd be trapped with a decent salary and benefits that would suck me into a life of red tape."

Kelly laughed, tapped ash from his cigar and declared, "No one hires anybody for only a year, unless it's a rare special project. A business has start-up expenses to train new employees. They don't want you to quit at the end of a year."

"These are all good issues," said Jack Radisch, now a deputy D.A. with Alameda County and part-time Maybeck teacher. "Sometimes ideals get battered by pragmatics. There's a desire here to become more closely involved with the students."

"But we can't do that when we are also administrators," said Stu. "We might consider liberating ourselves from doing all the administrative work and disciplinary hassles so we can establish better rapport with the students.

"We created a teacher-run school and we love our independence," said Stan. "We have no money to hire someone to tell us what to do."

"Stu," I said slowly, as I formulated my thoughts, "I've found that there's a 'halo effect' with anything new. Last year was fantastic and this year appears to pale in comparison. The bad moments from last year have been minimized. Selective forgetting."

"Yeah," said Radisch. "Like when Kelly's thermos full of liquid nitrogen exploded around a bunch of kids. Maybeck almost didn't have a second year.

"I can sense the tension," continued Radisch. "Last year's spirit, enthusiasm and creative energy has been replaced by school routines, class schedules, and tough decisions."

"We have problems with this school building that interfere with allowing students to have quality free time between classes," said Stu. "I support free time but many students simply don't have anything to do."

"We also have those who take advantage of the free time," said Stan. "They use the pianos, do extra reading, or even sit in on other classes when we have guests who are poets or politicians running for re-election."

"This Oakland location, near the corner of 35th Avenue and MacArthur, is not ideal for student free time," said Stu, opening his hands in an expectation of agreement. "Street people were in the pool room. Some kids threw eggs out the window. A student might sneak a cigarette on the back porch or, if they leave campus, the neighborhood is full of fast food joints. We need a richer environment."

"You're right about that," said Kelly, blowing his cigar smoke into the air. "We're not happy with at least one strict guy on the board of directors who wants our teenagers out of here. I say, let's go."

"I may have found the ideal place," said Stan. He held his head high, preparing to make an announcement. "It's another Methodist church right across from the University of California, just a block down from Bancroft and Telegraph. Our motivated students will have the resources of the university in their front yard. It may be available next year. Trinity Church. I'll look into it."

At this point we took a break, stretched our legs and engaged in a little small talk.

"I can't believe this building—Steppenwolf," I said. "It's only a white storefront with painted windows and no name or address on the door. How do people know about it?

"Only word of mouth," said Kelly. "We're surrounded by Berkeley liberals, radicals and hippies who took it over from the beatniks back when Max Scherr owned it."

"The guy who started one of the first underground newspapers, the Berkeley Barb, right?" I asked.

"Right." Said Kelly. "Rumor has it that he sold this place to start the Barb. It's crowded here every night."

"Before we get back to the meeting, I have a question. Is Radisch teaching his law course again for high school students?"

"No, not this semester," said Stan. "Radisch is volunteer teaching an early morning driver's education course. We needed to offer that this semester. He's still a Deputy District Attorney."

We resumed our meeting when Stu returned and said, "I have some specific suggestions. We've had good students but a few bad apples can do a great deal of harm to everyone in the school, taking up teacher time in dealing with problems they create. We have to be more selective in who we admit.

This is one of Stan's most eloquent statements on...

WHO SHOULD COME TO MAYBECK?

Since students are considered to be responsible persons, and are treated that way, it is important that they be responsible for themselves. Our experience has been that students who are interested in school, and reasonably mature, but do not like the usual authoritarian and impersonal atmosphere at large schools, usually get a great deal out of Maybeck. It offers them opportunities and experiences they would never have in the usual high school. On the other hand, a person who is not interested in classes and just wants to "get through" should probably consider another high school: Maybeck is not a "free" school. Its informal structure can do more harm than good if a student is not mature enough to handle it.

MAYBECK HIGH SCHOOL

"We've had this dilemma before you came on board," said Kelly. "If we have to expel students for bad behavior and harming others, we will. We had to expel a few last year."

380

"We have never turned down anyone who wanted to attend Maybeck," said Stan as he frowned a bit to think about what he said. "That does not mean, however, that we have selected only the best students or that we didn't make mistakes.

"New students give us new opportunities to grow," continued Stan. "It's the returning students, however, who reward us the most with their decision to return to Maybeck. This is an awesome validation. Their positive gesture is the most encouraging I can imagine."

I remembered an article I read. "Some students interview well but don't perform as expected. Others may not star in an interview but they diligently absorb their classes and take a leadership role in the school. Success can't always be predicted."

"What other suggestions do you have, Stu?" asked Stan.

"I think we should spend more time with students outside of class," said Stu. "Sometimes, only Dave and I are the only teachers here after school."

Kelly shifted a bit in his chair. "Well, I'm helping my brother in his business production business. After a year and a half of Maybeck, I need the income."

"And I go back to my home where I have to tend to curriculum planning, class schedules and corporate chores of the school," said Stan.

"I'm a substitute teacher and newspaper carrier driver, two part-time jobs," I said. "Also, I can't afford the extensive allocation of my time and energy. My kids need to know who their daddy is. I still do freelance writing and singing now and then. I didn't have 100% to give to students."

"What other suggestions do you have, Stu?" asked Dave.

"I think we should change the image of the school to be more in line with what we're doing. Let's drop the word 'alternative' and not try to fit into concepts like 'environmental school' just to be funded.

"Didn't we decide this?" asked Stan. "We're not an alternative school. That label has drop-out connotations. We don't need that."

"But we are an environmental school," I said, "because that's what we do. We fit into that language. Look, if I picked up my guitar to jam with you guys, we'd all have to use the language of music. Like, let's do a 12-bar blues in the key of E. Foundations, and education in general, understand environmental schools. We communicate to them by using their language, like it or not."

"Stu," said Dave. "Didn't you have a point about students who are developing a standoffish attitude about particular classes and school activities?"

"It's like it's unfashionable to be enthusiastic about what one is learning," said Stu. "Even one or two students in a class can strongly influence others that school isn't cool."

"It's not just Maybeck," I said. "I see it in the public schools where I substitute teach. Kids in gangs can influence others into thinking that it's not cool to do your homework, be on time or participate in class. They do the minimum to just barely pass. This problem transcends Maybeck."

"Is there anything we can do about it?" asked Dave.

"The cool kids are peer leaders," I said. "It takes time to turn them around, give them ownership in the class, work with them individually and get their support. And, frankly, it doesn't always happen."

"I must say, it appears we have a case of the year-and-a-half syndrome," said Stan, as he raised his shoulders to signify a new awareness of our situation.

"That's right," blurted Kelly. "We've seen it before. When Stan and I were checking out the other new—if I can use the term— 'alternative' schools last year while we were planning Maybeck, we discovered that a whole lot of those schools either didn't make it past a year and a half or they faced a crisis that put them to the test."

"Too many of those schools depended on one charismatic leader. When he or she quits, the schools sometime fall apart," said Stan. "This won't happen to us. We started with four veteran teachers who have been together for six years. Although August left, our two new teachers are as committed to continuing this school as we were to creating it."

"Okay Stu, you rascal," quipped Kelly. "Now that you've got us all riled up—what else is on your mind?"

Stu quickly responded. "The school is creating its own momentum. One feels a kind of inevitability about Maybeck's heading in the same direction as other schools: developing all the paraphernalia like hall monitors, tardy slips, and rigid class structures. Maybe there's little we can do except to let the school evolve."

"Agreed," said Kelly. "Sometimes nature will take its own course. Yosemite showed us that last year."

"Institutions evolve into whatever they have to become," said Stan. "And even our best plans run into unexpected consequences like they did at Yosemite."

"A few students put up an incredible resistance to what was planned in Yosemite and threatened to make the program unworkable," said Stu.

Dave shook his head is disagreement. "We came face-to-face with the forces of nature and survived a very real threat. A tree nearly wiped out our entire school, it rained and we had to evacuate camp and bears ripped up a tent."

"At Big Basin, at the beginning of this school year," said Stu, "there appeared to be a slight increase in the small number of students who used drugs. That trip makes me reluctant to go on another all school trip because we might be providing a situation where students take drugs or involve students who normally wouldn't use them."[37]

"Stu. What are you saying?" cried Kelly, throwing his hands up. "This is Oakland. Home of the Hell's Angels. They've been known to deal drugs. And we're right next to San Francisco and Berkeley, sister psychedelic cities."

"I feel this has been a productive discussion," said Stan, closing his folder, looking across the table and lifting his chin. "I don't feel we have to make any major decisions at this time. We're still a work in progress. We have flaws but the truest reality, I believe, is that we're developing, we're moving forward and ultimately we will become a school that reflects the best of our teachers and students."

"It's difficult to disagree with that," said Dave.

We all left. I chugged back to Oakland in my old VW bug. I remained on the board of directors but I truly missed my teacher friends, Maybeck's students, classes, and adventures. I felt alone.

Epilogue

MAYBECK'S THIRD YEAR (1974-75). In October, I dropped by Maybeck's new school site on Bancroft Avenue in Berkeley: Trinity United Methodist Church, right across the street from U. C. Berkeley. I had resigned from the Maybeck board the previous April because I was just plain burned out.

"We took the entire second floor: classrooms, office space, restroom and storage," said Stan as he expansively spread his arms while we walked down the hall to his classroom. "The only defect is that the building is old, shall we say, rustic, and it has no lab for biology or chemistry."

Maybeck's new location was simply remarkable. No high school, public or private, operated closer to U.C. Berkeley. Across the street stood Cal's Harmon gym that bustled with activity during basketball season. Zellerbach Hall, a world class venue for performers, was merely a block away. University resources were everywhere.

"The entire University is now just a few steps from Maybeck," Stan said proudly. "The opportunities for intellectual adventures are incredible. Free time is far more exciting for our students now than at any time in our first two years in Oakland."

Maybeck is just about a block-and-a-half below Dwinelle Plaza and the student union, the epicenter of university life. And Telegraph Avenue is right there—a parade of students, street performers, craftsmen, artists, homeless folks and Cal instructors. It's a microcosm of society and Maybeck's in the middle of it.

"And we are slowly growing," added Stan. "We welcomed 20 new students to Maybeck this fall. That brings our little student body up to 52 students, the vast majority of whom followed us from Oakland."

We entered Stan's classroom. It was after school and a few students were around working on homework or playing ping pong. "You guys are still doing the special programs, right? I said.

Stan pulled up a chair. "Yes," he said, as he flipped through the notes he took from his over-sized, well-worn, leather brief case. "Those programs make Maybeck unique."

"Did you all go to Yosemite to kick start school at the beginning of this year?"

"No," Stan replied. "It was our Feather River program. We called it, 'On the Skies.' An extraordinary experience."

Feather River is in rural Northern California, up near Quincy. That drive along the river winds through granite walls above and the wild rapids below. It's one of the most scenic roads I've ever driven in Northern California. My mind jumped to the immediate surroundings and I changed the subject. "This is an old but elegant building. Is it a Bernard Maybeck original?"

"Maybeck built a church in Berkeley, but this isn't the one," said Stan. "I wish it were. We have the entire second floor here. Church offices and the auditorium are below."

Remembering our problems with previous churches, I asked, "Have you guys received any complaints from folks who don't like teenagers?"

Kelly came in and joined us. "August! Where've you been? Complaints? In Berkeley? Hah! Who's going to complain?"

I laughed. "So you guys ventured into the far regions of Northern California to study the skies over Feather River."

"Yes, indeed," replied Kelly with raised eyebrows and a big Irish grin. "We had a good time playing shuffleboard, preparing our own meals, sharing cabins and making learning fun. Our students have even invented their own game, puff-pingo, where a Ping-Pong paddle fans the ball."

"Feather River wasn't all fun and games," observed Stan. "We organized a rigorous academic program. We considered the origins of the universe, the philosophical implications of astronomy and the evolution of human thought."

"As well as the more practical realities of NASA and space travel," added Kelly. "These kids now know the difference between red giants and white dwarfs, quasars and pulsars, black holes and the Big Bang. I'd say that every kid who went to Feather River came back knowing more than they ever expected to know about the universe in which they exist."

We sat around the table in Stan's classroom that had about 12 chairs. Stan had yet to organize a student crew to begin working on his wall murals. "Paul," said Stan, turning to me. "We have two excellent additions to our staff this year. Ela Youbaki, our new office manager, is also studying cello and Eastern Music at the Center for World Music. Kathleen Wolfe, our new Spanish teacher, is a guitarist and former Peace Corps worker in Nepal. Since we're now so close to U.C., we have a potential wealth of talented part-time teachers who can tolerate a low salary or even volunteer their time and energy to Maybeck."

"Tell him about independent study," said Kelly, gesturing to Stan with an unlit cigar. "It continues," said Stan. "In the past we've placed students in the community at sites like KPFA-FM where one young lady prepared scripts, hosted interviews and taped public service announcements. She's headed for a career in the media. This year we're placing students with the American Conservatory Theater, the United Farm workers and a few students in other schools assisting teachers in physical education, tutoring bilingual third graders and helping preschoolers in a day care center."

"We also have more than a couple of truly unique classes," laughed Kelly, raising his right hand and lowering his head. "Real grabbers."

Stan picked up the Maybeck catalogue of classes and began leafing through it. "Yes, here, Dave Kinstle's aerodynamics of kites."

"You got a class in flying kites?" I asked, incredulously.

"It's much more than that. First, students build these massive tetrahedron kites."[38]

"Whatever that is," I said.

"They fly them from the Berkeley Marina," said Stan. "It's more complicated than I care to explain. Another unique course is 'The Ocean.' Stuart Haynes takes students to the coast on selected weekends and uses the U.C. swimming pool for PE during the week. And Kelly and Stu are teaching a wild course called exobiology."

"Huh? I've never heard of that before. You guys are giving me an inferiority complex."

"It's about studying life forms other than those on Earth," said Kelly, with a wide smile and a mischievous gleam in his eyes. "And since there are no known extraterrestrial life forms, we'll use physics and biology to discuss the astronomical and physiological basis for life here on Earth. And Stan is too humble to tell you he has classes in oil painting and film study."

"Maybeck is amazing," I said. "How can you fit all these Maybeckian projects in around the usual algebra, English, math, and science requirements?"

"We build on who we are," said Stan. He continued to flip through the Maybeck catalogue as he spoke. "Our enthusiasm is contagious. This year, students are taking Greek, taught by Kathleen Tillinghast, fantasy and science fiction, taught by Gretchen Griswald, Calculus by Kelly and I'm teaching a new graphics class. It's really quite a full schedule."

"I've been away from Maybeck for too long," I said. "You've got teachers I don't even know."

Deja vu. Here I was leaving Maybeck again, being proud that I helped turn an idea into what Maybeck is now. And so, my dear reader, this ends book one of the Mindworker series. Book Two will begin during the summer after I left St. Liz. I'll take you with me through experiences that, at first, I'm not too anxious to return to. You'll find me diverted into another lifestyle but I'll always be in touch with Maybeck. After my first and only full-time year at Maybeck, my life took a new direction. The second book of my autobiography, *Maybeck: Ghostwriter,* takes the reader into the public schools where I encounter misadventures quite unlike my life at St. Liz or Maybeck.

After Words

MAYBECK, ABOUT 35 YEARS LATER, was recognized by San Francisco's KRON TV-4 as the "Best High School in the East Bay." This book commemorates Maybeck's 40th Anniversary.

Maybeck is still a teacher-run school. The director is hired by a steering committee, which is comprised of three teachers who are elected by the teachers and staff. Maybeck School reappears in parts of the next four Mindworker books.

Thanks for reading,
Paul August, Mindworker
End of Book One

Acknowledgements

I T'S NOT POSSIBLE FOR ME TO IDENTIFY or even remember all those who helped me bring this book back to life after 40 years of remission. First, I'm grateful to my parents who had a farm that my sister Patricia and I could use as a playground during our childhood.

If I had a dedication for this book, it would go to Muriel, my wife, and our children: Kristi (with granddaughter Chynna), John Paul and Wendy. Thank you all for tolerating my writing and music mania while I survived 38 years of teaching in Oakland.

I'd like to recognize all my Catholic schoolteachers, good and bad. Those who helped me most were Sister Regina in the sixth grade, Sister Mara, high school Spanish, and Sister Gerald, U. S. History (aka Sister Marie in the book). Father Emery Tang, my high school principal, used a firm hand in directing me to go to college. At Saint Mary's College, I came into contact with classmates from all over California who gave me a better understanding of my rural, wage-earning roots.

At San Francisco State I entered the creative writing department for help on a novel. I caught criticism for writing like a newspaper reporter. They advised me to take entry level creative writing courses. Instead, I went into journalism. I became a "post-baccalaureate special admissions student," a fancy phrase meaning I could take any journalism courses without getting a degree. My teachers included my mentor, Carl Nolte, ace newspaper columnist whose writing fills up most of page two of Sunday's San Francisco Chronicle.

As a full-time teacher and part-time writer, I depended on writing groups to refine my writing. Penny Warner led one of the best groups from her home in Danville, California. Her quick wit and dazzling presence made every group laugh and learn. When I got to Nevada City, California, Donna Hanelin led a similar group from her home. Her most unforgettable writing conference was when we all spent a week in Kalani, a tropical retreat in Hawaii, not far from the glowing red-orange night light of an active volcano.

Tracy Deliman, of the Sierra Writers, recommended that I join the group that helped her publish: BAIPA, the Bay Area Independent Publishers Association. David Colin Carr, an informal BAIPA leader and freelance editor, introduced me to members of this excellent Marin County group. Our meetings, on the second Saturday of the month, brought me into contact with a bunch of experts who shared more information than I could ever use. A year and a half after joining BAIPA, this book became a paperback and an ebook thanks to the expertise and experience of Ruth Schwartz, my book's midwife. We call her "The Wonderlady." (thewonderlady.com) Also thanks to Ruth, this book is available through a multitude of online book retailers.

Other Sierra Writers generally helped my writing. Jan Westmore opened her beautiful home in Nevada City, California, to a monthly nonfiction writing group who gave me insightful comments on all of my writings, at the time, especially with my occasional op-ed columns for *The Union*, our local Nevada City newspaper.

My editor, Susan Gabrielle, president of the Sierra Writers, found solutions to parts of my story where I needed another set of writer's eyes to find the flaws and fix the prose. In order to finally get this published, in 2014, Susan and I met one hour a week for months. If the reader sees any editing flaws, it's merely because I failed to make the changes she suggested. Daniel Bernick, former teacher and now an artist, gave a final reading to the "final" version of *Mindworker: Maybeck* before production began.

In fact-checking my material I used the *S. F. Examiner*, the *S. F. Chronicle*, the *Oakland Tribune* and weekly newspapers that no longer exist. I found articles from Berkeley High and Bishop O'Dowd. I have old photos I don't remember taking. The American Federation of Teachers (AFT) newspaper provided their coverage. Needless to say, I also drew from countless documents, brochures, flyers and minutes from all too numerous meetings.

Stan Cardinet took most of the candid teacher photos and Muriel took the personal photos of me and the children. I regret that I no longer have the documented details of who else did what. In one article I did for *Rolling Stone*, "Epitaph for Indian Joe." Stan took photos that were mistakenly credited to me. So, I want to set the record straight. Stan Cardinet took those *Rolling Stone* photos, not me. Throughout this book, selected articles, brochures, catalogues and other documents about the early Maybeck years were almost all created by Stan Cardinet.

Sue Matthews, a former St. Liz student who spent most of her life teaching at Maybeck, created the front cover painting of the four of us who were fired and resurrected as Maybeckians. What better person to engrave our images on the front of this book? R. L. Crabb, the editorial and political cartoonist for *The Union*, Nevada City and Grass Valley's local newspaper, created a visual conclusion at the end of the book. Maybeck, indeed, is: "Out of the indoors. Into the outdoors."

A special thanks to Wayne and Judy Harshbarger, our Sierra neighbors. They've come to our rescue more than once. Muriel and I owe them a debt of gratitude for years of help and friendship.

All the musicians I've worked with are also too numerous to mention here. Readers will find credits on my website for those who appeared on my two CDs: *Mindworker* and *Welcome to Nevada City, God's Country*. Many of those songs are alluded to in this book. All songs are owned through Kristi Music, BMI and produced by Mindworker Productions, LLC.

Here's a list of partial songs in this book. To hear samples of any of these songs, go to **Mindworker.net**.

Country Boy, City Blues
Fat Lab Rat
High School Athlete
The Rites of Spring
Picket Line,(aka) On Strike
The A. F. U. C.
Betty of the School Board
The Cardboard box Brigade

Mindworker
One Time
Black Man, White Man
Mrs. Abraham's Jesus
Grantwriter
Big Max
Psychology

My dear friends and colleagues: I expect to have a second edition to this book, so don't hesitate to contact me if you find any egregious errors or if I failed to credit you in any way. I want to be fair and accurate. This book is about teachers and so I have very few references to students. I can only say that you kids at St. Liz and Maybeck were among the best students that I have ever encountered.

Endnotes

[1] **Dad was a high school dropout:** No, actually he dropped out after the 8th grade. He never entered high school.

[2] **The statue of St. Anne:** (coincidentally, the mother of St. Liz): This was the sexiest statue of any saint that I've ever seen anywhere: pointed breasts, shapely figure, sensuous neck, one leg bent forward, and perfect feet. We adored her. She's no longer in the chapel but old-school Gaels like me know where to worship her in the woods just behind campus.

[3] **Catholic:** I'm not a Catholic anymore. I began "falling away" in college as I came to understand the philosophical, historical and irrational influences that created Catholicism. While teaching at St. Liz, I attended a Mass at St. Anthony's parish where the priest preached that, "The more you suffer on Earth, the higher your place will be in heaven." To my young college-educated mind, this was a perfect example of the Marx and Engels concept—religion is opium for the masses. This is not what I wanted to hear in church.

[4] **The Orange Bar:** They had so many bars in the casino that they just named them with colors: red bar, green bar, orange bar, etc.

[5] **Sierra/Sierras:** California's eastern mountain range is the Sierra Nevada. It's acceptable to shorten this to the Sierra. Locals like me, however, prefer Sierras. You'll find both forms here depending on who's talking.

[6] **Payola:** Pay-for-play. Some record labels made under-the-table payments to deejays so they would play their music on the radio, make the tune a hit and earn massive sales. Records that got no airplay generally did not sell and were considered by insiders to be a "stiff."

[7] **Nuns and priests:** All belong to a particular order. The emphasis here is on the individuals and personalities. The religious order doesn't matter.

[8] **Intersessions:** These creative activities happened twice a year at St. Liz. At the end of the first semester, we stopped regular classes for special events. We repeated this at the end of the second semester.

[9] **SCUFO**: As a reminder, it's the Society for Communications with Unidentified Flying Objects. In reality, Kelly used this to have fun with science and as incentive to fire up teens interested in astronomy, physics, and astrophysics.

[10] **Banning tennis shoes:** This was not just an issue about style or comfort. In those days, tennis shoes were far more affordable than any other kind of footwear. Banning tennis shoes would create additional money problems for students whose families were already hard up.

[11] **The student park:** The nuns' old convent, a huge two-story stucco building next to school, suffered from rusty pipes, a leaky roof, and a moldy foundation. The parish decided to build a new nunnery across the street and planned to demolish the vacant convent and use the land for a student park. After the nuns moved into their new home, a single-story structure with a tile roof and modest garden, the parish didn't have enough money left to demolish the old nunnery. So for over a year, the vacant building, partly boarded up, slowly deteriorated into broken windows, weeds, and decayed stairs.

It was Tom Rowe who described what happened next: "It seems that one of our illustrious varsity football players found that the bedrooms of the old convent still had beds with rusty box springs. He used this to his advantage and then shared his hedonistic knowledge with his teammates. At one point, several members of the team indulged in some rather unfortunate physical activities with a sophomore girl who was new to St. Liz. This happened on more than one occasion.

"At any rate, the neighbors complained about late afternoon shenanigans and Father Edward found out. The girl, whom the nuns classified as emotionally disturbed, was expelled. Three of the first-string players were also expelled, and several other football players were suspended. The *Tribune* said that the guys were, in the glib words of the press, 'contributing to the delinquency of a minor.'

"After that incident, they managed to find the money to demolish the vacant convent and lay the sod for a student park. It's amazing how things get done around here."

[12] **WASC:** Western Association of Schools and Colleges. Every five years or so, an outside group of educators visit schools all across the nation and help teachers evaluate themselves. This results in endless hours of paperwork writing up what we already know, discussing the same problems without solutions and adding to our overworked work load.

[13] **Sister Clem:** She's like a character out of the movie "Sister Act." Whoever cast that fictional group of sisters must have been at St. Liz when I was there as a teacher. On Bravo's list of the 100 funniest movies, this film is rated #83 out of 100. It's number one on my list of sister movies. Anyone who has ever earned an old school Catholic diploma will respond with "LOL."

[14] **Bingo/bingo:** Take your pick. After a while I got tired of capitalizing it. A perceptive reader might note that it is capitalized when used by those who defended it as important. When considered unimportant, I used lowercase. After a while, I got tired of doing that, too.

[15] **"He smoked cigarettes... "** It wasn't uncommon, during the seventies, to smoke cigarettes, cigars and pipes in faculty meetings or the faculty room but, supposedly, not in the classrooms.

[16] **California State University, Hayward** is now known as Cal State East Bay.

[17] **The Perpetual Chess Game:** Actually, they kept score. Kelly won 205 games. Stan won 45.

[18] **The second collection:** This refers to the ritual of donations at the Catholic Mass. The first collection during Mass is usually for basic needs to support the local church. The second collection is for a more specific purpose such as missionaries or food for the poor.

[19] **Confession:** Catholics went to church, kneeled in a little confessional and confessed their sins to a priest. They began by saying: "Bless me Father for I have sinned."

[20] **The Caldecott Tunnel** separates Alameda County (Oakland and Berkeley) from Contra Costa County (suburbs).

[21] **"Grab your picket sticks...:"** These lyrics are the start of a song that evolved into another song later on. Most of these lyrics are from songs on my CD, *Mindworker*.

[22] **Stan Cardinet:** Stan's grandfather founded the Cardinet Candy Company in Southern California.

[23] *Confession:* Like any songwriter, my inspirations were written on pizza stained napkins and stray pieces of paper. It took years for this song to mature into these lyrics. I invoke poetic license.

[24] **"...no correlation between class size and learning."** Dixon often repeated this as fact but it defied the experience of every teacher. Years later I found that study. It proclaimed that a class of 55 learned about the same as a class of 35. Nonsense.

It's false to compare a big class of 35 to a bigger class of 55. The primary objection to lower class size is money. Bureaucrats can hire one teacher for 50 students in a class instead of two teachers for two classes of 25 students.

[25] **Sadie Hawkins dance:** At the time, the Sadie Hawkins dance was a yearly event based on the Li'l Abner cartoon strip where the Dog Patch women could chase and marry the guy they caught on a certain day each year. The high school version allowed a female teen to invite a guy to this dance.

[26] **Mindworker:** Actually, I wrote this song several years later. I needed it in this scene because it's the title of the book and my CD.

[27] ***"Child is father to the man:"*** The astute reader will notice that I borrowed a line of poetry for my song, *One Time,* from William Wordsworth's poem: "My Heart Leaps Up."

[28] **"Hey, hey, LBJ. How many kids did you kill to-day?"** In my memory, this is the most intense chant from the protestors of the Viet Nam War era. The mistake I made was in remembering an incident that happened when Nixon was president. I really can't recall what the students were chanting but I do know my memory isn't always accurate.

[29] **VICARIOUS??:** "Vituperative" is an adjective that I had applied to her writing.

[30] **Work for free:** Ironically, years later at a school back east, a group of teachers agreed to work for free. It got media attention and a private foundation stepped up and paid their way. Maybe it wasn't such a crazy idea after all.

[31] **The Candle Class:** I did this once a year on Halloween. I'd put a candle in a bottle in the middle of the room. The students sat in a circle. After a brief funny lecture about how the sun is but a mere reflec-

tion of the moon, I'd pass out fresh pumpkin seeds. We'd discuss myths, symbols, omens and ritual. Then I gave them the assignment. Sit quietly and stare at the candle in the middle of the room. After a while, before class ended, I asked, "Do you see the reflection of the flame on the floor? If you do, point to it."

They were surprised to find that no one saw the same reflection in the same spot. Everyone saw it reflected only in front of them. This resulted in a discussion about the subjectivity of experience and how we do not see what others see. Most students were fascinated, amazed and grateful for the class where, for the first time in any class, they sat with their peers in silence. A few were bored, turned off and felt it was a waste of time and their parents' tuition.

[32] **Alternative school**" In those days, "alternative" was synonymous with "counter-culture" or away from the mainstream. These days it has the connotation of a "continuation school" for drop-out prevention. Maybeck, of course, is the former.

[33] **The Mass.** This is the standard Sunday Catholic ritual complete with candles, incense, Holy Communion, altar boys, and sermon. What hurt me the most here was my past belief that nuns sacrificed their lives for Christ's sake. To be denied Mass, per se, met nothing to me but the denial felt like a symbolic betrayal of my childhood beliefs.

[34] **Unforgivable:** I got over it. Long ago I made peace with the nuns, priests and others who fired us. Using that word in this context was a bit of a hyperbole. Sorry about that, sisters. I forgive you all.

[35] **The Maybeck salary:** Our salary at St. Liz, in 1972, averaged $10,000 a year, about $1,000 a month. Our Maybeck salary would be $100 a month—a 90% decrease. We subsidized the school by taking practically no salary. Kelly, altruistically, took ten dollars less so I could have ten dollars more, given my family

and three children. So, Kelly got $90 and I received $110 a month. Thank you, Kelly.

[36] **Dave Kinstle:** He would spend the next two years teaching at Maybeck as a volunteer without pay. Then we hired him and he never left.

[37] **Drugs:** Maybeck later evolved into making a "no drugs" policy their number one rule. A rules committee of two students and two teachers were selected to enforce student behavior. When five students were caught in the backyard of Maybeck smoking pot, they thought they had nothing to fear. But the committee expelled all five out of the small school population of 52, at the time. Maybeck's student body was reduced by 10% and the tuition budget took a serious hit.

[38] **Tetrahedron kite:** This is a giant box kite shaped like a pyramid. In 1907, Alexander Graham Bell built one that was 200 feet long and it weighed 200 pounds. It carried a man about 50 yards high above water.

About the Author

After PAUL AUGUST left Maybeck, he entered the curious realm of the Oakland Public Schools. He became the director of Castlemont High's night school and two years later he became a ghostwriter for Oakland's first black female superintendent. Read about it in book two of his autobiography, ***Mindworker: Ghostwriter.***

Over the years, his 300+ freelance articles have appeared in numerous publications, including: *San Francisco Chronicle* ("Neither – One Teacher's Angst"); *Oakland Tribune* ("Teaching: Not Your Ordinary 9-to-5 Job"), *Rolling Stone* ("Fat Eddie and the Rent-A-Cop"), *Songwriter Magazine* ("I Wanna Hold Your...Computerized Analyzed Hand"), *People's Almanac* ("Bio of the Beatles"), *Glimpse Magazine* ("Teacher War in Oakland"), *TAO Quarterly* ("San Quentin

Alumni"), *Classroom Teacher* ("Interview With Ruth Love"), *The Oakland Post* ("Disneyland in Oakland?"), *The Sacramento Observer* ("It's Only Words"), *The Montclarion* ("Suicide at Sixteen"), and *The Sun Reporter* ("The Expensive Bargain").

In addition to producing two CDs (*Mindworker* and *Welcome to Nevada City, God's Country*) and the songs in this book, August often participated in musical political events. When Tom Bates put on a Buddy Holly night as a fundraiser, Paul *was* Buddy Holly. Tom, a state legislator at the time, went on to become Mayor of Berkeley.

For more, go to Mindworker.net.

47831195R00232

Made in the USA
Lexington, KY
14 December 2015